The Soul of a Nation

The Soul of a Nation

America as a Tradition of Inquiry and Nationhood

Christopher R. Altieri

FOREWORD BY

Paolo Savarese

PICKWICK *Publications* · Eugene, Oregon

THE SOUL OF A NATION
America as a Tradition of Inquiry and Nationhood

Pickwick Publications
An Imprint of Wipf and Stock Publishers
199 W. 8th Ave., Suite 3
Eugene, OR 97401

www.wipfandstock.com

ISBN 13: 978-1-4982-2549-6

Cataloguing-in-Publication Data

Altieri, Christopher R.

The soul of a nation : America as a tradition of inquiry and nationhood / Christopher R. Altieri ; foreword by Paolo Savarese.

xviii + 218 p. ; 23 cm. Includes bibliographical references and index.

ISBN 13: 978-1-4982-2549-6

1. National characteristics, American. 2. United States—History—Philosophy. I. Savarese, Paolo. II. Title.

BL2525 .A57 2015

Manufactured in the U.S.A.   11/03/2015

The sacrifices of my wife, Ester Rita, and my son, Joseph Matthew, have made this work possible. Not only: their love and devotion, constant patience and unfailing support kept me sane, grounded, hopeful and happy through thick and thin. From them, more than from any other source or combination of sources, have I learned the true meaning of federal union. I dedicate this work to them, though all that is good and worthy in it is already theirs.

Contents

Foreword

THE WORK BEFORE THE reader at present, which Christopher R. Altieri successfully defended as his doctoral dissertation on May 13th of 2010, and now presents for publication, is the result of a weave of problems both of content and method, which required a lengthy and a severe labor of decantation, selection, and reordering that were propadeutic to the formulation and elaboration of the theses, or rather *the* thesis, which constitutes the lodestar of the work.

The first step in the process was to bring into focus the initial idea, or better, the initial *insight*, according to which *America* is a notion and a model of "public space" that informs and directs the way of thinking about and putting into practice—or conducting—the political and juridical institutions that were created in order to safeguard the foundations of that public space in time. It was not possible to unravel the skein of problems by reordering the material gathered according to theme and content. To untie the knot, as it were, it was necessary to extract a theoretical axis capable of polarizing, within the more than merely abundant material, the hermeneutical project and the basic idea of the thesis regarding America. The problem required a strategy in and for which the elimination of background noise would be accomplished by constant attention to and contact with the basic idea, and the possibility of distilling the—initially hypothetical—theoretical valence, to the point at which it could be formed into a hermeneutical principle of political experience.

In other words, it was necessary to maintain the research project and the connected reflection distinct from that, which is concretized in various disciplines, which also examine and reconstruct the event of American independence and the institutions born of that event. I am thinking of the history of political institutions and doctrines, of constitutional law, and of political science in the sorry para-sociological state into which it has been confined, having once been a splendid philosophical discipline.

Precisely this was at stake in the dissertation: the recovery of the discourse of political science, in the classical sense of a philosophy of the *polis* or of the *politeia* that harken back at least to Plato, reinterpreted through the Voegelinian lens, which was one of the great chapters of the general science of *order* in human history. The distinction of the orders of discourse, in fact, is certainly a necessary element in any such project as this one, but the project itself—or the question it addresses—can find a response, even an inchoate one, only if it is not dissociated from its theoretical tenor, from which it can alone receive its orientation—if you will, the indications of direction and meaning. Let it be clear that the recovery of the classical acception of political science is in no wise a matter of nostalgia. Rather, it introduces a difficult and exacting task, namely, that of rethinking an historical experience, the rethinking of an historically well-identified way of reading the problem of order in and of society, in order to discover whether there is in that society something meaningful not only in the sense of an American self-understanding, so to speak, but also for other political and institutional experiences and traditions.

A project so ambitious in its theoretical claim could not fail to come to grips with the need prudently to select and re-forge its instruments. Altieri addressed the problem by choosing a few travelling companions in the re-reading of the work of the Founding Fathers: Voegelin, McIntyre, Cavell, Thoreau, (and, I would add, Emerson). It was here that the idea of rereading the public space called America as a tradition of inquiry took shape—a tradition of inquiry being fundamentally a conversation, one at once open to and conscious of the risks it must encounter and the ambiguities that it must not fail to identify in its presuppositions and in its way of exercising them, so as to assure continuity with that tradition's constitutive principles, or rather, if you will, to safeguard itself as a tradition of nationhood.

One might say that Altieri's work is an attempt to cut and temper an interpretive key of and for the Declaration of Independence and the Constitution of the United States, showing how they are the fruit of the intellectual cooperation of a group of men—the Founding Fathers and Framers, as they are styled there—who were aware of the problem of order that constitutes public political and juridical space, as such. In their preparation and enunciation, we observe the *differentiation* (to use Voegelin's word for it) of the conscience and consciousness of a people (in Italian, we have one word, «*coscienza*»)—and one may maintain that this is a philosophical event.

The project, and the hermeneutical thread that I followed in directing Altieri, placed notable problems on me as director—problems of comprehension, discernment, filtering, methodological impostation, clarification of the decisive and core problematic and the fundamental nuclei of truth to favor and draw into the light. The maieutic operation that was necessary in order to guarantee that Altieri's intuitions circa *The Soul of a Nation*—of his nation—translated themselves into a coherent thesis project and product, was truly challenging—and I must say that Altieri let himself be guided with docility, and at the same time, without ever losing his originality. In this, the direction of this dissertation was a real exercise in philosophical conversation. The initial insights thus progressively reached coherent, ordered expression, communicable in the public space that is proper to philosophical research, and his reflection on the notion of America explained itself in terms that are meaningful for other historical political and institutional traditions.

Perhaps the most important and far-reaching acquisition of the work that Altieri had to make for himself in his effort to give form to his initial insights, was precisely the progressive honing of his capacity to practice a method that we might describe with Plato as *anamnetic*. One could also formulate the idea in the language of the self-appropriation of the self-understanding in its rapport with the world, with differentiation and integration that is both history and institutional translation of that order, which emerges in the human experience, both singular and associate (social), and allows people to live in and through it with passion, dignity, and finally, hope. This self-appropriation, in fact, is at once an exercise in sonship and condition of paternity in its most enthusing fecundity—and—against this backdrop, the characteristic of the exercise of conversation among equals.

It is for this that I think that Altieri, in the end, has not in this work defined problems, so much as he has honed a method, perhaps even the rudiments of an *organon*, that will be cultivated and developed in all the future developments of his intellectual life—and perhaps not only his intellectual life.

Paolo Savarese

Preface and Acknowledgments

THIS WORK CONSIDERS AN actual, historical political society as an apt field of study in and for the general science of order. As such, it is an entirely methodological exercise. Following certain philosophical insights of the German-born citizen of the United States of America and political philosopher, Eric Voegelin, for whom, "The existence of man in political society is historical existence, and a science of politics that penetrates to principles must at the same time be a philosophy of history," the work shows how the people that was formed through common experience on the North-eastern littoral of the North American continent is particularly apt for this type of study. The need to have an actual, historical political society in existence as the field of investigation is inherent to the philosophical character of the work, indeed qualifies the work as properly philosophical. The aptness of the chosen historical society, however, becomes visible only during the course of the work, itself.

Specifically, that which will emerge during the course of the work is the (in modern times) peculiar relation of anthropological thinking to the debate over the kinds of institutions that are best for governing, which took place in the latter half of the eighteenth century among British colonists in the New World.

In the public square, the debate over the nature of man was intermingled with the debate over the right kinds of institutions for the specific mass of humanity that was living on or near the North-Eastern littoral of the North American continent. For those, who were actually conducting the debate, however, the anthropological question was prior to the institutional one; the debate was conducted in the awareness that institutions are for human beings living in society. Most importantly, the conduct of the debate in the British colonies during the second half of the 18th century was not an innovation. It was, rather, a real, historical, practical example of the insight with which Plato began the critical scientific reflection on politics: the city is a man writ large, while society is the cosmos in miniature. Thus, as a *point de depart* and at the same time, a *point d'arrive*, the work takes the symbol in and around which that group of humanity, which was present along and relatively close to the aforementioned littoral, began to develop consciousness of itself as a distinct people.

For that human society, the symbol in and around which their popular self-consciousness emerged and grew in articulation, was and is the name, "America". The reader will immediately note that that this designation, "America", has at once a geographical and a conceptual significance. Though the geographical significance is rightly applicable to a broader territory than that comprehended by either the original littoral or even the present continental expanse of the United States, the term nevertheless, as a matter of history, i.e., according to a logic of action (including, in the first place, the act of thinking), has acquired a peculiar acception in the physical space occupied and governed by those human beings, who have become the people of the United States.

While this state of affairs is today cause of (or at least occasion for) a great deal of hard feeling, it is no judgment on those feelings to note that philosophers have known at least since Aristotle wrote his *organon* that a single word can refer to many different things, and ought not to be scandalized by the phenomenon. Rather, driven as by an impetus internal to the science they practice, they—we—ought to seek to understand it. It is in this spirit that this essay takes "America" as its object.

This is not to deny that there are other conceptual spaces in the geographical area called America—e.g., Central America, South America, and perhaps most pertinently Latin America, which straddles the first two and constitutes a peculiar cultural-linguistic and political worldview. The point is that these are other conceptual spaces, with peculiarities and structures that qualify them as other than what citizens of the United States call "America", peculiarities and structures that are independent of the conceptual space of the United States.

This project is concerned with the generation of the conceptual space in and under which the people who created the United States came to recognize themselves as involved in a common way of life, to which they gave the name, "America". It is with the genesis of this name, in just this sense, that the present project is concerned.

The procedure, which neither starts with the specific in order to arrive at the general, nor begins with general observations in order to arrive at specific conclusions, but seeks to discover what Voegelin calls, "the unfolding of the typical in meaningful concreteness," is not an innovation in theoretical politics; it is rather a recovery. The reader will already have noted that the work is concerned with discovering and elaborating the structure of experience. This would, on its own, tend to place the work in the way of phenomenology. The work is also concerned with the development of a symbol, specifically, "America", and this, on its own, would make the work essentially hermeneutical. Taken together, however, the two moments of the work place it in the way of Platonic anamnesis.

This work pretends to render possible the search for the general principle of order within a given political society in historical existence. That political society is, as such, an expression of an idea of order, is an idea that has been with philosophy at least since Plato engaged the issue thematically in his *Republic*, discussing the city as a man writ large—an idea that creates the founding tension of political theory, which is the tension between the anthropological and the cosmological, i.e. between the idea of the city as a man writ large and the idea of society as the world writ small (368d7–369a5).

This work therefore seeks to establish a way of thinking about America—understood as above—in which the American founders' preoccupation with precisely this founding tension of political theory emerges as the real motive force behind the generation of America.

The way of thinking about America, which this work proposes to establish, is therefore at once essentially American and philosophical, since it will be (seen as) a fact of history that the genesis of America is nothing other than an exercise in this way of thinking, and this way of thinking is constitutively a conscious experience of the tension that is at the foundation of political theory, the basic concern of which is to order human affairs in concord with the order of the cosmos.

The impetus for this work came from a series of conversations with Prof. Giorgio Salzano, beginning in the late Spring of 2002, about six months before my wedding on October 5th. The first few conversations regarded philosophical and political questions, though they quickly passed into the realm of autobiography. In the sharing of stories, we found community of experience and discovered a spiritual *idem sentire* that led us to investigate the quality, in the strict, etymological sense, of our respective experiences of the place in which I lived the first 20 years of my life, a place that is in many important ways still home for me.

During the course of those early conversations, it became more and more apparent that existing treatments of American politics, whether in histories, political science tracts, economic interpretations, cultural surveys, *inter alia*, while extremely valuable and useful in different ways, nevertheless did not offer, whether taken singly or all together, an adequate theoretical expression of our experiences in America, which were at once of convergence, and conversion. If my friend and mentor discovered America by going there, I discovered America by leaving. Though each of us had his direction, it was by a peculiar way of indirection, called philosophical conversation, that we found ourselves more deeply than ever in a city that was, and was not of our making. It was a city of words, to borrow a phrase from Plato, and it seemed worthwhile to write it down and see what it came to.

If the impetus for this work is in my conversations with Prof. Salzano, the origins of it are to be found rather further back in my history. I recently discovered, for example, that the U.S. history text I studied during my junior year at Fairfield Prep contains a brief, but explicit discussion (it is one sentence, or perhaps an independent clause) of America as having at some point a geographical sense, though not yet any other. Since the idea that America is at once a physical and a conceptual space is central to this work, I could safely conclude I have been thinking about the issue since at least 1993. I believe, however, that there are good grounds for placing the beginning of my thinking about America in a way one of the writers who will shortly come into play calls, "thinking consecutively," rather earlier than 1993. I was reared as part of a household for which love of country was the proper and expected disposition, by parents for whom being responsible citizens meant being, first of all, upright persons and good neighbors. I was further blessed, from the very beginning of my formal school instruction, with inspired and inspiring teachers, especially my teachers of history and languages. Though I did not repay their inspiration by becoming a disciplined student, I did read everything I could get my hands on regarding the colonial era and especially the revolutionary period. Somehow, I have been thinking the thoughts that have become this work at least since I read *Johnny Tremain*.

What the work has come to is now beyond my competence to judge, though it would have come to nothing at all without Prof. Paolo Savarese, who generously shared his erudition and by his unfailingly patient good counsel showed me that true wisdom is knowledge informed by charity. Both during the writing of this project, and in the long period of editing and preparing the "finished" product—originally a PhD dissertation—for publication, I have been happily reminded of my indebtedness to scores of persons, many of whom may never know the extent of my debt. The names appearing here constitute an acknowledgment of some few of the specific debts I have incurred, though in no wise do they constitute a full account, nor ought acknowledgment of my indebtedness be in any wise construed as payment of my debts, which must remain outstanding.

My editor, Charlie Collier, paid extraordinarily careful attention to an unusually complicated manuscript under implausibly difficult circumstances, and answered my queries with unwarranted patience and gentleness. My typesetter, Calvin Jaffarian, guided me through the final stages of preparation with both expertise and graciousness. To them, and to everyone at Wipf and Stock, my gratitude.

My thanks to John L. Altieri, Eileen M. Altieri, John L. Altieri jr., Maudie T. Altieri, Sheila W. Altieri, Mr. & Mrs. Kieran G. Altieri, Mr. & Mrs. Kevin J. Altieri, Matthew O. Altieri, Anne E. Altieri, the Peter L. Altieri family, Msgr. Sante Babolin, Robert Bernier, Rev. Richard Cipolla, the Charles M. Collins family, Most Rev. C.J-N. de Paulo, Michelle DeRubeis, Maureen Diffley, Harry Evans, Rosanna Finamore, Kevin Flannery SJ, Patricia Graham, Bruce Jaffe, Raymond Koehler, Barbara Kolessar, Séan-Patrick Lovett, Elena Mannucci, Emer McCarthy, Nathan Morley, Lydia O'Kane, Msgr. Mario Pangallo, Chad Pecknold, Ann Pomeroy, Stephanie Reich, the Roberto Rita family, Laurence Ryan SJ, Louis A. Saracco, Niko Sprokel SJ, Msgr. Edward Surwilo, John Szablewicz, Barry Wallace, Christopher Wells.

CRA

Rome, August 20th, 2014

A Note on the Scholarly Apparatus

Excepting texts and materials for which there are other established methods of citation, the scholarly apparatus has been assembled essentially according to the indications for the humanities in the *Chicago Manual of Style* 16th Edition. There is one notable deviation in the scheme: the method of citing the works of Eric Voegelin. Unless otherwise indicated, the source for all citations of Voegelin is the Missouri edition of Voegelin's *Collected Works*. Several volumes of the *CW* group together different works, originally published as single volumes, e.g. Volume 4. When this is the case, I give the name of the original work, and the page number in the *CW* volume on which the quotation appears or on which the citation is to be found. I employ a series of abbreviations for specific titles cited, each of which I give at the first instance of a work's appearance in the scholarly apparatus. Thus, quotations and from and citations, of Voegelin's *New Science of Politics* shall henceforth be given as "Voegelin *NSP*, pp." In citing *Order and History*, I give the *CW* volume number in the first full citation only, and afterward give the volume number of *Order and History*, with the page reference to the corresponding *CW* volume. Hence, *Order and History: the ecumenic age* (Vol. 4 of *Order and History*) is given as *Order and History, volume 4: the ecumenic age* in *CW* 18:pp. Subsequently, the cite appears in the footnotes simply as *OH* 4:pp.

A few abbreviations are also employed, and are indicated in the footnotes. They are either standard, or self-explaining.

The footnotes contain bibliographical information, and all the usual scholarly trappings. In addition, they often contain brief discussions of titles that could be useful to various kinds of readers for various reasons. They therefore sometimes approach the tone or style of a running bibliographical commentary. This is not in lieu of a standard bibliography, but in addition to it, in the hope it might be useful to orient different kinds of readers in the history and development of the thought that is in the background of the work, while avoiding lengthy intellectual autobiography.

Words between Worlds

Thematic and Methodological Introduction

LIKE PHILOSOPHY, AMERICA IS a problem. Both philosophy and America need to be "worked out". The purpose of this essay is to show that, and to begin to show how, the working out of America cannot be completely achieved without ultimately involving the working out of philosophy. Presumably, the idea that both philosophy and America are problems will not be controversial. Even the idea that both America and philosophy are similarly problematic might avoid serious objection. The claim that this work undertakes to assert and defend, however, i.e., the idea that America is essentially a philosophical problem, so that whatever it is we call philosophy has therefore something to learn about itself from America, is less likely to meet with easy approbation. The words in the pages to follow seek to begin to make the case.

That America is a problem is readily observable. When one says, "America," it is not clear what one's object is. The word may refer to one continent, or two. Often enough, and even commonly in the U.S. English idiom, America is short-hand for the United States of America. If a German says, *er ist Amerikaner*, or if an Italian says *gli americani. . . .*, it is almost certain that the referent is a citizen or citizens of the United States, or perhaps even an action of the government of the United States. Even so, those who are not citizens of that country have a legitimate claim to the name, "American". It is in many international societies and social circles, therefore, a matter of good manners to be sensible of this fact and, in light of one's sensibility, to employ some other mode of diction in reference to oneself or others who are citizens of the United States of America, e.g. *citoyen des Etats Units* or *statunitense*.

With due regard for the well-founded sensibilities of our age, it is nevertheless a matter of equally pressing fact, that the employment of America as short-hand for the United States does persist in the common usage, not only of U.S. English, but of other languages as well. The question facing us has two moments: the first regards the origin of the usage; the second asks why the usage persists in the face of such sensibilities. This question, as posed, involves a series of further questions regarding at least the nature of idiom, and of language in general. Consideration of these and other, further questions cannot be postponed indefinitely if the present project is to make good on its claim to philosophy. For reasons that will only come into view in the course of the work to follow, the series of general questions regarding idiom, language, and most generally, the phenomenon of communicability, must receive treatment within the framework of a study of a given community of sense and meaning. Since the idiomatic peculiarity that is America began in the language proper to the political community that is the United States of America, and since the problem as posed would not really exist if that society did not exist, the political community of the United States of America shall be the particular field, from the study of which the more general problem shall be made to emerge and achieve a measure of relief.

When America is used as short-hand for the United States of America, it does not merely name a place on the Earth. Likewise, when a citizen of the United States describes himself (or is described) as an American, he is not necessarily suggesting, nor is he implying that the other places are somehow less American than the one from which he hails.

America names both a mass of land and a conceptual space. "American" qualifies things and persons in one, or the other, or both. Let these few examples from common usage illustrate the point: the protagonist of the original 1948 "Superman" serial battled for truth, justice and something the series' authors called the "American way"; Rick's Café Américain is in Casablanca; the Italian expression, *americanata* names a film of hackneyed plot, scant characterization, shallow interpretation and foregone conclusion; the United States House of Representatives created the Committee on un-American Activities, or HUAC, in order to investigate attempts to subvert the order of society in the United States; thirty-five years before HUAC's creation,[1] Katharine Lee Bates brought

---

1. In 1938, if one dates from the HUAC's immediate predecessor committee, chaired by Rep. Martin Dies Jr. D-Tx.

two decades of poetic composition to a close when she published the final version of "America the Beautiful,"[2] which sings of a place that is beautiful ". . .for pilgrims' feet / whose firm, impassioned stress / A thoroughfare for freedom beat / across the wilderness," and prays, "America, America / God mend thine every flaw / confirm thy soul in self-control / thy liberty in law." In each of the above uses, "American" refers to something that is not a land mass; in the very last instance, "America" refers contemporaneously to the physical space between Atlantic and Pacific and to the common experience of that mass of humanity, which was occupying an ever-increasing portion of that space.[3] It is with the generation of the conceptual space of America, that this work is concerned.

The field of investigation is admittedly vast, though the proposed work will be manageable if it is remembered that the documents of the American founding advance specific claims regarding the convictions of the persons, whose lives were to be ordered according to them, so that by focusing on those documents and on the debate regarding the meaning of the claims advanced in them, the bearing of the work will remain true, and the work will not be lost in the field.

The famous words of the Declaration of Independence, "We hold these truths to be self-evident. . .," and the perhaps less-widely known, though equally powerful words of the Preamble to the Constitution of

---

2. The short of it is that Katharine Lee Bates began composing "America the Beautiful" in 1893, after traversing the country and ascending Pike's Peak. The final version of the poem was published in 1913.

3. From Frederick Jackson Turner's essay on "The Significance of the Frontier in the American History" (in Turner, *Frontier in American History*, 1):

> In a recent bulletin of the Superintendent of the Census for 1890 appear these significant words: "Up to and including 1880 the country had a frontier of settlement, but at present the unsettled area has been so broken into by isolated bodies of settlement that there can hardly be said to be a frontier line. In the discussion of its extent, its westward movement, etc., it cannot, therefore, any longer have a place in the census reports." This brief official statement marks the closing of a great historic movement. Up to our own day American history has been in a large degree the history of the colonization of the Great West. The existence of an area of free land, its continuous recession, and the advance of American settlement westward, explain American development.

Turner gave his essay as a paper delivered to the July 12 meeting of the American Historical Society in Chicago in 1893. That city in that year was also host to the Columbian Exhibition, a precursor to the World's Fair. Katharine Lee Bates visited Chicago and the Columbian Exhibition on the same cross-country tour that brought her to Pike's Peak, from the summit of which she looked out and had inspiration to write her poem.

the United States, "We, the People . . . Ordain and Establish this Constitution . . . ," are words, the meaning of which continues to be a matter of
national importance, so that even in the present day, and perhaps more
now than ever, the meaning of America itself is an open question in the
national life of the people who claim the name of America as their own.
This book shall attempt to show that, and begin to show how, the achievement of the Founding Fathers, as they are styled in America, was the
establishment of a framework in which the debate regarding the meaning
of America's claims could continue to flourish.

There are, then, two principal documentary points of reference: the
Declaration of Independence and the Constitution of the United States.
This narrows the field to some degree, though the scholarly literature regarding the founding period, generally, and the documents of reference,
specifically, is enormous and constantly growing—practically endless.
This, however, is precisely the point. America, like philosophy, exists only
and entirely in an endless conversation. One cannot stop either; engagement in each is a matter of finding oneself (engaged) in it. No human
person need ever consciously and deliberately inquire into the ultimate
reason of things; nevertheless, the philosopher will always recall with awe
the moment in which he realized he was no longer merely the student
of a discipline, but a disciple in a way of life. A citizen may or may not
ever realize that his form of life,[4] his modes of living are not a matter
of indifference to himself and the world. If he does, and if he takes his
realization seriously enough, he will question his citizenship, and when
he finds himself doing that, he will have found himself engaged in that
kind of questioning, which has been the work of philosophy at least since
the moment Socrates stood in the Athenian Assembly and declared that
the unexamined life is not worth living (i.e., since Athens put Socrates,
and in him, philosophy, on trial).

In describing philosophy and America as endless conversations, it
is important to keep in mind that there are no endless conversants. Both
America and philosophy are the work of some in every generation. Philosophy and America are, so to speak, traditional enterprises, conducted

4. Cf. Cavell, *Claim of Reason*, 168–90. Cavell is there explicitly responding to
Wittgenstein's discussion of the human form of life, which, as Cavell notes in the title
essay to *This New Yet Unapproachable America*, is essentially talking. Cf. Cavell, *This
New Yet Unapproachable America*, 47. Cf. also, Wittgenstein, *Philosophical Investigations*, 88e (§241). Henceforth, references to the *Philosophical Investigations* shall be
given by section only, and shall come from the Blackwell edition, unless otherwise
noted.

by those who investigate the questions that constitute the conversations in which they find themselves engaged. Alasdair MacIntyre has described a tradition as:

> [A]n argument extended through time in which certain funda-
> mental agreements are defined and redefined in terms of two
> kinds of conflict: those with critics and enemies external to the
> tradition who reject all or at least key parts of those fundamental
> agreements, and those internal, interpretative debates through
> which the meaning and rationale of the fundamental agree-
> ments come to be expressed and by whose progress a tradition
> is constituted. Such internal debates may on occasion destroy
> what had been the basis of common fundamental agreement, so
> that either a tradition divides into two or more warring compo-
> nents, whose adherents are transformed into external critics of
> each other's positions, or else the tradition loses all coherence
> and fails to survive. It can also happen that two traditions, hith-
> erto independent and even antagonistic, can come to recognize
> certain possibilities of fundamental agreement and reconstitute
> themselves as a single, more complex debate.[5]

MacIntyre's discussion of a tradition of inquiry is more than simply useful in understanding intellectual dynamics. Application of MacIntyre's vision of traditions in conflict, of the genesis, development, disintegration and re-constitution of traditions of inquiry bears directly on the founding of American nationhood, when American nationhood is understood as a way of life ordered according to the conceptual space called America. A brief consideration of the issue of slavery, its presence, eradication, and enduring consequences, is apt to bring the point further into view.

Why was the question of slavery a matter of national importance? Was slavery compatible with America, or was it an abomination, the destruction of which was devoutly to be wished and ardently to be pur-sued by all? Why did that question, from the very inception of the new Constitutional order, threaten to tear the new Union asunder? Was the Union, as constituted, defective, so that a resort to arms was rendered by it inevitable? Race-based chattel slavery, to be sure, is incompatible with human liberty, so that any political society conceived and dedicated to the proposition "All Men are Created Equal" cannot coherently sanction and protect such an institution with the power of the state, unless those held in bondage are not men at all. So the question becomes, "What is a man?"

---

5. MacIntyre, *Whose Justice? Which Rationality?*, 12. Henceforth *WJWR*.

Since we know that learned Americans considered, "Government. . .[is] the greatest of all reflections on human nature, (let this also say, roughly, 'the City is man writ large')" it is reasonable to assume that the question was settled. Some of the political societies in America, however, did not see it that way. The abolition of race-based chattel slavery in several of the original states, and the subsequent exclusion of that institution on explicitly anthropological grounds by the people constituting new states in the Union made the federal government a *locus* of strife.

Two different and fundamentally incompatible understandings of the human constitution, i.e., of human nature, that is to say, irreducible and irreconcilably different understandings of what a human being is, found various, more or less geographically concentrated adherents, all of whom were vying for control of the larger society's representative apparatus. The point of contention, moreover, was the correct interpretation of what we might call the national ethos: all men are created equal. The words were the same, let us say, common among all adherents to whichever camp. The meaning each camp attached to or drew from the words could not have been more different. "They were," we say in English, "worlds apart." They were worlds apart, though sharing physical space, and, try as they might, they eventually ran out of ways to bridge the gap between their worlds of thought, between the conceptual spaces they created in response to their respective experiences and employed to order their daily lives, in response to which their competing conceptualizations arose. There were, in short, two different *saecula*, two different world orders, competing for control of that apparatus, which they had erected for the preservation and direction of their existence.

In short, under the name of America, the possibility of there being words between worlds is in question. Now, "to have words with somebody" means, in English usage, to quarrel with him. The having of "words between worlds" therefore suggests the presence of a communicative flow between persons whose understandings of the constitution of reality are somehow at odds with each other. In such a situation, i.e., one of querulousness—and especially just such querulousness—the conditions of discourse are precarious, for the slightest misunderstanding, any misstatement of a disagreement could lead to an interruption of the communicative flow. This dangerous potential in, or power of human speech, has been a question for philosophy at least since the writing of the *Euthyphro*, when Socrates names his interlocutor, "friend," and asks him what kind of disagreement causes hatred and anger[6]—though this kind of case illustrates only one particular way in which words may fail, or one particular mode of our failing our words. This power is but one intimation of the infinite responsibility we have for our words, taken together with the endless ways in which our words, let us say our language, might fail to convey or to achieve our meaning, our purpose.

Words establish our relations to people, and place us, and do many other things, as well, though how well they do the things we want them to do is not always, perhaps never, in our power to tell.[7] If it helps, the Harvard philosopher Stanley Cavell has described the issue as one of, "Word[ing] the world."[8] The expression is awkward, perhaps, though by no means is it arcane. It recalls our sense of the world's being given by language, and so at the same time our giving words to the world, or a world to words. If we allow "Word" to translate the Greek *logos*, then to word the world is to make it, to make the world (intelligible). In an old story, God gives sound to His breath, and speaks the being of the world: He gives us the power of speech, through which we can participate in (the intelligibility of) creation. Either we keep faith with the power that is bequeathed us, or we do not. To lose faith in the power is to despair of (knowing) the world.

When words fail, there can be parting, an end to friendship, say, or to marriage, which Milton calls a "meet and happy conversation"—an institution that is for him a symbol and metaphor of polity. When words have failed, and parting is not an option, there is war. The announcement of a *novus ordo seclorum* proclaims, not (only, not yet) a new order for the ages, but a new order for the worlds. The experiment called America

6. Plato *Euthyphro* 5c1–4, 7b6–7. Cf. also Cavell, *Cities of Words*, 25.

7. A boy can say, "I love you," to a girl, but if he says it to the wrong girl, or at the wrong moment, or even with just the wrong inflection, all might be lost; he can never know beforehand whether it is the right moment, and if she refuses him, he can never know whether it was – just – that the moment was not propitious. Whatever the result of his declaration, the world is changed utterly and irrevocably by and in and from the moment of his declaring. One can wrong a friend or a lover and offer an apology, and not be heard, or be heard too late –the one who welcomed his declaration has married another; one can cry out for help, and receive none; or have help come, only to discover that there was no danger, so that his trustworthiness – his standing to call for help – is itself called into question and even possibly destroyed, as in the tragedy of the boy who cried, "Wolf!"

8. Cf. Cavell, *In Quest of the Ordinary*, 154. Henceforth, *Quest*.

(the finding of the Founders) is an attempt (a way) to have words between the worlds.

If it seems odd, or even pretentious, to consider America not as one but, at its beginning, two worlds, whole and entire, then remember the first name (still in use in some circles) for the area of the globe that America encompasses, was the New World. More to the point, the idea that a political society should be a world unto itself is not new to philosophy. The German-born American thinker, Eric Voegelin made the point in his series of Walgreen Lectures in 1952:

> Human society is not merely a fact, or an event, in the external world to be studied by an observer like a natural phenomenon. Although it has externality as one of its important components, it is as a whole little world, a *cosmion*, illuminated with meaning from within by the human beings who continuously create and bear it as the mode and condition of their self-realization. It is illuminated through an elaborate symbolism, in various degrees of compactness and differentiation—from rite, through myth, to theory—and this symbolism illuminates it with meaning in so far as the symbols make the internal structure of such a *cosmion*, the relations between its members and groups of members, as well as its existence as a whole, transparent for the mystery of human existence. The self-illumination of society through symbols is an integral part of social reality, and one may even say its essential part, for through such symbolization the members of a society experience it as more than an accident or a convenience; they experience it as of their human essence. And, inversely, the symbols express the experience that man is fully man by virtue of his participation in a whole that transcends his particular existence, by virtue of his participation in the *xynon*, the common, as Heraclitus called it, the first Western thinker who differentiated it.[9]

Each of the aforementioned authors, MacIntyre, Cavell and Voegelin, is a thinker whose work has involved a considerable amount of reflection on various areas of intellectual inquiry and endeavor, all of which are either immediately identifiable as, or at least readily brought to bear on moral, political and metaphysical questions. Each is, in his own way, concerned with what we might call established philosophical questions, and at the

---

9. Voegelin, *New Science of Politics*, 109. Henceforth *NSP*. The work is to be found in Voegelin, *The Collected Works of Eric Voegelin*, vol. 5: *Modernity without Restraint: The Political Religions, the New Science of Politics, and Science, Politics, and Gnosticism.*

same time precisely concerned with the problem of America. There is, as we shall see in the course of the present work, a considerable area of overlap in their reflections. The program of this work, at once scholarly and speculative, is to show how these authors are in conversation with one another regarding the problem of America, a problem each addresses in his own way. Though the argument proper of the thesis is only to be accomplished in the ensuing chapters, a few preliminary points of conversation are already available. Illustration of these points will serve to bring the complexity of the proposed work further into view.

If the existence of a conceptual space called America must be given for the moment *causa argumenti*, the fact remains that the most recent settlers and conquerors of the continent that came to be called North America were Europeans. The critical usefulness of this observation depends on its not being taken merely to identify the geographical location of the provenance of the most recent settlers and conquerors, but also to indicate their social, cultural and intellectual heritage. If it is at least reasonable to understand Europe as a social, cultural and political phenomenon born of the encounter among historical claims advanced by devotees of a certain Hebrew sect who were the carriers of a particular Hebrew theology of history, with the Greek tradition of inquiry into the ultimate reason of things and the Roman system of social governance, then the settlement of that stretch of Earth, which came to be called, "America", will itself arguably be an historical phenomenon that stands necessarily in relation to the process of synthesis in which those who settled that tract of land were themselves involved. Said shortly, the question of America involves the question of Europe, and the question of Europe is an essentially philosophical question, so that the question of America cannot be indifferent to philosophy. MacIntyre, Voegelin and Cavell have ways of addressing the relation of America to the idea of Europe, and each finds that America stands in some relation to the different and conflicting visions of what philosophy is, which have characterized the intellectual, social and political climate of both Europe and America for many generations now. Indeed, a great deal of that conflict has involved and continues to involve the question of tradition's intelligibility, that is, whether tradition is properly a way of knowing the world and being in it.

Among the three authors, who, as it is hopefully becoming clear, will be the three principal interlocutors with whom the present work proposes to engage, Voegelin most forcefully identifies the problem as one of full-blown civilizational pathology in which:

> The corrosion of Western civilization. . .is a slow process extend-
> ing over a thousand years. The several Western political societ-
> ies, now, have a different relation to this slow process according
> to the time at which their national revolutions occurred. . . The
> American Revolution, though its debate was already strongly
> affected by the psychology of enlightenment, also had the good
> fortune of coming to its close within the institutional and Chris-
> tian climate of the *ancien régime*. Western society as a whole. . .is
> a deeply stratified civilization in which the American and Eng-
> lish democracies represent the oldest, most firmly consolidated
> stratum of civilizational tradition.[10]

MacIntyre has said that our culture is characterized by, "[A]n inability to
arrive at agreed rationally justifiable conclusions on the nature of justice
and practical rationality,"[11] and that this inability, "coexists with appeals
by contending social groups to sets of rival and conflicting convictions
unsupported by rational justification."[12] The result is that, "Disputed
questions concerning justice and practical rationality are thus treated in
the public realm, not as a matter for rational inquiry, but rather for the
assertion and counter-assertion of alternative and incompatible sets of
premises." MacIntyre argues that, in the present situation:

> What we need now to recover is. . .a conception of rational in-
> quiry according to which the standards of rational enquiry as
> embodied in a tradition, a conception according to which the
> standards of rational justification themselves emerge from and
> are part of a history in which they are vindicated by the way in
> which they transcend the limitations and provide remedies for
> the defects of their predecessors within the history of that same
> tradition.[13]

Cavell, in his turn, has phrased the matter in terms of philosophers' relations to the history of philosophy. Writing about Emerson, he describes
the history of philosophy as an edifice:

> Every European philosopher since Hegel has felt he must in-
> herit this edifice and/or destroy it; no American philosopher has
> such a relation to the history of philosophy. In the generation
> after Hegel has [*sic*] announced the completion of philosophy,

10. Cf. Voegelin, *NSP*, 241.
11. MacIntyre, *WJWR*, 5–6.
12. Ibid.
13. MacIntyre, *WJWR*, 7.

American writers must be free to discover whether the edifice of Western philosophy is as such European, or whether it has an American inflection.[14]

Supposing for the time being, and for the sake of argument, that the edifice of Western philosophy does have an American inflection (if the idea of a talking edifice seems strange, remember that edification is one of the reasons for speech, and that, in the philosophical context invoked by Cavell, education—the goal of philosophy—is a matter of "building up" before or as much as it is a matter of "leading out"), it becomes reasonable to wonder what philosophy might sound like in America.

By way of suggestion, and as a way further into the problem, consider the following lines from Terence Mann, the character James Earl Jones played in *Field of Dreams*, a film based on the W.P. Kinsella novel, *Shoeless Joe*:

> Ray, people will come Ray. They'll come to Iowa for reasons they can't even fathom. They'll turn up your driveway not knowing for sure why they're doing it. They'll arrive at your door as innocent as children, longing for the past. Of course, we won't mind if you look around, you'll say. It's only $20 per person. They'll pass over the money without even thinking about it: for it is money they have and peace they lack. And they'll walk out to the bleachers; sit in shirtsleeves on a perfect afternoon. They'll find they have reserved seats somewhere along one of the baselines, where they sat when they were children and cheered their heroes. And they'll watch the game and it'll be as if they dipped themselves in magic waters. The memories will be so thick they'll have to brush them away from their faces. People will come Ray. The one constant through all the years, Ray, has been baseball. America has rolled by like an army of steamrollers. It has been erased like a blackboard, rebuilt and erased again. But baseball has marked the time. This field, this game: it's a part of our past, Ray. It reminds us of all that once was good and it could be again. Oh, people will come Ray. People will most definitely come.[15]

The idea of there being one constant through all the years is one of the most problematic ideas, with which philosophy has wrestled since its inception, indeed in the thinking of which philosophy may be said to be

14. Cavell, *This New Yet Unapproachable America*, 108–9.
15. From *Field of Dreams*, dir. Phil Alden Robinson, Universal Pictures, 1989.

born. The thickness of memory, and the movement toward something, say a future, under the impetus of something past, in the hope of finding it there (though transformed utterly, as though an army of steamrollers had passed over it), when taken with baseball's power to remind what was good and communicate, let us say, name a hope for what could be good again, may call to mind the magnificent phenomenology of memory St. Augustine gives in Book X of the *Confessions*. One may no more be made to hear it, than could Ray Kinsella make his brother-in-law see the game being played a few feet away. Can a game provide the peace that is lacking in the human heart? If it is the right game, perhaps the game called contemplation of wisdom, some to whom the name of philosopher has been granted have thought so.[16] There is a further text of baseball from another Kinsella story, one that instances a way of thinking that, if not exactly the kind of thinking that is philosophy, is at least concerned with concepts that are the stock-in-trade of accepted philosophy:

> "Why not baseball?" my father would say. "Name me a more perfect game! Name me a game with more possibilities for magic, wizardry, voodoo, hoodoo, enchantment, obsession, possession. There's always time for daydreaming, time to create your own illusions at the ballpark. I bet there isn't a magician anywhere who doesn't love baseball. Take the layout. No mere mortal could have dreamed up the dimensions of a baseball field. No man could be that perfect. Abner Doubleday, if he did indeed invent the game, must have received divine guidance." "And the field runs to infinity," he would shout, gesturing wildly. "You ever think of that, Gid? There's no limit to how far a man might possibly hit a ball, and there's no limit to how far a fleet outfielder might run to retrieve it. The foul lines run on forever, forever diverging. There's no place in America that's not part of a major-league ballfield: the meanest ghetto, the highest point of land, the Great Lakes, the Colorado River. Hell, there's no place in the *world* that's not part of a baseball field.[17]

On the side of philosophy, the quoted text contains an explicit discussion of dreaming and wakefulness, which have been themes of philosophy since Heraclitus;[18] then there is the limitlessness of the field, which names

16. Cf. Thomas Aquinas, *Expositio librii Boetii de Hebdomadibus*, proemium, 267–68.

17. Kinsella, *Iowa Baseball Confederacy*, 44–45. Page references are to the Mariner edition.

18. Cf. Voegelin, *Collected Works of Eric Voegelin*, vol. 14: *Order and History: The World of the Polis*, 303. Henceforth *OH* 2.

quite literally the *apeiron*, and the convergence of time and always that might name the transformed condition of our world, into the history of which the *eschaton* irrupts; lastly, a reader may receive the invocation of hell, not as mere profanity, but as an admonition: the ballfield, and therefore America, and therefore the world (the whole of which is contained in an American ballfield) is a place in which we are playing out matters of eternal life and eternal death. Baseball is a serious game.[19] Of course, no reader need necessarily see these things, and any reader may experience something akin to outrage at the suggestion that baseball, which is so obviously an entertainment, ought even for a second be considered as somehow in relation to the giants of Western thought.[20] Perhaps no sane person would dare to suggest that W. P. Kinsella's baseball story should be treated as though it were philosophy. Even so, the text of the game may be taken to show that there is in America, in American practices, an inchoate awareness of the flux of time and infinity within the weave of the world, which could be theorized.

Consider for a moment more generally the importance of "marking the time," which arises in Stanley Cavell's *Senses of Walden*. Cavell is discussing a passage in Thoreau's *Walden*:[21]

19. Cf. Plato, *Republic* 424e3–425a7.

20. If I do not insist that you follow me in this reading, I do point out that I am not alone. Listen to a part of Brian W. W. Aitken's contribution to Charles S. Prebish's delightful and challenging collection of essays on *Religion and Sport*:

> Having been involved in sport for many years and having read what others have related about their sports experience, such as Ken Dryden in his book *The Game* and the wonderful books of W. P. Kinsella about baseball, my experience is that on occasion in sport we have a sense of being carried away, of losing track of time, of feeling awe and wonder, a deep sense of release and well-being, a feeling that everything is all right with the cosmos. With Charles Prebish I ask the question, If that is not an experience of the sacred, then what is? Sport in itself responds to deeply felt religious needs in human beings because it is itself a ritual that re-enacts eternal realities. And because sport is essentially a form of play it can occasionally lift us to a higher plane of reality.

As the Jesuit scholar Hugo Rahner has put it: "To play is to yield oneself to a kind of magic, . . . to enter a world where different laws apply, to be relieved of all the weights that bear it down, to be free, kingly, unfettered and divine." Rahner, *Man at Play*, 65; cited by Prebish, *Religion and Sport*, 211.

21. "In any weather, at any hour of the day or night, I have been anxious to improve the nick of time, and notch it on my stick too; to stand on the meeting of two eternities, the past and future, which is precisely the present moment; to toe that line. You will pardon some obscurities, for there are more secrets in my trade than in most men's, and yet not voluntarily kept, but inseparable from its very nature. I would gladly tell all

[T]he notching [that is both the mention of Emerson that Thoreau makes at XIV, 23, and a response to the prophetic] must
mark not simply the occurrence of time but the improvement
of it. So in this case the act of marking must itself be the improvement. There is an earlier notice of a visitor whose name the
writer is "sorry [he] cannot print. . .here" (VI,8). For me, these
curiosities come together in Ezekiel's vision which contains the
myth of the writer (Ez. 9:3-6).[22] The writer's nameless marking of
Emerson is done in order to preserve him and, simultaneously,
to declare that his own writing has the power of life and death in
it. America's best writers have offered one another the shock of
recognition but not the faith of friendship, not daily belief. Perhaps this is why, or it is because, their voices seem to destroy one
another. So they destroy one another for us. How is a tradition
to come out of that? Study of *Walden* would perhaps not have
become such an obsession with me had it not presented itself
as a response to questions with which I was already obsessed:
why has America never expressed itself philosophically? Or has
it—in the metaphysical riot of its greatest literature?[23]

With prudent disregard for the question of the status of W.P. Kinsella's
baseball stories as great literature, it is nevertheless beginning to appear
more and more likely that a search is underway for a way of thinking in
America that could provide America with a way of expressing what wisdom there may be there. In his 2005 work titled *Cities of Words: Pedagogical Letters on a Register of the Moral Life*, specifically in the first chapter
of the book, on Ralph Waldo Emerson, Cavell places the issue as follows:

> I myself experienced, especially after writing a little book on
> Thoreau's *Walden*, a sort of cringe in trying to get back into Em-
> erson, a recoil from what struck me as his perpetual and irritat-
> ing intertwining of lyricism and cajoling. Yet I was convinced,

that I know about it, and never paint 'No Admittance' on my gate." Thoreau, *Variorum
Walden*, 35. "There was one other with whom I had 'solid seasons,' long to be remembered, at his house in the village, and who looked in upon me from time to time; but I
had no more for society there." Ibid., 221.

22. "Then He called to the man dressed in linen with the writer's case at his waist,
saying to him: Pass through the city (through Jerusalem) and mark an X on the fore-
heads of those who moan and groan over all the abominations that are practiced
within it. To the others I heard him say: Pass through the city after him and strike!
Do not look on them with pity nor show any mercy! Old men, youths and maidens,
women and children–wipe them out! But do not touch any marked with the X; begin
at my sanctuary." From the USCCB-approved New American Bible.

23. Cavell, *Senses of Walden*, 32–33.

from my experience with *Walden*, that *some such mode of writing may lend itself to a systematic thoughtfulness in a way only the name of philosophy suits* [emphasis mine – CRA]. And, since it is obvious that *Walden* is in conversation with Emerson's writing in every page, and since nothing before Emerson in America is philosophically ambitious and original on this scale, it is reasonable to conclude that what we have in these two writers is nothing less than the origins of the American difference in philosophical thought, as this enters into a new well of American literary ambition on these shores.[24]

Allowing the obvious conversation of *Walden* with the writing of Emerson to stand unchallenged, or allowing it as articulated in *The Senses of Walden* to be sufficient to justify the deployment of the adverb, "obviously," it shall eventually become necessary in part to concur with, and in part to contest (not to say, "dissent" from), Cavell's assertion that Emerson and Thoreau are the writers in whom we find the origins of the American difference in philosophical thought. Whatever the results of further conversation with Cavell, Voegelin and MacIntyre might be, the concern of the conversation with them is that of recovering the American tradition as an intelligible object. That tradition will emerge during the course of the work as one that is at once of inquiry and of nationhood.

The previous discussion began with a presentation of the points of reference in the proposed conversation of recovery, and passed rapidly through the presentation of a series of cultural artifacts in which the possibility of thematizing America in its relation to the patrimony of Western thought was raised. Though the proposed work of recovery cannot avoid consideration of these and other such artifacts, neither can it start with them, for America is, as we have said, the short-hand name for a political community, the constitutions of which are presumably erected in view of preserving the way of life in which any cultural artifact will be recognizable as such. At the time of the American founding, neither baseball nor Boston transcendentalism existed, at least not in the forms that have acquired significance for a critical investigation of America. Such artifacts—like Jazz and the Hollywood talkie, to name some others—if they are American in a critically useful sense, must be shown to stand in some relation to the founding of American political community, the authoritative expression of which is in the Declaration of Independence and the Constitution. The investigation must therefore begin with

24. Cavell, *Cities of Words*, 20.

the cultural and social milieu of the founding generation, for it is, in the first, the self-understanding of that generation, which the Declaration and Constitution represent.

Thus phrased, the question may well appear rather more suited to a faculty of history than a philosophy faculty. History faculties, however, are about a different business. The eminent historian of the American founding, Forrest McDonald, has phrased the matter in the following way: "In a burst of creative scholarship," writes McDonald in the preface to his 1965 work, *E Pluribus Unum*, "[Historians] unearthed an array of long-forgotten facts. . .and devised a new interpretation of the national origins that would accommodate this information."[25] At the midway point of the first half of the 20th century, the number of empirical facts from the remote past available to historians increased exponentially. Historians began to conceive their task as essentially that of constructing entirely new narratives on the basis of the vastly expanded and ever-increasing body of empirical facts at their disposal. The vastly improved field of empirical knowledge would guarantee the comprehensive character of the new narrative, though McDonald admitted that the new task presented itself as "gargantuan."[26] Quite apart from the size of the enterprise, there were two other difficulties. One of them was a psychological accident, and therefore potentially visible to and corrigible by historians themselves. The other is a larger problem, one that inheres in the epistemic structure of the historical discipline thusly conceived. It eludes the historian *qua* historian. He cannot, *qua* historian, correct it.

First, the psychological accident: writing in 1965, McDonald notes that most of his contemporaries by that year had, in the main, "shaken loose the fetters of the old [i.e., those of Charles A. Beard, Carl Becker & co.[27]] generalizations about American history." He continues:

> [Historians] have not [however] *entirely* freed themselves from the old dogmas. The old dogmas, the philosophy of the New Historians in retreat, postulated that all judgments are subjective and therefore (1) that all truth is relative to the point of view of the observer, (2) accurate knowledge of the human past is not knowable [*sic*] and (3) not worth seeking.
>
> Now any sophomore student of logic should be able to perceive that it is indefensible to draw such inferences from that

25. McDonald, *E Pluribus Unum* , 19.

26. Ibid., 20.

27. Cf. ibid., 18–24.

premise, but historians, even the modern ones, have somehow managed to believe that if the premise is sound the rest necessarily follows.[28]

The second, larger structural problem is aptly and amply illustrated by McDonald, as well, so we need to circumscribe it. McDonald says that history is like a map, at least according to the historical enterprise as it was conceived a half-century ago.[29] McDonald admits the new narratives would be "mere made up stories." Properly drawn, however, "Their contours would reflect those of past reality." They would reflect the past, "Much as a map. . .reflects topographical reality—and not the immediate needs or aspirations of the present or any other generation." Here, the problem begins to come into view.

The fruits of academic historians' labors, would be like a map, then. Historical writing would be to the founders' *forma mentis* what a comprehensive schematic of a given stretch of country is to a vacationing hiker or an invading general. Until recently, however, those who lived in the United States were also at home in the conceptual space they called "America". Like anyone who lives his whole life in one place, "Americans'" knowledge of the conceptual space in which they were "at home" was at least as good and sometimes better than the Founders' own; certainly, their knowledge of the space was more broad, subtle, nuanced, detailed and profound than any intellectual map's portrayal of those same spaces could hope to be. The American story was already meaningful to those who were making it in the second half of the eighteenth century, and it was still meaningful to those we might call "ordinary Americans" long after the founders were dead and gone. It was not, however, a static meaning, sealed in amber, as it were. The symbology of the founding was being constantly revised and adapted as the experience of those who lived in the order it established grew in their understanding of themselves and of the founding events. Said simply, Americans interpreted their common existence in light of the founding; simultaneously, they interpreted the founding in light of their common experience.

A brief survey of 19th and early 20th century political texts will serve to illustrate the point. Consider firstly Ralph Waldo Emerson's "Concord Hymn", the first and last stanzas of which are:

---

28. Ibid., 21.
29. Cf. ibid., 20–21.

By the rude bridge that arched the flood,
Their flag to April's breeze unfurled;
Here once the embattled farmers stood;
And fired the shot heard round the world.

O Thou, who made those free men dare
To die and leave their children free,—
Bid Time and Nature gently spare
The shaft we raise to them and thee.

The poem was composed in 1837, and was an occasional piece to be sung at the ceremony dedicating a statue at Old North Bridge a few miles outside Boston where the battle of Concord was fought on April 19th, 1775. By 1837, the youngest sons of those who remembered the day on which that fight took place were passing middle age. The importance of the text above is to be found in the fact that, by the year of the poem's publication, the action of which the poem sings had become the seminal moment in a series of events of world-historical importance. At the time the events took place, however, they were understood merely as the armed continuation of a constitutional crisis within the British Empire: a skirmish between colonists jealous of their place in the British Empire and anxious to defend the rights they purported to enjoy by virtue of their subjection to the British Crown, and royal troops sent to press the supposed right of the British Parliament to legislate for those colonists.

Abraham Lincoln's speech of July 10th, 1858 signs another important moment in the development of the founding narrative as ordinary Americans inherited and lived and understood it:

> We find a race of men living [at the time of the founding] whom we claim as our fathers and grandfathers; they were iron men; they fought for the principle that they were contending for; and we understood that by what they then did it has followed that the degree of prosperity which we now enjoy has come to us. We hold this annual celebration to remind ourselves of all the good done in this process of time, of how it was done and who did it, and how we are historically connected with it. . .There is something else connected with it. We have besides these, men descended by blood from our ancestors—among us, perhaps half our people, who are not descendants at all of these men; they are men who have come from Europe—German, Irish, French and Scandinavian—men that have come from Europe themselves, or whose ancestors have come hither and settled here, finding

themselves our equals in all things. If they look back through
this history to trace their connection with those days by blood,
they find they have none, they cannot carry themselves back
into that glorious epoch and make themselves feel that they are
part of us, but when they look through that old Declaration of
Independence, they find that those old men say that "We hold
these truths to be self-evident, that all men are created equal;"
and then they feel that that moral sentiment taught in that day
evidences their relation to those men, that it is the father of all
moral principle in them, and that they have a right to claim it as
though they were blood of the blood, and flesh of the flesh, of
the men who wrote that Declaration; and so they are.[30]

Lincoln's words attest to the achievement, in ordinary Americans' day-
to-day life, of an understanding of the human and the citizen that goes
beyond anything previously seen in the mundane existence of peoples.[31]

Whatever it is, Lincoln's historical connection with the founding
is not "history's" connection with it, when history is McDonald's discipline. Lincoln's speech went on to call the sentiments expressed in the
Declaration the "electric cord. . .that links the hearts of patriotic and
liberty-loving men together, that will link those patriotic hearts as long
as the love of freedom exists in the minds of men throughout the world."
Immigrants' ability legitimately to claim the heritage of the Founders as
their own, indeed the fact that their claim is set out and defended by
a representative, suggests that American society had already more than
begun to become a society of persons such as an American author had
envisioned at the time of the founding:

He is an American, who, leaving behind him all his ancient
prejudices and manners, receives new ones from the new mode
of life he has embraced, the new government he obeys, and the
new rank he holds. He becomes an American by being received
in the broad lap of our great Alma Mater.[32]

30. Basler, *Abraham Lincoln*, 401–2. The full speech runs 385–404.

31. The attentive student of history will object to this diction, and cite in support
of his objection the gradual extension of the Roman citizenship to virtually all those
living within the bounds of the Empire, beginning with Augustus' extension of the
citizenship to all free males on the Italian peninsula. Granted some superficial similar-
ity, with due recognition of the American Founders' intimate knowledge of Roman
history and politics, the paragon will not hold. We shall explore the question in some
detail later in our work. For now we only make note of the objection and of our intention to address its merits.

32. Crèvecœur, *Letters from an American Farmer*, 43.

These lines are taken from the third of Michel Guillaume (Hector) St. Jean de Crèvecœur's *Letters From an American Farmer*, which were published in 1782.[33] By 1858, Lincoln was able plausibly to claim that over half of his audience responded to Crèvecœur's description. The men Crèvecœur and Lincoln described and addressed had no need of intellectual maps to help them navigate the remote past of the founding, because the founding did not exist conceptually in a remote past. They were conscious participants in the unfolding of that order, which was present to the mind of Emerson's audience (however implicitly or as yet *in nuce*) when he composed his hymn. The founding notions of America were a living reality, an ordering force in the soul of the nation.

To use a slightly modified version of McDonald's metaphor, the Founders' *forma mentis* was the individual citizen's intellectual *forma urbis*. Americans at home are neither visiting hikers, nor invading soldiers—and though a newly-arrived American or even a long-time resident may from time to time consult with profit a topographical map or a city plan—people in general have no need of a map to get around their home town. If one does not know the ins and outs of his home town, then we cannot reasonably expect a map to be of use to him.

The upshot of all this is that, if we accept the essential soundness of McDonald's understanding of the historical discipline's method, purpose and possible usefulness, then we must recognize that such a conception of history, such an estimation of its usefulness thusly conceived, can only occur to an historian who writes for an audience no longer able to negotiate the Founders' conceptual space unassisted. If McDonald were writing for fellow historians only, then the difficulty would be easily dismissible as one of the periodic quirks to which the academy is so susceptible. McDonald, however, writes neither exclusively nor primarily for fellow historians. One of the great strengths of his prose is its stylistic vivacity, which recommends his work so admirably to the generally erudite reader. We might take this to indicate that the audience for whom McDonald

---

33. "Our records of that life are in the highest degree inexact; he himself is wanting in accuracy as to the date of more than one event. The records, however, agree that Crèvecœur belonged to the petite noblesse of Normandy. The date of his birth was January 31, 1735, the place was Caen, and his full name (his great-grandson and biographer vouches for it) was Michel-Guillaume-Jean de Crèvecœur. The boy was well enough brought up, but without more than the attention that his birth gave him the right to expect; he divided the years of his boyhood between Caen, where his father's town-house stood, and the Collège du Mont, where the Jesuits gave him his education." Ibid., viii.

and those of his bent write, i.e., the citizen of average instruction, to the extent he finds historical writing useful, has need of a map to navigate the very conceptual space in which those institutions have their origin, which are responsible for the ordering of his daily life, the tutelage of his rights and the direction of the energies of the society to which he belongs. Whether this state of affairs does in fact obtain is an important question to which we shall turn shortly. It is a fact, however, that the discipline of history is methodologically incapable of treating the founders' *forma mentis* as anything more than an artifact to be described (more or less manualistically).

Nor is the phenomenon confined to academic history departments. In fact, for nigh on half a century, sociologists, social psychologists, economists and most importantly, political scientists have been dedicating their best energies and devoting their dearest resources to understanding the American founding. After nearly five decades of constant attention, however, perplexity continues to abound regarding the truth of the American founding.[34] The attention has been constant, and increasingly intense. In a recent article examining the role of rhetoric in the creation of political union in America, Rogan Kersh offers a brief statement and overview of the situation, in which he notes that the academy does not remain without a satisfactory explanation for the founding of the United States for want of trying:

> Americans' original movement toward a unified polity has been explained in various ways, usually following disciplinary lines. Economists emphasize the effect of inter-colonial trade, while political scientists and historians cite the binding force of nascent institutions, or of events like war and tax increases. Ideological historians reconstruct various paradigmatic "pattern[s] of ideas and attitudes" that informed colonists' decisive steps towards unity.[35]

Those who have made efforts to understand the founding period are not wanting in intellectual power. Beyond the obvious increase in our empirical knowledge of the colonial period and especially of the second half of the eighteenth century, the work of the past five decades has led to greater, though still partial and fragmentary understanding of the revolution the founders effected. The reason for the present perplexity even in the face

34. Cf. Kersh, "Rhetorical Genesis of American Political Union," 229.
35. Ibid., 229–30.

of obvious advancement is built into the very structure of inquiry that has fostered it. Each of the disciplines named above must, for reasons of methodological rigor and epistemic economy, assume a certain structure in which given types of fact will be meaningful and certain others will not be. Thus, the economist does not deliberately downplay the importance of the English constitutional tradition in explaining, e.g. American resistance to the Stamp Act. He simply spins a story in which that particular aspect of the crisis does not come into play much. The political historian, on the other hand, cannot give his account of the episode without reference to that tradition.[36] The *annales* historian[37] does not mention George Washington, except to say what effect the genesis of his mythology had on the American psyche, while Washington's biographer writes to the effect that Washington's personal characteristics were largely responsible for the continental army's ability to weather all manner of adversity.[38] The problem, further, is not simply that both what we might call "economic factors" and what we might call "political factors" contributed to something we might call the "American Revolution".

What a "political factor" or an "economic factor" is, i.e., what the terms mean in contemporary scientific discourse, is something inherently resistant to the kind of narrative the American story already is. This is not an indictment of science. It is not even the beginning of a criticism of contemporary science's self-interpretation. The point is that the science of politics as this is understood by "Poli Sci" departments throughout the country today is a qualitatively different affair from the "science of politics" that informed the Founders' thought and action. The Founding Fathers were about the business of "Provid[ing] for a government . . .by laws that conformed to the genius and circumstances of the people."[39]

As those circumstances changed, the popular genius adapted, altering certain ways of societal organization and cultural practice. Sometimes violently, often contentiously, and always imperfectly, the American people have sought to order their lives together according to the Founders'

---

36. McDonald, *Novus Ordo Seclorum*, 9–53. Henceforth *NOS*.

37. Cf. Boorstin, *Americans: National Experience*, 337–56.

38. Cf. Ellis, *His Excellency: George Washington*, 125–89; see also McCullough, *1776*.

39. McDonald, *NOS*, 260. See also Montesquieu, *Spirit of the Laws*. Good introductory discussions of Montesquieu and of the Founders' appropriation of Montesquieu are still to be found in the essays by David Lowenthal and Martin Diamond, respectively, in Strauss and Cropsey, *History of Political Philosophy*, 513–34, 659–79.

vision, in the belief that they were and are the heirs to and carriers of that vision in history. In the present day, however, and as MacIntyre has noted, there are rival, incompatible understandings of what that founding vision was, so that the question as to how Americans ought to understand and apply that vision cannot be reasonably raised without great difficulty. An example from recent history will illustrate the point.

In 1973, the Supreme Court of the United States decided that a state legislature's power to regulate conduct does not extend so far as to permit the state to impede a woman intent on terminating a pregnancy. Some at the time, and more in greater numbers in the decades to follow, believed that the question at stake was whether the law of the land protects children in the womb. More discerning observers considered and continue to consider that the question was rather whether a state legislature may, in a manner consistent with the federal Constitution, enact measures that treat unborn children as persons. This was and is a formulation closer to the crux of the matter. In any case, the Court reasoned that the silence of the Constitution regarding the question as to when, exactly, the onus of a gravid uterus becomes a human being, means that the Constitution treats the beginning of human life as a matter of individual opinion. The Court further reasoned that, since it is an established principle of Constitutional law and general legal theory that human positive law cannot force a person to be of one opinion or another, human positive law is accordingly powerless to prevent a person from acting on his or her opinion vis à vis when a new human life begins, even when acting on the opinion in question could directly result in the death of another human being.

At its most basic level, Justice Blackmun's opinion in the case of *Roe v. Wade*[40] established that the Constitutional order in the United States is one in which a state is powerless to impede a person bent on acting in a way that might bring about the death of a human being. The rationale for the decision is essentially that, since law has no power to force opinions on people, a woman is free to terminate her pregnancy, and a legislature is powerless to stop her.

Needless to say, not everyone agrees. Some people hold that, while it is true that no man-made law can compel a person's assent to a given opinion, yet a government must be able to regulate conduct in order to fulfill its duty to protect life; in a regime such as the American one, where the power to make law rests with an elected legislature, that legislature

40. 410 U.S. 113 (1973)

is not only competent, but duty-bound to enact laws based upon the informed consensus its members reach regarding opinable questions such
as the proper age to drink, the maximum permissible speed at which a
motor vehicle may move, and when human life begins. One may wonder
whether those who so consider the matter obey the state, not out of a
considered opinion of the justice of its law, but for some other reason.
Readily identifiable reasons for obeying the commands of the state are
fear of punishment, and desire to avoid an evil that is greater than the
one caused by disobedience. The teenager refrains from drinking in a
bar because he is afraid of the local policeman (and/or the barman, who
probably knows and will likely bring the teenager's transgression to the
attention of the teen's parents). The man on a lonely stretch of highway
keeps to (or close enough to) the established speed limit because he
somehow understands that capricious disobedience of the law corrodes
order in society. It is not easy to see, however, how reasons such as these
can account for the obedience of citizens who maintain the absolute
dignity of human life from conception to natural death, who make the
protection of innocent human life thusly understood to be the purpose of
all government, and hold that effectiveness in providing such protection
is a criterion of a state's legitimacy. To say that many Americans think this
way is not too controversial. It therefore becomes reasonable to doubt
whether such citizens as fit the above description actually consent to be
governed by a civil authority committed to the use of its power for the
protection of persons engaged in the organized destruction, on a massive
scale, of human life. If all those who claim the name of Americans hold
in the self-evident truth of the proposition that governments derive their
legitimacy from the consent of the governed, then the question as to what
constitutes consent and whether Americans as a whole are still committed to government thereby, presses itself upon the national consciousness
with a palpable urgency.

Though the question of consent arises in America, its pertinence is
not restricted to the American political community. Indeed, the founding generation of Americans was mindful of the universal import of the
events unfolding on the Eastern littoral of the Columbian continent, if
the words of one Founding Father are to be taken seriously:

> It has been frequently remarked, that it seems to have been re-
> served to the people of this country, by their conduct and exam-
> ple, to decide the important question, whether societies of men
> are really capable or not, of establishing good government from

reflection and choice, or whether they are forever destined to depend, for their political constitutions, on accident and force. If there be any truth in the remark, the crisis, at which we are arrived, may with propriety be regarded as the æra in which that decision is to be made; and a wrong election of the part we shall act, may, in this view, deserve to be considered as the general misfortune of mankind.[41]

The work to follow is the beginning of an attempt to recover the genius of those who first approved of the American experiment in governance as one worth pursuing, so that the reasons for approving of the structure of government they erected for themselves may once again become clear, and possibly defensible.

There have always been those who have found, and there are today many who find America—what it was at the beginning, what it is now, what it might become—indefensible, and there are reasons. If, however, the persons who held the equal creation of all men and the rights to life liberty and the pursuit of happiness to be self-evident, the persons who ordained and established the Constitution, were able at all to make such a declaration and establish an ordinance for the protection of their declared understanding of human being, then our judgment of them must be based, not on disagreements with the policy of one or another administration's exercise of America's constituted governing machinery, but on our understanding of what the founding generation of America understood itself to be doing. Only then will the other questions that may or may not arise under America be amenable to criticism—whether from America or philosophy. The single, over-riding question with which we are faced, then, is precisely that of what America represents, in light of the founding of the political community that takes its name from it.

41. Alexander Hamilton, James Madison, John Jay, the *Federalist* papers, #1. All page citations of the *Federalist* in this work refer to Ball, *Federalist with Letters of Brutus*. The cited passage is on 1. Henceforth, the practice shall be to give the number of the *Federalist* paper and the page cite to the Ball edition, e.g., *Federalist* #1, 1.

CHAPTER I

Pretexts of Declaration

The Crisis of Representation in America

REPRESENTATION IS THE BASIC problem of political science. In the thought of Eric Voegelin, political science names the general science of order, which emerges from critical reflection on the social life of human beings in history. The period in American history from 1763 to 1775, the period of the Stamp Act crisis and its aftermath, was one in which the crisis of British imperial order emerged in America precisely as a crisis of representation, and therefore as an adequate field for the study of order. In the task of establishing this thesis, the first order of business is to clarify the senses of representation, i.e., the ways in which representation occurs in human society.

The Senses of Representation in Voegelin

In two very dense chapters of *The New Science of Politics*—these present remarks give only their conceptual skeleton—Voegelin points out the two meanings of representation implicit in its elemental sense:[1] that a society "exists" by way of representation; that it only exists in an idea, so to speak, of order.

There is an important sense in which representation is the direction of social energy through political power structures. Organs of power (e.g. a king, a Parliament, a Congress, a Council) are erected over a society, in

1. "Representation and existence"; "Representation of truth".

26

order to harness the energies thereof and to bend them to some purpose, thus making a society active in history.

In this elemental sense, any social power structure, from a small, pre-historic tribal society to the Pharaonic order of ancient Egypt, from the Italian Republic to the constitutional regime in the U.S. State of Connecticut, is representative of the society, the energies of which it directs, precisely to the extent that it succeeds in directing the energies of the society. An elemental representative must command the habitual obedience of those over whom it is erected; the success with which an elemental representative commands habitual obedience is identical to the measure in which we may say of a government that it is constituted.

In the post-Machiavellian political paradigm, perfected by Hobbes,[2] to be in power means only to have force enough to command the obedience of a number of persons sufficient to accomplish, in a sufficient number of cases, the will of the person, whether a single natural person or a group of individuals acting as an artificial person,[3] who have taken or to whom is assigned responsibility for the direction of social energy.

Voegelin shows this elemental sense of representation to be unable on its own to help us in parsing the differences among types of regime. In the elemental sense, it is impossible adequately to distinguish, e.g., the representation secured by the elements of the United States from that secured by those of mainland Communist China. If it is to be critically useful, any distinction among, red China and the United States (e.g.) on the ground that the United States has "representative institutions," must

2. See Strauss, *Political Philosophy of Hobbes*. Also Voegelin, *NSP*, 212–38.

3. From Hobbes, *Leviathan* II.16 "Of Commonwealth": "This is the generation of that great LEVIATHAN, or rather, to speak more reverently, of that *Mortal God*, to which we owe under the *Immortal God*, our peace and defence. For by his Authority, given him by every particular man in the Common-Wealth, he hath the use of so much Power and Strength conferred on him, that by terror thereof, he is enabled to form the wills of them all, to Peace at home, and mutual aid against their enemies abroad. And in him consists the essence of Common-wealth; which (to define it,) is *One Person, of whose Acts a great Multitude, by mutual Covenants one with another, have made themselves every one the Author, to the end he may use the strength and means of them all, as he shall think expedient, for their Peace and Common Defence.* And he that carries this Person, is called SOVEREIGN, and said to have *Sovereign power*; and everyone besides, his SUBJECT.

"That attaining to this Sovereign Power, is by two ways. One, by Natural force…The other, is when men agree amongst themselves, to submit to some Man, or assembly of men, voluntarily, on confidence to be protected by him against all others." Hobbes, *Leviathan*, 119. I have modernized the spelling.

be claiming something more than will emerge from a mere rehearsal of the external characteristics of their governing machineries.[4]

Representing the Truth of Existence

A society is made of human beings who, by outward bodily signs, recognize themselves as belonging together; through habitual usage that becomes customary, bodily signs acquire the character of marks of fellowship; bodily signs thus become symbols, i.e., signs that effect the fellowship they represent.[5] By finding its representation, in customs and symbols as well as in the organs authorized to act and speak in the name of all, society finds its existence: it acquires what Voegelin calls a form for action in history.[6] Thus, the order of society is constituted for the purpose of providing for the subsistence of the society from generation to generation of its membership. In this regard, Voegelin speaks of the "articulation" of society, and points out that it is a process, by which societies come to be more or less articulated, with greater or lesser distances between and differences among the rulers and those who are ruled.

In medical parlance, "articulation" is the growth of a limb or an organ within an organism. This specialized jargon still occurs in everyday language, where there is talk about the "members" of society, as the different "parts" with a function or role into which society is articulated.[7]

While any number of interlocutors might disagree about what, exactly, society owes each member and what each member owes society, to be a member of society is in any case to stand in a certain relation with other members and with society as a whole. The process of "articulation" gradually transforms a society's self-understanding. Voegelin therefore uses the word to describe the process by which a society develops new organs; it is the process by which classes and then individuals become

---

4. Cf. Voegelin, *NSP*, 113–17. The general problem encompasses questions that the economy of the present project will not allow us to address. Two works by Prof. Paolo Savarese are extremely helpful in approaching and dealing with the general problem. See Savarese, *Il diritto nella relazione*; see also Savarese, *La possibilità nella regola*.

5. Think of Fourth of July barbecues and fireworks, of Thanksgiving dinner, of Opening Day and the October Classic. Think also of pledging allegiance and singing songs, of saying to a person for the first time, "Friend."

6. Voegelin, *NSP*, 116 *et passim*.

7. This evokes other times and places, from the old Hindu scriptures to Plato, in which political society is depicted as a *meganthropos*, a human being writ large. Cf. Plato, *Republic* 368d7–369a5.

representable units, i.e., members of society. In its articulation, then, a society represents its members' common understanding of human nature.

Convention and Nature in British America

When the members of a given society do come to understand themselves as responsible participants in the social effort, they begin to seek and demand recognition from the ruler of society, and often so as condition of their continued assent to (recognition of) the ruler's right to rule. Voegelin gives the example of the movement from the default language of absolute royal representation in England up to *Magna Charta*, through the later events of English constitutional history at the origins of what we call, *causa argumenti*, American order. It is worthwhile to mention at least the starting point of his discussion of that history.

Voegelin begins with a fragment of the *Magna Charta* in which Parliament is named, *commune consilium regni nostri*. He proceeds to analyze the history in which the Great Charter is symbologically intelligible. "In a first phase," writes Voegelin:

> [T]he king [of England] alone is the representative of the realm, and the sense of monopoly of representation is preserved [in the Charter] in the possessive pronoun attached to the symbol.[8]

There then proceeds a second, historically well-documented phase in which the various communes within the king's realm begin, "to articulate themselves to the point where they are capable of representing themselves for action." This second phase culminates in the articulation of the *baronagium*, one of the two principal parties to *Magna Charta*. "The weight of representation,"[9] however, would remain with the king in the centuries immediately to follow. This is evidenced by the fact that the articulated representatives remain possessions of the kings, whilst those persons, who are not included (yet) in the representative scheme are "of the realm" or city. Throughout the two centuries following *Magna Charta*, further, "Ordinary individual members of the society are plainly 'inhabitants' or 'fellow-citizens of the realm,'"[10] and, "[t]he symbol 'people' does

8. Voegelin, *NSP*, 38.

9. Ibid., 39.

10. Ibid. While king Edward I did summon to his Model Parliament 2 knights from each county, 2 burgesses from each borough and 2 citizens from each city, those names (borough and city, at least) were only then acquiring their political significance, and so largely as a result of their having been summoned to Parliament.

not appear as signifying a rank in representation."[11] Voegelin finds an apt discussion of the emergence of a politically significant sense of "people" in a text of Sir John Fortescue, whose discussion of the symbol Voegelin describes as an attempt to theorize the problem of articulation. In his *De laudibus legum Angliae*, Fortescue describes England as a *dominium politicum et regale*, and suggests that this *dominium*, a very specific form of *regnum* or realm, *ex populo erumpit*.[12]

Society's articulation down to the last individual human being makes society, in Voegelin's words,[13] representative of itself, which is to say each member of society stands in a relation of responsibility to every other member. It is worthwhile to note that Voegelin cites Abraham Lincoln as the person responsible for the differentiation of the language symbol that expresses this level of articulation:

> When articulation expands throughout society, the representative will also expand until the limit is reached where the membership of the society has become politically articulate down to the last individual and, correspondingly, the society becomes the representative of itself. Symbolically this limit is reached with the masterful, dialectical concentration of Lincoln's "government of the people, by the people, for the people." The symbol "people" in this formula means successively the articulated political society, its representative, and the membership that is bound by the acts of the representative. The unsurpassable fusion of democratic symbolism with theoretical content in this formula is the secret of its effectiveness. . . .[T]he transition to the dialectical limit presupposes an articulation of society down to the individual as a representable unit.[14]

11. Ibid.

12. Voegelin describes Fortescue as criticizing what he calls, "St. Augustine's definition of the people as the multitude associated through consent to a right order and a communion of interests." This is not Augustine's but Cicero's definition (and this fact is itself of considerable theoretical significance, though to pursue its implications is beyond the purview of this investigation, at least at this juncture). Cf. Cicero, *De re publica* I.xxv.39. The cited text is from Cicero, *De re publica. De legibus*, 64. Henceforth *DRP*. Page references for both *DRP* and *De legibus* are to the 1994 reprint.

13. Voegelin, *NSP*, 119. In Fortescue's formula, the people remains largely inarticulate in its individual membership. To answer the otherwise interesting scholarly question whether the lack of articulation is in Fortescue due to the historical character of his purposes or some theoretical deficiency on his part, is for our purposes unnecessary. Theoretically, it is only important to note that Fortescue finds the people to be the (albeit inchoate) source and end of political power.

14. Ibid., 119-20.

The common notion of what human being is, then, will be reflected in the structure, or order of society. When every member of society participates in the symbol of the human, the order of society can no longer be set above each member's existential requirements for life in it. That which is just is consonant with human nature, so that a society's attempt to guarantee justice to its members will itself constitute a claim, even if only an inchoate one, regarding human nature.

The question, "What is justice?" arises in society; the answer to the question consists in a claim about what is just for human beings, so that the questions, "What is justice?" and "What is a man?" are not really two questions, at all, but one question in two distinct moments.

Existential representation brought down to the last individual member of society does not exhaust all questions; it rather opens the question of how the individual human being should be conceived in his relation to society and to the knowledge passed from generation to generation of society. Whoever acts and speaks for all men, whether a few representative men or an everyman, claims to tell the truth about their common existence, about what can make their lives orderly in accordance with the order of the universe, or, if you like, the cosmos.[15]

Voegelin is concerned with the way in which representation of order occurs through the more-or-less elaborate symbolism of the all-encompassing *cosmos*, a symbolism in and through which a society has knowledge of itself and justification (or indictment) of its structure. These symbols, taken together, constitute a claim about how things are. In sum, the symbols through which the order of a society becomes intelligible to its members are meant to be true, so that the representation of order is the representation of a truth regarding the nature of things. At its most basic level, representation of order is representation of a truth claim, or simply, the representation of truth.

An example of such a differentiation, to which Voegelin dedicated one of the volumes of *Order and history*, is the breakthrough represented by the historical emergence of the Hebrew order, over and against the old

---

15. Different conceptions of truth divide one society from another, and sometimes even split a single society in two. One need only think of the great divide separating Byzantium and the Caliphate, or the divisions within revolutionary France, or those within America before the Civil War. European history, to the problems of which the symbol America attempts to reply and (to the extent possible) resolve, has in recent centuries been characterized by a struggle between those who would separate, on the one hand, and those who resist, on the other, the separation of Europe's present from its past.

order of the Pharaohs' Egypt. Hebrew order emerges in a specific historical moment: the Exodus. When the Hebrew tribes under the agency of
Moses go out of Egypt, Egypt's ruler sends his army to stop them. The
ruler of Egypt was Pharaoh, the manifestation of Ra, the Heavenly Lord.
Ra was chief among the heavenly bodies, and in charge of the maintenance of Order[16] in the world of the living. The God of Israel, YHWH,
intervenes to thwart the plans of Pharaoh, and He succeeds in doing so
by causing Pharaoh's army to be swallowed by the Red Sea. Thus, YHWH
is proclaimed *Adonai Sabaoth*, the LORD of Hosts, which is to say, the
lord who is above the order of the heavens. This example is not very far
away from America, given the fact that the Biblical record of that event
was exemplary in shaping the experience of the people coming to eastern
shores of the North American continent. The importance of this nearness
will become clear only in later moments of this work, especially in the
remarks between chapters three and four. At present, the reader is invited
to keep the story in mind, as the work progresses.

Opening Passes: The Great Seal and its Problems

The Great Seal of the United States of America bears two inscriptions
on its reverse.[17] The first, *annuit coeptis*, is recognition on the part of the
American Founding Fathers that the prayers of pilgrims have been answered. The second, *novus ordo seclorum*, is a bold pronouncement of
the New World's having come into its own. Each of the expressions is a
modified version of a Vergilian text;[18] both recall, in some wise, the working presence of providence; together, they constitute a claim regarding
the significance of the series of human events that was already in course
when the English Crown granted a Charter to the Virginia Company of

16. The Egyptian word is Ma'at or Maat. For a brief discussion of the concept, see
Hart, *Dictionary of Egyptian Gods and Goddesses*, 116.

17. Adopted by Congress on June 20, 1782: "Reverse. The pyramid signifies
Strength and Duration: The Eye over it & the Motto allude to the many signal interpo-
sitions of providence in favour of the American cause. The date underneath is that of
the Declaration of Independence and the words under it signify the beginning of the
New American Æra, which commences from that date." Charles Thomson, "Report
to Congress," June 20, 1782. From the *Congressional Record*, in *The Great Seal of the
United States*, U.S. Department of State Handbook, Septempter 1996, Appendix C.

18. Cf. Vergil, *Aeneid* IX.625: *Iuppiter omnipotens audacibus adnue coeptis*; cf.
Idem, *Eclogues* IV.5: *magnus ab integro saeclorum nascitur ordo*.

London in June, 1606 and did not end with continental victory at York-town in October, 1781.

In recalling the favorable judgment of Divine Providence on their undertakings, the symbol recalls contemporaneously the events that manifest the favorable judgment. In claiming a providential intelligence at work in those events, the Great Seal is recalling an intelligible structure of the peculiar experience of those who recognize themselves in the symbol under our consideration. In short, the Great Seal is an historical symbol.

The Great Seal itself represents the new order of civil society that emerged on the eastern littoral of the North American continent in the second half of the eighteenth century, so that those who recognize themselves in the seal are able to do so by virtue of their participation in the order it represents. The society of those who recognize themselves in the seal is, in its turn, represented by a government that is responsible to the people within the scope of its power and representative of the people to themselves and to the world, at large. In sum, the Great Seal is a political symbol.

Politics and History

In representing the political, the Great Seal recalls a series of events that constitute an history, which is, under the Seal, or rather, in the order and the government[19] erected for the tutelage thereof, and of the participants therein, which the Seal represents, the history of a people; so in the particular symbol presently under our consideration, history and politics coincide in an acknowledgement of the manifest presence of the Divine in His providential works. This, at any rate, is the claim advanced by a particular group of human beings in a peculiar moment of a series of events that that group claimed (claims?) as its very own story. If this state of things will admit generalization—this is what this work is after—then something that might for various reasons come to be called or receive the name "America" is an instance of the following generalization: the political presupposes history, and history has the political as its own mode of interpretation (at least).

---

19. "The seal heretofore used by the United States in Congress assembled shall be the seal of the United States." 4 *USC* 41 (15th Sept., 1789).

The employment of such language in the exposition of a political symbol ought not, in any case, come as a surprise. Indeed, Voegelin explicitly acknowledged the root of his conviction regarding the need for a recovery of political science to be in his experience of 20th century politics, an experience that included persecution at the hands of the Nazis, as well as refuge and citizenship in the United States;[20] at the midway point of the last century he thus formulated the problem:

> The existence of man in political society is historical existence; and a theory of politics, if it penetrates to principles, must at the same time be a theory of history.[21]

That is to say: the question of how justly to order the lives of men and women, of human persons, cannot be resolved without reference to the historical circumstances of the human society in which and for the members of which the problem of representation arises. The balance of *The New Science of Politics* is an outline of Voegelin's program for the recovery of political science as enunciated in the lines above. The need for such a recovery of political science is itself an enormous question, running through the whole of Voegelin's work, from his early studies in jurisprudence to his unfinished project of *Order and History*, which occupied the last thirty years of his life.

At a very early point in his consideration of the question, Voegelin's work turned from a "political science" of which Machiavelli[22] is the putative father, to embrace a thorough investigation of how the very question of science arose and became a constitutive element of a cultural and (therefore) intellectual tradition, which recognized the question of science as one inherently and essentially and inseparably related to the experience of the enunciation of laws as the necessary determination of the just way for human beings to live together.[23]

The Great Seal of the United States declares a *novus ordo saeclorum*, co-eval with the independence of American society. It is no longer clear (if ever it was), however, what social order the Great Seal represents,

20. Voegelin, *Autobiographical Reflections*, vol. 32 of *CW* (Columbia: Univ. of Missouri Press, 1999). See esp. p. 93: "The motivations of my work are simple, they arise from the political situation."

21. Cf. Voegelin, *NSP*, 88.

22. Viz. "modern" political science. For the history of modern political science as beginning with Machiavelli, see the "Machiavelli" essay in Strauss and Cropsey eds., *A History of Political Philosophy*, 296–317.

23. Cf. Cooper, *Eric Voegelin and the Foundations of Modern Political Science*, 65.

because the proper order of American society is not immediately apparent, even to those who claim to participate in that society as its present constituents. This "opacity of order"[24] suggests that the ability of contemporary political reality effectively to interpret itself is rather attenuated, so that the order of society is not, or no longer, readily available to society's participants. This is to say that there is general social disorder, or the constant threat of it; that this threat of disorder is characteristic of societies affected by the growth of modernity; this is, in turn, a further obstacle to the recovery of political science.[25]

The one encouraging aspect of the present crisis of order in American society, is that there is still a general attachment to the notion that there exists an idea that guides and has guided the society of human beings organized under the representative organs called states and united in the political union called the United States. As the full style of the union explicitly states, the name of the guiding idea is, "America." The Great seal, by representing the government of the United States, also symbolizes, though in a mediate way, the conceptual space called America.

On this reading, America names an experience that makes a difference. To name is to speak in a certain way about a certain object under certain circumstances. To name is to do something with words.[26] Other activities plainly at issue in the present investigation amount to nothing more (and nothing less) than doing things with words, e.g. declaring independence and saying what the law is. These are the classical problems of politics (or the *loci* of them); they also name some of the normal, everyday employments of language.

24. Voegelin, *NSP*, 89.

25. To be modern is to be *mox hodie*, "just today", which is to say without history, so that modernity itself is constituted by a rejection of the very idea that the human mind can penetrate to principles of order; at its most extreme, modernity denies that there are such principles. "[T]he very historicity of human existence," which Voegelin describes as, "the unfolding of the typical in meaningful concreteness," makes "a valid reformulation of principles" impossible if such a reformulation is attempted by means of a return to the contents of previous political theory; much is to be learned, however, "from the earlier philosophers concerning the range of problems," interesting to the political theorist as such, "as well as concerning their theoretical treatment. Cf. *NSP*, 89.

26. Cf. Austin, *How to Do Things with Words*, 5 *et passim*. Austin's essay is considered the *locus classicus* for the founding statement of "Ordinary Language" philosophy. The present appeal to that philosophy assumes an inherent connection between its own method of philosophical practice and that of Aristotelian political theorizing, in that each is an attempt to clarify the ways in which language is used by real people in everyday circumstances. Cf. also Voegelin, *NSP*, 109–12.

Take, for example, the word, "order". The term occurs daily, in manifold contexts, with myriad significances. A few examples were in order: one might order a cup of coffee, or get money from the bank, in order to do the grocery shopping, or put one's papers in order; an orderly might bring coffee to a doctor or an officer in the military; a mathematician might be charged with the discovery of the order of a sequence; a teacher might explain ordinal numbers to her class. In fine, all of the aforementioned activities are quite ordinary. That each of the activities named above is ordinary is itself surprising and even bewildering, upon reflection; to stop so long as to think about what all those ordinary activities might have in common, is to occasion wonderment.

Returning to the Seal

The Great Seal of the United States is not an existential representative. It is a symbol of the government of the United States, the elementally representative structure responsible for the existential representation of the people of the United States. The question is not simply whether the United States of America represents an idea of man, i.e., whether it is a man writ large; the question is rather, "What is the truth represented by the United States of America?" A question of this type raises a series of further ones. The series of questions regarding the United States of America must be made to emerge, however, from reflections on the concrete situation of American humanity. Reflection on the concrete situation of American humanity requires, indeed consists in the consideration of those symbols, which order daily life in the United States.

The claim of the Great Seal is in essence that the word, "America" names the experience of a difference from which the need for a new theoretical formulation of the questions of man and society becomes apparent. America, in other words, is the name of a peculiar logic, where logic here most especially denotes the presence of a peculiar narrative, in which new modes of human life on the North American Continent are ordered.[27] For anyone interested in understanding America, the question would therefore be, "How were they ordered?"

---

27. This language is plausibly Machiavellian. J. G. A. Pocock has explored the founding as a "Machiavellian Moment". Though the Founders did read extensively and un-squeamishly in Machiavelli, Pocock's reading remains partial, though extremely useful. See Pocock, *Machiavellian Moment*.

Toward the Crisis of Colonial Order

One immediate consequence of Voegelin's articulation of the basic problem is that the political and the historical will interpret one another in reality, illuminating each other and informing one another in a process of development and refinement of the whole civil and civilizational symbology, as this occurs in reality. The significance of this basic fact is that critical science shall not ever be able to say something about the one without its diction's bearing also and equally and simultaneously on the other.

The American Theory of Representation: Historical Notes

In the American case, the theoretically pertinent problem of representation emerged historically as a dispute over which of two competing constitutional orders was to be the sole legitimate representative of American society. Any claim to represent American society needed to recognize and protect effectively (or at least have some reasonable chance of effectively protecting) the social relations among individuals into which American society was articulate. In other words, the crisis of representation in America occurs when Americans recognize that an adequate representative of articulate American society must represent the terms of American social articulation. The problem of representation, however, is not merely that of deciding who or what is to represent whom and for how long and in what things, but is the question of representation's very own constitution, i.e., what representation is, and what becomes of it when society comes to be articulate down to the individual.

The problem is complicated by at least one important historical fact, namely: that "American society" is, at least at first glance, something of an abstraction. The basic political structure in America at the time of the revolution was the state (sometimes the township within the state).[28] It was through the correspondence among townships within the individual states regarding the British threat to local governance, and the correspondence among the states themselves regarding the same, that the first awareness of a common American problem possibly requiring a common American response grew. Historians have made great strides toward reconstructing the nuts and bolts, as it were, of this particular phase

28. Cf. McDonald, *NOS*, 143–50.

in history, and the magisterial works are well known.[29] Following John Fiske,[30] Forrest McDonald calls the period from 1783 to 1789 "the critical period" in American history. Fiske characterized the years between the conclusion of peace and the ratification of the Constitution as critical in response to Thomas Paine's premature proclamation of the end to crisis in America following the Versailles Treaty. Both McDonald (Fiske) and Paine have incomplete visions of the American crisis. The twelve years beginning in 1763 and ending with the Olive Branch Petition saw the beginning of the "critical period" in colonial history, and as such, comprehend the first articulate phase in the crisis of America, which was and is a crisis of representation.[31]

The Crisis of Representation:
The Stamp Act Crisis

The document in which American colonists began to differentiate a distinctly American area of representation, was the Declaration of Rights and Grievances drawn at the Stamp Act Congress, held in October of 1765 at New York City. The Congress was the first concerted action of a

---

29. In our discussion, we shall rely primarily on the work of Forrest McDonald. The reason for this decision is twofold: firstly, the facts of history that are pertinent to our theoretical discussion are generally known, so that reconstruction or recapitulation of scholarly investigation and debate is largely unnecessary; McDonald's narrative style and critical acumen are such that he approaches, as far as it is possible to approach from within the discipline of history, the theoretical problems associated with a critical clarification of the problem of representation in history.

30. John Fiske (1842–1901) was a Darwinian-Spencerian in biology and sociology, who sought to show how religion (as he understood it) and science (as he understood it) are already perfectly harmonious and therefore in no need of reconciliation. Fiske was also a prolific writer of historical works, including a *fin de siècle* history of the years intervening the conclusion of peace at Versailles and the ratification of the constitution. Fiske chose "The Critical Period" as the title of that work, on the basis of his estimation that Thomas Paine's suspension of *Crisis* on the grounds that, "The times that try men's souls are over," was mistaken, and that the years from 1783 to 1789 were at least as important for the history of America as were the years of the revolution's military contest. Cf. Fiske, *Critical Period of American History, 1783–1789*, viii *et passim*.

31. More recently, in his volume on the revolution for the Oxford History of the United States series, Robert Middelkauff recognized the revolutionary period as beginning in 1763 and ending in 1789, with the ratification of the new federal Constitution. Originally published in 1982, MiddelKauff's history has recently appeared in a new, revised and expanded edition (2005).

majority of colonies.[32] That document[33] contained a theoretically significant series of declarations, first among which was:

> That His Majesty's subjects in these colonies owe the same al-
> legiance to the crown of Great Britain that is owing from his
> subjects born within the realm, and all due subordination to
> that august body, the Parliament of Great Britain.

Regarding their relation to the crown, then, the colonists assert their articulation into representable units. Further, by acknowledging the debt
of all *due* subordination to the Parliament of Great Britain, they raise
the question as to what subordination, precisely, is due the Parliament
on the part of *colonists*. It is also important to note that in the second
declaration, the colonists assert their enjoyment of rights as subjects of
the crown, owing to their participation in the political life of the colonies.

In point of fact, they are already separate from the political life of
the state of England, though they enjoy some, at least, of the same rights
as the king's subjects in the mother country:

> That His Majesty's liege subjects in these colonies are entitled to
> all the inherent rights and privileges of his natural born subjects
> within the kingdom of Great Britain.

The third, fourth, fifth and sixth declarations claim rights regarding the
tutelage and disposal of property, specifically regarding the power to tax.
The third declaration contains a further, theoretically pertinent assertion:

> That it is inseparably essential to the freedom of a people, and
> the undoubted rights of Englishmen, that no taxes should be
> imposed on them, but with their own consent, given personally,
> or by their representatives.

Two things emerge from this declaration. The first: to declare as inseparably essential to the freedom of a people, that no taxes should be imposed,
but with the people's consent, is an important step toward theoretical

32. Only nine of the thirteen colonies elected to accept the invitation of Massachusetts to discuss the Parliament of Great Britain's "supposed acts of legislature." New
Hampshire, Virginia, North Carolina and Georgia sent no delegates. Delegates from
Connecticut, New York and South Carolina were not authorized to act as attorneys
for their respective colonies (i.e., they were not empowered by their colonies to sign
eventual documents issuing form the proceedings.)

33. Thoroughly reliable texts of the Declaration of Rights and Grievances are
widely available, both in print and in electronic versions. I am quoting from the text as
it appears in Angle, *By These Words*, 38–42.

generalization and the first sign of the existence in America of a way of thinking about the general problems of governance that, while rooted in the English tradition, is distinctly American; the second thing to emerge is that the colonists claim not only those rights and privileges, which are common to all the subjects within the kingdom of Great Britain, but also and specifically the rights of Englishmen. The fourth through sixth declarations[34] specify the English traditions of governance in which the American claims are rooted:

> That the people of these colonies are not, and from their local circumstances cannot be, represented in the House of Commons in Great Britain.
>
> That the only representatives of the people of these colonies are persons chosen therein, by themselves; and that no taxes ever have been or can be constitutionally imposed on them but by their respective legislatures.
>
> That all supplies to the crown, being free gifts of the people, it is unreasonable and inconsistent with the principles and spirit of the British constitution for the people of Great Britain to grant to His Majesty the property of the colonists.

Anyone who knows anything at all about the American Revolution is aware that the British Americans were roused to indignation regarding certain exercises of Parliamentary power, which they considered improper: specifically, the power to tax. "No taxation without representation!" was the slogan on Americans' lips. In British North America from 1765,[35] forward, it was a maxim of the American colonial resistance to Parliament.

In the English tradition, taxation was a free gift of the people to the public coffers, rather than a requirement of the government upon the people.[36] Practically, the working of government required frequent gifts

---

34. The ninth through twelfth declarations give reasons of prudence, rooted in legal principle, for the speedy repeal of the Stamp Act. A close reading of them is not immediately necessary, and therefore omitted for reasons of economy.

35. The year of the Stamp Act crisis.

36. Cf. McDonald, *NOS*, 24–28. The power of lay taxation effectively passed from the king to Parliament in 1362, when by statute it was established that Parliament must assent to all taxation. In 1407, Henry IV acknowledged that lay taxation must initiate in the Commons (the current Constitution of the United States provides that money bills must originate in the House of Representatives).

of a sum commensurate with the necessities of governing. Appropriate sums were determined by the people's representatives in Parliament.[37]

Properly understood, therefore, the famous American maxim, "No taxation without representation!", was not a claim to the effect that government cannot take from citizens unless those citizens be adequately represented. Rather, "No taxation without representation!" meant that, unless citizens are represented adequately, then government cannot tax them, but only take from them. Add to this certain facts of English constitutional law, to wit: government has no power, no authority to take property from law-abiding subjects (unless under the law of eminent domain, which provides for just compensation); government may compel property from subject peoples. Take these together, as they were given to the British Americans by custom, combine them with the English Parliament's acts at the end of the 7 Years' War, which, without respect to the question of their legitimacy, directly challenged and indeed tended entirely to vacate nearly a century of uninterrupted political usage in British America, and the sum of it all is a socio-political crisis of the first order.

There is a further aspect to the socio-political crisis that began to emerge in the Stamp Act, addressed in the seventh and eighth declarations, which regard the right to trial by jury. The right to trial by jury, previously enjoyed by the colonists and protected in the colonial courts, had been seriously curtailed, first by the Proclamation of 1763, and later by the Sugar Act and the Stamp Act. These acts of Parliament took the power to try cases of supposed violation of the aforementioned acts out of the hands of the civil courts, and handed power to try such cases to the Courts of Admiralty. This irked the colonists for a series of reasons, starting with the often far-removed venues for trials at Admiralty.[38] The procedural rules in trials at Admiralty were quite different and much more favorable to the prosecution. There was no general right to counsel, and the rules of evidence were not designed to facilitate defense. Most irksome to the colonists, however, was that trials at Admiralty were bench trials: there was no jury to decide the facts of the case.[39] The colonists protested:

37. Ibid., 25.

38. England's maritime courts sat in several different places throughout British North America. Often, a person accused in New York would stand trial in Nova Scotia or even England.

39. Cf. Bodenhamer, *Fair Trial*, 33–46. The book is a readable overview of the state of British law in the late eighteenth century, and offers a picture of colonists' reaction to Parliamentary provisions regarding their rights.

That trial by jury is the inherent and invaluable right of every British subject in these colonies.

8th. That the late act of Parliament entitled, "An act for granting and applying certain stamp duties, and other duties in the British colonies and plantations in America, etc.," by imposing taxes on the inhabitants of these colonies, and the said act, and several other acts, by extending the jurisdiction of the courts of admiralty beyond its ancient limits, have a manifest tendency to subvert the rights and liberties of the colonists.

Already in the 1760s then, the right to jury trial inhered by ancient usage in the subject of the crown. The specific way in which the extension of Admiralty jurisdiction had a manifest tendency to subvert the rights and liberties of the colonists is rooted in the same ancient reasons for the institution of jury trials.

The history of the right to trial by jury was already long and complex by 1764, and its details are beyond the scope of this study. Suffice it to say that at the time of the Stamp Act crisis, the role of the jury in criminal proceedings was generally understood, both in the colonies and in Great Britain, as a safeguard against the tyrannical exercise of powers proper to the state. A subject was to be tried by a jury of peers.[40] The Braintree, Mass. lawyer, John Adams had the following to say:

[T]he most grievous innovation of all, is the alarming extension of the Courts of admiralty. In these courts, one judge presides alone! No juries have any concern there! The law and the fact are both to be decided by the same single judge, whose commission is only during pleasure, and with whom, as we are told, the most mischievous of all customs has become established, that of taking commissions on all condemnations; so that he is under a pecuniary temptation always against the subject. . .What can be wanting, after this, but a weak and wicked man for a judge, to render us the most sordid and forlorn of slaves![41]

The jury's purpose was and is to act as a bulwark against the improper exercise of the state's power. The colonists' jealousy of their right to trial by jury was rooted in their understanding of the terms of their relation to the

40. For a survey of the development of the jury system within the broader context of English constitutional and legal history, see Smith, *A Constitutional and Legal History of England*, 1955.

41. John Adams, "Instructions of the Town of Braintree to their Representative, 1765" in Diggins, *Portable John Adams*, 229–30.

royal power.[42] The colonists' understanding of their relation to the crown is key to understanding the emergence of American self-consciousness.

Representation and Rights: The Individual Case

The colonists understood their relation to the crown at once corporately and individually: they understood the colonies to be incorporated in the British Empire; at the same time, each colonist claimed and understood himself to be an English subject of the British Crown. To be an individual person subject to the king of England is not simply to be under his power, but to be in a sort of relation from which flow certain privileges and to which are attributed by king and subject alike, certain duties according to the proper station of each and in whom inhere particular characteristics called "rights" and "liberties" by those who enjoy them.

Such a state of affairs did not always obtain between ruler and ruled in England. The state we have described, which did at any rate obtain in 1765, was rather the result of a process of articulation. In British America, a separate process of articulation was underway, though it took the Stamp Act crisis of 1765 to make the American colonists even dimly aware of it.

By 1763,[43] in addition to the symbolic representation of all British in the person of the king, the articulate members of English society enjoyed existential representation in one of the two Houses of Parliament. Parliament claimed, further, to represent also the colonists of North America, and it is at this point that the first difficulties began to arise. Colonists elected no Member of Parliament, directly or otherwise. This fact, on its own, was not particularly troubling to colonists, whose local councils and colonial legislatures effectively provided them with representation of a kind analogous to that provided by Parliament to the articulate members of English society, i.e., existential representation in the Voegelinian sense. In short, colonists provided for their own existential representation through the colonial legislatures. What is more, colonial legislatures sat and conducted their business in the presence of the king's responsible minister. The crisis of representation in America occurs when the articulate representative of one society, i.e., the English King-in-Parliament,

---

42. Cf. ibid., 228–31.

43. The year in which the 7 Years' War ended.

makes existential claims on a society that has already erected existential representatives.

Existential Representation
in British America

The claim of the King-in-Parliament hinged on the reduction of Americans' rights to representation in the king (whose office was the symbol of the unity of the Empire) and in the body of Parliament. The British essentially claimed that American colonials were represented existentially in Parliament. The American colonists responded that indirect representation is not necessarily effective existential representation, and that representation under a symbol of order (i.e., the King-in-Parliament) was no existential representation, at all. Existential representation was adequately provided only by the colonial legislatures. The claim of the King-in-Parliament to represent colonials, not only in their membership in the British order of empire under the crown, but also existentially, through the Parliament, could not but have failed, because it was an argument directly repugnant to English law, itself.

Either the American legislatures were illegitimate, or the supposed authority of Parliament to tax British America did not exist. Parliament claimed "virtually" to represent all subjects in America, so the American self-understanding that began to emerge during that political struggle was rooted in Americans' discovery of the inadequacy of the Parliament's claim to represent them, or, if you will, the inadequacy of the representation that the Parliament of Great Britain provided. The American colonists, therefore, came to understand that the king in Parliament considered the colonists to be so many subject peoples, whose goods and labor were, in principle, forfeit to the Imperial authority. This understanding was at odds with colonists' self-understanding. At issue then, was precisely what constituted adequate representation according to the customs and political practice of the colonists.

This is as close to an explicit formulation of the question, "What is representation?" as anyone is like to find. The question of representation is one that does not emerge from abstract and isolated theoretical reflections, but from colonists' acute awareness of and close attention to the concrete circumstances of life in colonial society, especially to colonial modes of organization as these were rooted in and therefore outgrowths of the older English tradition.

Further Development of American Self-Consciousness

The lawyer, farmer and congressman, John Adams of Braintree in Massachusetts, and the lawyer, a planter and burgess of Albemarle County in Virginia, Thomas Jefferson, each offered a developed statement of the colonists' self-understanding. The first source is Jefferson's *Summary View of the Rights of British America*, which Jefferson wrote while on his way to a session of the Virginia House of Burgesses, called to discuss Parliament's punitive legislation against the city of Boston and all Massachusetts for the act of resistance now known famously as the Boston Tea Party. More generally, though, the colonies were organizing resistance to the notion, which the British Parliament had put forth at the time of the Stamp Act's repeal in 1765, that Parliament had the power to legislate for the colonies in all cases, whatsoever.[44] As Jefferson explained, the purpose of his *Summary View* was:

> To represent to his majesty that these his states have often individually made humble application to his imperial throne to obtain, through his intervention, some redress of their injured rights, to none of which was ever an answer condescended; humbly to hope that this their joint address, penned in the language of truth, and divested of those expressions of servility which would persuade his majesty that we are asking favours, and not rights, shall obtain from his majesty a more respectful acceptance. And this his majesty will think we have reason to expect when he reflects that he is no more than the chief officer of the people, appointed by the laws, and circumscribed with definite powers, to assist in working the great machine of government, erected for their use, and consequently subject to their superintendence.[45]

The first thing to emerge from this passage is its description of the colonies as "states", a juridical and political term that, in 1774, at least strongly

---

44. Cf. Jefferson, *Summary View of the Rights of British America*, ix–xiii. The *Summary View*, which argues the diametrically opposite case, was published without Jefferson's permission, first at Williamsburg and then at Philadelphia.

45. Ibid., 5–6 (spelling modernized).

suggested, even if it did not imply or entail internal autonomy. When the time comes to consider the debate over ratification of the proposed constitution in 1787, the importance of this consideration will achieve a greater measure of relief, for then it will be coupled with the apparently novel notion of "divided sovereignty" or, *imperium in imperio*. In light of these present considerations, it shall be possible then to see (especially in chapter 3, with Forrest McDonald, when we explore the Constitution) that the doctrine of *imperium in imperio* is really rooted in, and in conformity with colonial experience—or rather in and with an important interpretation thereof. Of more immediate importance, however, is the following consideration: in this passage, Jefferson is not engaging in political theory; he is giving the king a lecture in English constitutional government. The circumscription of the powers of the imperial throne, once again, is constitutionally effected by the existential representative of the English, i.e., by Parliament, without whose approval the king may make no law.[46] In America, the American legislatures effect the circumscription—or so the argument runs. For this reason, Jefferson, recalling but one of the episodes in what he would call, two years later, a, "long history of usurpations," laments that:

> [B]y an assumed right of the crown alone [the lands rightfully held by American colonists] were [given over to the favorites of the crown, who were] erected into distinct and independent governments [independent of the colonists over whom they ruled]; a measure which it is believed his majesty's prudence and understanding would prevent him from imitating at this day, as no exercise of such a power, of dividing and dismembering a country, has ever occurred in his majesty's realm of England, though now of very ancient standing; nor could it be justified or acquiesced under there, or in any other part of his majesty's empire.[47]

The erection of such puppet governments in the colonies, whether by act of the crown alone, or by the King-in-Parliament, should have been unconstitutional; the king had no constitutional authority to act by exclusive royal *fiat*. As Jefferson himself would argue later on in his *Summary*

---

46. "[T]he written laws of the kingdom. . .are statutes, acts or edicts, made by the king's majesty by and with the advice and consent of the lords spiritual and temporal and commons in parliament assembled." Blackstone, *Commentaries on the Laws of England*, 85.

47. Jefferson, *Summary View*, 8.

View, "The true ground on which we declare these acts void is, that the British Parliament has no right to exercise authority over us." The reason, once again, for which the British Parliament has no such right, no such power, no such authority, no such competence, is to be found in the fact that the British Parliament did not at that time, nor had it at any other time, represented existentially the British subjects in America. Jefferson's argument is essentially the following: Parliament, while representing existentially the People of England and participating in the English political symbol of order, "King-in-Parliament", was not and could not be the adequate existential representative of the British subjects in America.

As a matter of fact, there were, and had been in many of the colonies for more than a century, colonial legislatures. Considering the king as the representative of the unity of the empire, present to those legislatures in the person of a responsible minister (usually a colonial governor), Jefferson argued that the sole legislative authority in any colony rested in the king-with-legislature:

> One free and independent legislature. . .takes upon itself to suspend the powers of another, free and independent as itself; thus exhibiting a phoenomenon [*sic*] unknown in nature, the creator and creature of its own power. . .Shall these governments be dissolved, their property annihilated, and their people reduced to a state of nature, at the imperious breath of a body of men, whom they never saw, in whom they never confided, and over whom they have no powers of punishment or removal, let their crimes be ever so great?...[W]e do earnestly entreat his majesty, as yet the only mediatory power between the several states of the British empire, to recommend to his parliament [*sic*] of Great Britain the total revocation of these acts. . .By the constitution of Great Britain, as well as of the several American states, his majesty possesses the power of refusing to pass into law any bill which has already passed the other two branches of legislature.

Jefferson urged the king to exercise his constitutional veto power, in order to correct Parliament's unconstitutional exuberance. According to Jefferson, the American colonies of Britain were, if not from the very beginning, at least owing to circumstances retreating into the dim past of British America, free and independent states, tied to the British Empire by their voluntary subjection of themselves to the person of the king, whose sole person was the representative of imperial unity. The subordination due the Parliament is, according to Jefferson, nil. In light of the

1765 Declaration of Rights and Grievances, in which the colonists recognized themselves as owing all due subordination to the British Parliament, this claim will itself appear as a change in American understanding
of the colonies' standing vis-à-vis Great Britain, and at least possibly as a
further development of American consciousness.

Jefferson was, however, somewhat disingenuous in urging the king
to exercise his veto power. The royal veto power, a definite legislative
power proper to the king's office as that office was constitutionally defined in 1774, was a power that no king of England had used for nearly
70 years.[48] The general understanding was that the king would no longer
veto any law Parliament proposed for England or the general governance
of Great Britain. Jefferson, therefore, in asking the king to employ the
veto in favor of American rights as British subjects, was essentially committing a not-too-subtle *petitio principii*. The question-begging consisted
in the following: Jefferson assumed that the king's employment of the
veto in favor of British America would not violate the settlement because
the law that his veto would abrogate should never have been passed on
the pretense of its being a law of England; this assumes, however, both
the historical accuracy of Jefferson's claims of fact and the constitutional
legitimacy of the colonial legislatures; these were the very things at issue
in the dispute. The king could not employ his veto without committing
a constitutional act reducing doubly, with but one stroke, the legislative
power of Parliament. Given the diffuse, if not general idea that there was
in fact a royal desire issuing forth in a tendency to reduce the subjects
of the Crown, everywhere, to slavery;[49] given the king's desire not to an-
tagonize Parliament, on whose good grace he had come to depend for the
finance of his foreign policy (read: wars); the king was not about to employ his veto over a sorely needed money bill for enforcement of which
Parliament had not even provided explicit funding and that required a
negligible portion of American colonists' income in order to cover, in

48. The case was that of the Scottish Militia Bill, 1708, vetoed by Queen Anne,
who doubted that the militia would have been loyal. Wilfrid Prest has argued that the
veto became largely unnecessary, due to the effective ministerial management of tension between the crown and parliament. Cf. Prest, *Albion Ascendant*, 131–33. It could
equally be urged that the ministerial management of tensions was the happy response
of human genius to political necessity, created by the establishment of parliamentary
supremacy. Whether out of principled deference to the terms of the settlement, or
prudent desire not to upset the political balance of constitutional powers, George III
would not exercise the veto to protect the interests of his subjects in America.

49. Cf. Bailyn, "Central Themes of the American Revolution," 12 *et passim*.

part, the costs of a war prosecuted in order to preserve British supremacy in North America, upon the supremacy of which the protection of colonists' liberties supposedly depended.

The extent to which Jefferson was aware of the intricacies of English politics in 1774 is uncertain and debatable. What is certain is that Jefferson came as close as anyone else, with the exception of John Adams, to articulating both the American question as essentially one of authority in America, as well as the impossibility of a constitutionally unproblematic solution to the American question (by explicating for his Majesty's grace the political tangle that the only possible remedial action would necessarily create).[50]

Science and Nature:
Understanding and Domination

Beyond its usefulness in illustrating the American understanding of the constitutional crisis in the Empire in the years following the Seven Years' War, this passage from Jefferson also contains a pertinent instance of the American *forma mentis*. When Jefferson says that Parliament's supposed legislation for the colonies exhibits, "A phenomenon unknown in nature," he is suggesting that Parliament's supposed act of legislature is illegitimate *insofar as it is manifestly contrary to the natural order*. This is not only to say that government is naturally limited in the scope of its power. It means that in America, the power to make laws inheres in the natural order of things, so that the human power to make laws is essentially the power, hence the responsibility, to explain and express the order of relations inherent in the members of society, which exists as an integral part of an ordered universe. Two years later, Jefferson would write:

> When in the course of human events it becomes necessary for one people to dissolve the political bands which have connected them with another, and to assume among the Powers of the earth, the separate and equal station to which the Laws of Nature and of Nature's God entitle them, a decent respect for the opinions of mankind requires that they should declare the causes which impel them to that separation.

50. Pauline Maier makes substantially the same point in her rightly renowned study of the Declaration. Cf. Maier, *American Scripture*, 21–23.

One excellent commentator on the rhetorical structure and contents of the Declaration, Stephen E. Lucas, seizes upon the term, "necessary," in order to alert the reader to a particular intellectual tendency that was quite strong and growing ever stronger in the second half of the eighteenth Century. That tendency, a defining characteristic of the American intellectual climate, was one of wide reading in all the sciences, on the part of all learned men. Their wide reading in all the sciences lent itself to a greater deal of intercourse and inter-play among developing and not yet crystallized scientific vocabularies. "Necessary," for example, had certain connotations in physical science, connotations that would have been immediately present to the educated reader, and that are largely either absent or only present to the contemporary reader upon reflection.[51]

The meaning of "nature" was likewise in flux at the end of the eighteenth century. In Aristotelian-Ptolemaic physics, the object of inquiry was movement in general, understood as change of any kind. With Galileo and Newton, however, the study of physics had begun to confine itself to the study of the local motion of material bodies With Galileo first, and then with Newton, there occurred a differentiation of the object of "natural philosophy" or "physics", accompanied by a change in method. While physics had once been the study of all kinds of change, e.g. the movement of the stars and also the orientation of souls toward ends, the science eventually came to be the study of the local motion of bodies. This methodological change had taken place by 1776. Nevertheless, the old habit of considering *ta physika* as bearing on *ta politika* was not yet completely undone.

Thus, when Jefferson appealed to the "Laws of Nature and of Nature's God," in a political tract, he was speaking in the political idiom of his day and simultaneously recalling that older tradition and recognizing its ordering, harmonizing presence in the conceptual space he was at once constructing and interpreting in the Declaration itself. If a claim for the presence of such a theoretically ambitious project seems rather far-fetched, remember that Jefferson, when asked about his ideas as they are found expressed in the Declaration, denied that the ideas therein expressed should be considered properly his, at all:

---

51. Cf. Lucas, "Justifying America," 75–76. One might wonder whether Jefferson was conscious of this tendency, and whether he was deliberately playing on it. The point is that the tendency was there: Lucas's assessment of the sensibilities of Jefferson's audience is at least plausible.

> Neither aiming at originality of principle or sentiment, nor yet
> copied from any particular and previous writing, it was intended
> to be an expression of the American mind, and to give to that
> expression the proper tone and spirit called for by the occasion.
> All its authority rests then on the harmonizing sentiments of
> the day, whether expressed in conversation, in letters, printed
> essays, or in the elementary books of public right, as Aristotle,
> Cicero, Locke, Sidney, etc.[52]

A list containing the whole canon of revolutionary and pre-revolutionary
"Books of public right," would run to considerable length, and cannot be
attempted here. The first important thing to note is that there was such
a canon. The public man in America was expected to be conversant in
several subjects, and to know at least a few of several books relating to
each subject. The second half of the eighteenth century was *epoch d'or* for
pamphleteering. Jefferson's appeal to the ready availability of newspapers
and pamphlets is testament to the presence in North America of a lively
public conversation that embraced, in one form or another, all the arts
and sciences.

Jefferson's appeal to Aristotle, Locke, Sydney, etc. is an important
key to the lock guarding the door to the minds of the men of the founding generation: those authors[53] were not generally read as part of a university curriculum. Instead, they were read by men having such leisure as
would permit them to read. A truly surprising number of American men
and women found time to read, not only the pamphlets, but also what
Jefferson called "elementary books of public right," i.e., books that penetrate (or claim to) to the elements or principles of the laws that govern
and direct, i.e., that order public life. Inquiry into the principles of order
governing political society, however, is political science.

Voegelin has noted that a science of politics that penetrates to principles must become a philosophy of history.[54] He cites Plato as the thinker
who first differentiated the concepts of politics and history[55] to the point

52. "Jefferson to Henry Lee—2nd May, 1825," in Bergh et al., *Writings of Thomas Jefferson*, 16:118–19. The expression "[T]he harmonizing sentiments," rings awkward in the contemporary ear. Idiomatically, the statement as quoted means, in good contemporary grammar, ". . .rests on the harmonizing [of] [the] sentiments of the day." So, the claim is that the authority of the Declaration rests in the document's creating a harmony of the sentiments of the founding generation.

53. Aristotle excepted.

54. Cf. Voegelin, *NSP*, 88.

55. The recognition of Thucydides' *Peloponnesian War* as the first work of history

of their being useful for science. Neither all, nor even a majority of the American Founding Fathers were facile in Greek (though Adams and Jefferson were). They were, however, steeped in the Latin classics, and, as Forrest McDonald has noted, had, nearly to a man, a *forma mentis* largely classical in its structure:

> [E]very educated Englishman and American knew Latin, Eng-
> lish words were generally closer to their Latin originals than
> they are today, and sometimes, as with the use of the subjunc-
> tive, it is apparent that an author is accustomed to formulating
> his thoughts in Latin (passages in Daniel Defoe's novels,[56] e.g.,
> read often like literal translations from Latin).[57]

That such classical works were so widely read in pre-Revolutionary America; that Americans considered conversation with those books to be essential to the integrity of a person's education; are telling facts. Jefferson's admission, then, coupled with the state of education in British America during the second half of the eighteenth Century, places Americans in the living center of that which Alasdair MacIntyre has called a "Tradition of enquiry." A tradition of inquiry (to adopt the orthography more commonly used in the American idiom) is, in a word: a way of seeking truth, in which certain authors are authorities to the extent that the problems those authors discover and to which they address themselves in their work are commonly recognized as fundamental problems in the search for truth.[58]

---

is accurate and correct in the Platonic sense. *HISTORIA*, or, "Study," is the search for the logic of action in human affairs and events. In this sense, then, Thucydides, who "[W]rote the Peloponnesian War," created a literary *genre* with that work. The idea, however, of a logic of action, i.e., that human activity is essentially political, is Plato's, without which Thucydides could not have written his work. This is not to say, of course, that Thucydides read and made a careful study of Plato's *corpus*, in order to master the platonic understanding of politics, and to proceed thence toward the writing of history. It is to say, rather, that Plato identified a concept that was at work in the Greek *forma mentis*.

56. Defoe's 1719 novel, *Robinson Crusoe*, was, in British America, a more widely tapped source of "Lockean" political ideas, especially regarding the "Lockean" state of nature, than were Locke's two treatises on government, themselves. A brief discussion of this is found in McDonald, *NOS*, 60 n.6; for a more fulsome discussion of the theme, see Jay Fliegelman, *Prodigals and Pilgrims*, 1982.

57. McDonald, *NOS*, xi.

58. Cf. MacIntyre, *WJWR*, 349–69.

In other words, American nationhood is traditional in a way that is analogous to the way in which inquiry is traditional. America is a symbol of order that grounds, that constitutes the American tradition of nationhood. America, as the conceptual space of American nationhood, is erected by means of an investigation that has all the trappings of an effort to overcome a conflict of traditions of inquiry. America brings Aristotle, Cicero, *inter alia*, into conversation with Locke, Sydney, etc.

When Jefferson speaks of, "Harmonizing sentiments," there are two things to hear, simultaneously: there is the immediate and immediately recognizable invocation of the semantics of sovereignty that the European powers inaugurated at Westphalia in 1648; there is also a theoretical assertion regarding the nature of man and the origins of civil society. In this second, there are discernible echoes—or better—counterpoints to certain specifically Ciceronian notes, which were also and equally present to the Founding Fathers, generally. First, the passage from Cicero:

> *Nam sic habetote, nullo in genere disputando posse ita patifieri, quid sit homini a natura tributum, quantam vim rerum optimarum mens humana contineat, cuius muneris colendi efficiendique causa nati et in lucem editi simus, quae sit coniunctio hominum quae naturalis societas inter ipsos. His enim explicatis fons legum et iuris inveniri potest.*[59]

Investigation of "Nature's gifts" and "such natural society" is the exercise that coves the "*intima philosophia*,"[60] in which one discovers the *fons legum*; the point is that, at bottom, philosophy and politics share a starting point, which is the question of authority—a question that involves, though by no means is limited to issues such as who can speak legitimately for whom, and regarding which questions, and for how long, and to what extent.

---

59. "You must have this clear, then, that in no other kind of discussion is it possible to feel out what Nature's gifts to man are, what a wealth of excellent possessions the human mind contains, what the cause is of his striving to accomplish, for which we are born and brought into the light, what it is that conjoins men to each other, what natural society there is among them. Only once these things have been explicated is it possible to discover the font of laws and right." Cicero, *De legibus* I.v.16.

60. Atticus follows the speech we cited with a question. He asks whether Cicero holds, as Atticus has understood, that the study of law (*iuris disciplina*) is to be drawn from the "most intimate depths of philosophy." Cicero answers in the affirmative.

The Contribution of Adams

John Adams wrote a series of letters under the pen name, *Novanglus*, in response to the pseudonymous *Massachusettensis*,[61] who defended the British policy toward the colony of Massachusetts particularly, and the British colonies generally. The eighth *Novanglus* letter, in particular, contains an important enlargement of the discussion of the American condition in relation to Great Britain. Adams's discussion is theoretically important for two distinct though connected reasons. Adams makes a thorough and rigorous distinction between rights held under nature and rights held under human positive law; Adams grounds his distinction in a consideration of American experience, rather than a consideration of existing political theory in abstraction. This is not to say that Adams was ignorant of the history, especially recent and contemporary history of political thought. Quite the contrary: he knew Hobbes, Locke and Sydney by heart; for fun and relaxation, he read Cicero and Thucydides in the original. This makes it all the more telling, that Adams turned to look for the circumstances of the very first settlement of the colonies in order to judge the question as to where the right to speak for the colonies in matters touching the common weal (i.e., the power to legislate) should be found:

> When a subject left the kingdom by the king's permission, and if the nation did not remonstrate against it, by the nation's permission too, at least connivance, he carried with him, as a man, all the rights of nature. . . Our ancestors were entitled to the common law of England when they emigrated, that is, to just so much of it as they pleased to adopt, and no more.[62]

If Adams's claim seems bold and reckless, it is only because its readers and interlocutors from Massachusetts would have understood it's ground implicitly. The ground was the Mayflower Compact. Adams relies on that political act in his subsequent presentation of the American case for independence and the conditions of continued participation in the constitutional order of British empire. The Compact reads, in full:

61. *Massachusettensis* was the young Massachusetts lawyer, Daniel Leonard. For a dated, though thoroughly enjoyable and, as regards the basics, perfectly adequate sketch of Leonard and many other Massachusetts loyalists, see Stark, *The Loyalists of Massachusetts*, 1910. This essay also includes a lucid discussion of the reasons and reasonability of the loyalist position.

62. Adams, *Works of John Adams*, 4:122. Henceforth *WJA*.

In the Name of God, Amen. We, whose names are underwritten, the loyal subjects of our Dread Sovereign Lord King James, by the Grace of God, of Great Britain, France, and Ireland, King, Defender of the Faith, etc., having undertaken, for the glory of God, and advancement of the Christian faith, and honor of our King and country, a voyage to plant the first colony in the northern parts of Virginia, do by these presents, solemnly and mutually in the presence of God, and of one another, covenant and combine ourselves together into a civil body politic, for our better ordering and preservation and furtherance of the ends aforesaid; and by virtue hereof to enact, constitute, and frame such just and equal laws, ordinances, acts, constitutions, and offices, from time to time, as shall be thought most meet and convenient for the general good of the colony, unto which we promise all due submission and obedience. In witness whereof we have hereunto subscribed our names at Cape Cod the eleventh of November, in the reign of our Sovereign Lord, King James of England, France, and Ireland the eighteenth, and of Scotland the fifty-fourth. *Anno Domini*, 1620.[63]

As Adams continues, he practically paraphrases the Compact, itself:

By a positive principle of the common law they were bound, let them be in what part of the world they would, to do nothing against the allegiance of the king. . . [O]ur ancestors, when they emigrated, having obtained permission of the king to come here, and being never commanded to return into the realm, had a clear right to have erected in this wilderness a British constitution, or a perfect democracy, or any other form of government they saw fit [which is, of course, precisely what they did].[64]

The reason for this lengthy disquisition is that *Massachusettensis* had claimed the colonies were somehow annexed to "the realm" of England. Adams proceeded to show the falsity of that claim, pointing out that such annexation could only come about by one of two ways: concurring acts of Parliament and each of the colonial legislatures, or, as in the case of Ireland, conquest. Since America had never been conquered; indeed, as Adams pointed out, the first colonizers bought the land on which they founded their political societies; since the offensive acts of Parliament in question specifically mention America, and do not pretend that other of its acts hold sway over America, which would be the case if America

63. Angle, *By These Words*, 4–5.
64. *WJA*, 4:123.

were annexed to any of the realms comprising the British Empire; since acts and public records generally distinguish among the realm of Great Britain (created by the act of union) and other of the royal dominions; the claim of *Massachusettensis* is patently false:

> This is the first time that I ever heard or read that the colonies are annexed to the realm. It is utterly denied that they are, and that it is possible they should be, without an act of parliament [*sic*] and acts of the colonies. Such an act of parliament cannot be produced, nor any such law of any one colony. Therefore, as this writer builds the whole authority of parliament upon this fact, namely,—that the colonies are annexed to the realm, and as it is certain they never were so annexed, the consequence is, that his whole superstructure falls.[65]

As a matter of fact, the colonial charters contained various provisions, guaranteeing the rights of Englishmen to the colonists and their progeny. Adams builds on this, attacking the language of *Massachusettensis*, who argued, "[T]hat in denying that the colonies are annexed to the realm, and subject to the authority of Parliament, individuals and bodies of men subvert the fundamentals of government, deprive us of British liberties, and build up absolute monarchy in the colonies." Adams responds:

> When he says, that they subvert the fundamentals of government, he begs the question. We say, that the contrary doctrines subvert the fundamentals of government. When he says, that they deprive us of British liberties, he begs the question again. We say, that the contrary doctrine deprives us of English liberties; as to British liberties, we scarcely know what they are, as the liberties of England and Scotland are not precisely the same to this day. English liberties are but certain rights of nature, reserved to the citizen by the English constitution, which rights cleaved to our ancestors when they crossed the Atlantic, and would have inhered in them if, instead of coming to New England, they had gone to Otaheite or Patagonia, even although they had taken no patent or charter from the king at all. These rights did not adhere to them the less, for their purchasing patents and charters, in which the king expressly stipulates with them, that they and their posterity should forever enjoy all those rights and liberties.[66]

65. *WJA*, 4:124.
66. *WJA*, 4:124.

The crux of Adams's argument is therefore that the opportunity of maintaining allegiance to the king is entirely rooted in the king's effective protection of colonists' natural rights. Colonists' possession of those rights is a matter proved not only, nor even primarily, by the fact that they are explicitly guaranteed in documents of right and record, but because colonists have always exercised them. What is more, colonists know they possess their rights precisely *because* they have exercised them. Adams's contention is therefore that the American colonists claim their independence of Parliamentary legislation on the basis of their having established a way of life for themselves that is incompatible with Parliamentary authority over them.

Writing years after the Revolution, in responding to a query as to who the true author of American independence was, Adams responded:

> We might as well inquire who were the Inventors of Agriculture, Horticulture, Architecture, Musick [*sic*] . . . [The] only true answer must be the first emigrants. The Revolution was effected before the war commenced. The Revolution was in the minds and hearts of the people; a change in their religious sentiments of their duties and obligations.[67]

So long as they were left to dispose of their lives and goods in consonance with their own best estimations of the requirements that their common existence placed upon them, indeed, in the measure they were left to do so, and protected in their right to do so, which they had by virtue of the fact that they had always done so, they were happy to maintain their allegiance to the king. Parliament's claim to legislate for the colonies in all matters was essentially a denial of their right to determine the course of their common life, a right that was grounded on the fact of their having made such determinations for many generations. When the king consistently supported Parliament in the efforts that so threatened the colonists, a fundamental question pressed itself upon the colonists: who shall speak for us, if we do not do so ourselves?

After exposing at length the documentary evidence of a plan to break the power of colonial legislatures, and so under the color of right, i.e., by denying the authority of such bodies to legislate for the colonists, Adams wrote:

---

67. Adams to James Madison, July 25th, 1818; Adams to James Tudor, Nov. 7th, 1816; Adams to Hezekiah Niles, Feb. 13th, 1818 as cited in Ellis, *Passionate Sage*, 103–5.

Now, let me ask you, if the Parliament of Great Britain had all
the natural foundations of authority, wisdom, goodness, justice,
power, in as great perfection as they ever existed in any body of
men since Adam's fall; and if the English nation was the most
virtuous, pure, and free that ever was; would not such an unlimited subjection of three millions of people to that parliament
[*sic*], at three thousand miles distance, be real slavery? There
are but two sorts of men in the world, freemen and slaves. The
very definition of a freeman is one who is bound by no law to
which he has not consented. Americans would have no way of
giving or withholding their consent to the acts of this parliament, therefore they would not be freemen. But when luxury,
effeminacy, and venality are arrived at such a shocking pitch
in England; when both electors and elected are become one
mass of corruption; when the nation is oppressed to death with
debts and taxes, owing to their own extravagance and want of
wisdom, what would be your condition under such an absolute
subjection to parliament? You would not only be slaves, but the
most abject sort of slaves, to the worst sort of masters![68]

To be bound by a legislature in all cases, whatever, is not to be represented
at all, but to exist in a state of slavery. The issue, therefore, really does
center—not only, though really, nonetheless—on the questions of who
may represent whom, and in what matters, and to what extent in time
and space.

Adams says Americans would not be able to give, nor would they be
able to withhold their consent to laws, if Parliament were the sole legisla-
tor for them. This is to say, Americans would have no voice, no say in the
making of laws. Political thinkers have known at least since Aristotle's
day, that possession of language is the condition of political life. Parliament, in advancing its right to legislate for the colonies in all cases, was
not establishing control over the American political societies loyal to the
crown. Parliament was attempting to annihilate those political societies, by denying, in effect, that the members thereof were possessed of
voice, i.e., denying that they were political animals (another name for
human beings).

68. *WJA*, 4:122–128.

CHAPTER 2

Standing to Declare

Reading in America from Adams to Cavell

IN THE LAST CHAPTER, we observed the emergence of an American self-consciousness in opposition to British claims regarding the locus of responsibility for colonial order. America emerged as more than a simple geographic designator. America named a conceptual space created by people living in a physical space of the same name. The conceptual space was essentially a way of thinking about, of interpreting and ordering the common experience of life in the physical space called America. Americans' ability to recognize themselves as such, i.e., as Americans, emerged as a result of a challenge or threat against their way of life, a threat that arose from within the representative structure Americans had erected for their preservation. The threat could not be removed but by secession from the British Empire.

The reason for which such a drastic action became necessary was that the question at stake in the critical period of colonial history, the question that led to the outbreak of hostilities and the Declaration of Independence, was in fact the basic question of the authority of the human voice, prior to all positive law and the source of theoretical discourse,[1] the discovery of the American inflection[2] of which was rooted in the American colonists' common experience.

The question of voice, articulated in terms of the power to give and withhold consent, was the essential anthropological question driving

---

1. Cf. Cicero, *De legibus* I.v.16–17; cf. also Cavell, *Cities of Words*, 51 *et passim*.
2. Cf. Cavell, *This New Yet Unapproachable America*, 108–9.

colonists' self-interpretation. The question of voice was thematized in the colonists' debate with each other and with the imperial power over the right to give or withhold consent. Colonists' reflections on their condition led some of their number to explicate an understanding of order in the colonies that depended, not upon the King-in-Parliament, but upon the authoritative expression of certain commonly held tenets regarding human nature, inherent in the colonists' traditional modes of providing and maintaining order in their lives together. In short, we saw how colonists' critical reflection on the problem of representation began to provide a specifically and explicitly American way of thinking about the problem, a way that was rooted in American colonists' long experience of governance. Following Eric Voegelin and Alasdair MacIntyre, we say we observed the emergence of an American tradition of inchoate nationhood that provided the fertile ground, out of which an American tradition of inquiry into the principles of politics could, and in fact did grow. The purpose of this chapter is to move us further in the direction of an American science of politics, that is, toward the critical articulation of that science of politics, which lives in the American tradition of nationhood. Our principal interlocutor is Stanley Cavell.

The Concerns of Cavell

Cavell is explicitly concerned with the problem of America, and specifically with the problem of American philosophical expression. Cavell's earliest explicit expression of concern for America is in his *Senses of Walden*, published in 1972. There, Cavell finds himself explicitly wondering "Why has America never expressed itself philosophically? Or has it—in the metaphysical riot of its greatest literature?"[3] Considering the question more than two decades after he first explicitly stated it, Cavell said he finds it reasonable to hold that the origins of what he calls the American difference in philosophical thought are to be found in the writing of Henry David Thoreau and Ralph Waldo Emerson:

> I myself experienced, especially after writing a little book on Thoreau's *Walden*, a sort of cringe in trying to get back into Emerson, a recoil from what struck me as his perpetual and irritating intertwining of lyricism and cajoling. Yet I was convinced, from my experience with *Walden*, that some such mode

3. Cavell, *Senses of Walden*, 33.

of writing may lend itself to a systematic thoughtfulness in a way only the name of philosophy suits. And, since it is obvious that *Walden* is in conversation with Emerson's writing in every page, and since nothing before Emerson in America is philosophically ambitious and original on this scale, it is reasonable to conclude that what we have in these two writers is nothing less than the origins of the American difference in philosophical thought.[4]

We cannot accept Cavell's location of the origins of the American difference in philosophical thought in the writing of Emerson and Thoreau. Those themes, the concern with which characterizes what Cavell calls, "the American difference", were already present in the writing of Jefferson and Adams (as we began to see in the last chapter and shall continue to see in the present one). The last chapter, however, shows us in implicit agreement with Cavell's idea that that there is, in America, a tradition of thinking that calls for the name of philosophy, owing to the character of its thoughtfulness. There is a further point of agreement. American thoughtfulness will call for philosophy, that is, will demand the name of philosophy for itself, in its own language. If American thoughtfulness is already philosophy, so that its demand for the name of philosophy is (as Thomas Jefferson says of the Colonies' olive branch to George III) the requirement of a right and not the begging of a favor, then American systematic thoughtfulness will already speak in the language of philosophy; it will stake its claim in what we might call philosophy's American dialect.

Whether America has a language of its own, a voice and a literature, is an open question, the answer to which shall depend at least in part on how we conceive philosophy (to conceive philosophy will always, though not only be to have an idea of what philosophy is):

> I understand [philosophy] as a willingness to think not about something other than what ordinary human beings think about, but rather to learn to think undistractedly about things that ordinary human beings cannot help thinking about, or anyway cannot help having occur to them, sometimes in fantasy, sometimes as a flash across a landscape; such things, for example, as whether we can know the world as it is in itself, or whether others really know the nature of one's own experiences, or whether good and bad are relative, or whether we might now be dreaming that we are awake, or whether modern tyrannies and weapons and spaces and speeds and art are continuous with

4. Cavell, *Cities of Words*, 20.

the past of the human race or discontinuous, and hence whether the learning of the human race is not irrelevant to the problems it has brought before itself.[5]

Cavell's questions as to whether modern tyrannies, etc., are continuous with the past of the human race or discontinuous, and hence the question of the relevance of the learning of the human race to the problems it faces in the present of his writing (in 1984, and also today, as we read his writing), find explicit and systematic address in a seminal essay by John Adams, *A Dissertation on the Canon and Feudal Law*. Consideration of a few salient passages from that essay will serve to establish that the writing, hence the thinking that was done during the political crisis in America, provides an instance of exactly what Cavell considers to be philosophy.

Educating America (1): the colonial college

If undistracted thinking about problems that commonly occur to human beings may be taken as the end (or one of the ends, at least) of higher education, then the founding of such an institution or institutions may be understood to have been taken with a view to precisely this end. The decision of a given political community to found a college or university, will therefore at least arguably tell us something about the kind of people they understand themselves, or aspire, to be. In his *Dissertation on Canon and Feudal Law*, John Adams discusses the early Massachusetts settlers' decision to found a college:

> They were convinced, by their knowledge of human nature, derived from history and their own experience, that nothing could preserve their posterity from the encroachments of...tyranny... but knowledge diffused generally through the whole body of the people. Their civil and religious principles, therefore, conspired to prompt them to use every measure and take every precaution in their power to propagate and perpetuate knowledge. For this purpose they laid very early the foundations of colleges, and invested them with ample privileges and emoluments.[6]

It is true that Adams conceives the tyrannical threat to be concretely located in the systems of canon and feudal law.[7] While this cannot be

5. Cavell, *Themes Out of School*, 9.
6. Diggins, *Portable John Adams*, 217.
7. Cf. ibid.

irrelevant to any argument, such as the present one, which would place Adams in precisely the tradition of inquiry that produced those two systems, neither does it defeat the thesis. For reasons that will become clear as the work progresses, discussion of how and why the fact itself does not foreclose the argument, must nevertheless wait until the fourth chapter. Presently at stake is the political import—the theoretical significance—of colonists' decision to found colleges. The importance of this is further attested in the following lines from his *Dissertation*:

> We have a right to [liberty], derived from our Maker. But if we had not, our fathers have earned and bought it for us, at the expense of their ease, their estates, their pleasure, and their blood. And liberty cannot be preserved without a general knowledge among the people, who have a right, from the frame of their nature, to knowledge, as their great Creator, who does nothing in vain, had given them understanding, and a desire to know; but besides this, they have a right, an indisputable, unalienable, indefeasible, divine right to that most dreaded and envied kind of knowledge, I mean, of the characters and conduct of their rulers. Rulers are no more than attorneys, agents, and trustees, for the people; and if the cause, the interest and trust, is insidiously betrayed, or wantonly trifled away, the people have a right to revoke the authority that they themselves have deputed, and to constitute abler and better agents, attorneys, and trustees.[8]

With regard to Cavell's search for a tradition of thinking in America, we can say, in light of this passage, that it was quite literally present at the creation, say, at the foundation, of those political societies, which came to call themselves American. We can further see how the conceptual space called America characteristically has this dedication to undistracted thinking about questions of order.

With regard to the question of American independence, we see that Adams is essentially claiming, throughout the texts we have just read, that Americans were as a matter of fact independent of the crown precisely because they knew how to live together, and had provided for the permanence and furtherance of that knowledge within the body of the people. Knowledge of how to live together almost says, "political science." Knowledge of how to live together is *techne politike* in Greek. *Episteme politike* differs from *techne politike* in that *episteme* is knowledge of principles. The justification of American *techne politike* required an

8. Ibid., 218–19.

articulation of the principles of American politics. What we are proposing, with Voegelin, is that a science of politics apt to understand America
must give critical articulation of and account for the principles animating
the American genius for governance.

Cavell and the Placement of a Quarrel

Returning to Cavell, it is also important to note that his understanding
of philosophy as learning to think undistractedly about ordinary human
things, arises out of a resistance to his express desire to claim Thoreau
and Emerson as philosophers, and specifically as philosophers of America. Cavell describes his response—his resistance—to this resistance, as a
quarrel[9] with the profession of philosophy, and describes the terms of
his quarrel as follows:

> That this is a quarrel means that I recognize the profession to be
> the genuine present of the impulse and the history of philoso-
> phy, so far as that present takes place in our (English-speaking)
> public intellectual life. . . I might indicate how hard it has be-
> come for me to conduct my quarrel with the profession, to find
> common ground for it. The difficulty is epitomized by my grow-
> ing insistence on receiving Emerson and Thoreau as philoso-
> phers, figures who from the beginning of the professionalization
> of American philosophy have been regarded as philosophical
> amateurs.[10]

If it is defensible to receive (and here it is worthwhile to note that receiving is an essential, perhaps the essential, act of participation in tradition)
Emerson and Thoreau as philosophers, it is only so insofar as they are
demonstrably part of an already existing tradition. In fact, the origins

9. In order to provide a little historical background to the circumstances of his
quarrel, Cavell adduces a book by Bruce Kucklick, titled, *The Rise of American Philosophy*, which cannot for reasons of economy receive the treatment it deserves here. That
book essentially traces the achievement of a professional philosophical academy in
the United States to Harvard University's expulsion of Emerson from the ranks of its
professional philosophers. This fact of history is especially pertinent to our discussion,
since the college at Harvard Yard in Cambridge is precisely the institution to which
Adams referred in his exposition of the American tradition of governance, so that the
founding moment of what is, on one reading, the present epoch of philosophy's life in
America, will be, on the same reading, the deliberate break with at least some of the
roots of the American tradition of thinking (as we have begun to find it).

10. Cavell, *Themes Out of School*, 31–32.

of the American difference in philosophical thinking reach farther back even than Adams and those of his day; they go back, as even Emerson and Thoreau will say, to the learned men who were the first settlers of the American wilderness, and back even further, to wherever they all sought what wisdom they were after. Just as Cavell encountered resistance in the American academy to his claim that Thoreau and Emerson should be considered philosophers, so has the American academy resisted recognizing the presence of a science of politics in the founding generation. The present unwillingness to let Emerson and Thoreau be philosophers, as well as the resistance to recognizing the political science of the Founding Fathers, is due to a peculiar feature of the American political conversation, which is intimately connected to the circumstances of Cavell's questioning, his querulous-ness, and so the circumstances of his quarrel.

Educating America (2): The American Roots of a Quarrel

Two years after Adams's death, in 1828, the second-oldest institution of higher learning in the United States, the Yale College in New Haven, Connecticut, commissioned a report on the opportunity of a revision of the college curriculum. Another eulogizer of the transformed university, Lawrence W. Levine, offers this documentary discussion of the intellectual milieu at the time of Adams's passing:

> The Yale Report of 1828 rejected the [proposed "modernization"] out of hand. The end of a college education, it asserted, was "the discipline and the furniture of the mind; expanding its powers, and storing it with knowledge," with the emphasis always upon discipline rather than information, and for this purpose there was nothing equal to the classical languages and mathematics. The study of the classics, the report's authors insisted, "forms the most effectual discipline of the mental faculties. . . . Every faculty of the mind is employed; not only the memory, judgment, and reasoning powers, but the taste and fancy are occupied and improved." Should Greek and Latin ever be given a "secondary place" in the curriculum, Yale College would "sink into a mere academy," its degrees "would become valueless," and it would become "directly accessary to the depression of the present literary character of our country."[11]

11. Levine, *Opening of the American Mind*, 38.

There are two points of interest in this passage. The first is that Levine recognizes the emphasis of the older curriculum as being on the discipline
of the mind. Admittedly, discipline of the mind is an ambiguous idea.
On the one hand, it might be a euphemism for brainwashing, or at least
indoctrination. On the other hand, it might stand to indicate something
like instruction in (a way of) thinking that is apt to render the thinking
subject capable of properly employing his mental faculties. To be sure,
there were schools then, as there are now, which do not educate, but
only indoctrinate. The importance of the language of the Yale study that
Levine quotes, however, is precisely its statement of an understanding of
the purpose of a university, which is much closer to the understanding of
discipline as instruction in thinking.

Let "the discipline of the mind" name the project and process of
thinking and learning to think undistractedly, then the American schools
were entirely dedicated to it, and so in view of what the Romans called
the *salus rei publicae*, the health (and also the salvation) of the republic.
That the American institutions of higher learning were founded with this
end in mind is not incidental to their constitutions and curricula, which
Levine describes in the following manner:

> Throughout the colonial period, American colleges were char-
> acterized by a homogeneous model; they were, as one student
> of education has called them, "copies of copies": the American
> rendition of the English adaptation of the Renaissance revision
> of the medieval curriculum. Institutions of higher education in
> America began their existence suffused with a religious ethos
> and purpose and firmly in the grip of the classical curriculum,
> which consisted of Latin, Greek, sometimes Hebrew, math-
> ematics, natural philosophy, moral philosophy, and logic. All
> students studied the same subjects at the same time with the
> class in which they entered college.[12]

In light of this, the second clause of the first quoted text from the Yale
report, regarding the teaching of classical languages, is particularly telling. The study of classical languages was, in the estimation of the Yale
report's authors, apt to impart (or, to use a verb then current), to *actuate*
all the faculties of the mind: memory, judgment, reasoning powers, taste
and fancy. This last is extremely important. "Fancy" is an old way of saying, roughly, "imagination". Imagination is useful to the informed thinker
only when the structure of knowledge is assumed to be essentially open

12. Ibid., 37.

and unlimited. When all the faculties of the mind are together actuated, the subject in whom they are may become a kind of man the Greeks called *spoudaios*, a mature or complete man, or, if you will, a "well-rounded human being." The danger in shifting the focus of university education from the formation of such persons is also clearly stated: the college would become a mere academy, i.e., a place outside the city, which is to say, politically insignificant, or useless, detached from the common good.

All of this hinges on the presence of an idea of science as principled knowledge, rather than as something determined by the mere formalities of methodological rigor, without regard for the subject matter to which the method is applied. The authors of the Yale report believed that the purpose of higher education was to teach how to recognize what is important in life and what is not, how to achieve important things and not to be bothered overmuch by that which is, in the scheme of things, less important. In such a scheme, questions of what actually is important must necessarily arise, and critical discussion, exploration of criteria will inevitably come into play. The choice of a life devoted to exploration of one or another branch of human inquiry is by no means denigrated, nor are there external limits placed on the mode to be employed in the pursuit of a given branch of inquiry. A student who, having completed his course of study, should decide on a career in physics, or chemistry or geology or what have you, is to be approved, applauded, admired, seconded and even actively supported.

Such a choice, it was assumed by the authors of the report, would be taken with sufficient deliberation, with the graduate's awareness of his own capacities and aptness to contribute by prosecution of such a course, to the general good. More to this, a society with a sufficient number of members thus formed and actuated, would readily provide for such as would choose to dedicate themselves to life in pursuit of truth through study. Thus, it was not in disparagement, but rather in light of the worthiness of the vocation to science, that the Yale authors argued for the maintenance of the older *ratio studiorum*. Said shortly, education, and especially higher education, was in America education in citizenship. American citizenship was citizenship in a free society, so that education in America was education in and for freedom. This commitment has remained a characteristic of higher education in America until very recently, and remains an idea with considerable purchase, even in the present day, when much of what passes for higher education seems to be little more than rote job training and skill-acquisition exercise. If we accept, for the sake of argument, that this is the case, and that higher education as workforce preparation is the genuine present of the educational project in America, then the question arises as to whether—and if so, then how and to what extent—that project is still related to its American original, or whether there has been a break. The key to resolving this conundrum is to be found in the unpacking of a peculiarity of the American political conversation, as that conversation is conducted in American public intellectual life.

Jefferson and the (Up)rooting of the American Tradition

The peculiarity currently under consideration has been present in American public intellectual life from before the time of the founding of the American republic. The Founding Father who gave this peculiarity its first formal characterization, however, was Thomas Jefferson: the principal draftsman of the Declaration of Independence, and of the statutes of the University of Virginia. Jefferson confessed himself an "Epicurean" to several different interlocutors during the course of his life. Jefferson indeed used to call Epicurus his master.[13]

Jefferson's Epicurean Syllabus

When Jefferson composed a letter to William Short in 1819,[14] he included a syllabus of Epicurean doctrine, which he had drawn up some years previously.[15]

Jefferson's Syllabus[16]

Physical.—The Universe eternal.

Its parts, great and small, interchangeable.

---

13. Cf. Koch, *Philosophy of Thomas Jefferson*, 4.

14. Jefferson died on July 4th, 1826, within hours of his friend John Adams, whose last words were, "Thomas Jefferson still lives," or words to that effect.

15. Jefferson says the syllabus was composed twenty years previously. This testimony would place the composition of the syllabus at some point during the height of Jefferson's powers, either while he was seeking the presidency most actively, or just after he achieved it.

16. The syllabus appears here as it appears in Appleby and Ball, *Thomas Jefferson, Political Writings*, 316.

Matter and Void alone.

Motion inherent in matter which is weighty and declining.

Eternal circulation of the elements of bodies.

Gods, an order of beings next superior to man, enjoying in their sphere, their own felicities; but not meddling with the concerns of the scale of beings below them.

Moral.—Happiness the aim of life.

Virtue the foundation of happiness.

Utility the test of virtue.

Pleasure active and Indolent.

Indolence is the absence of pain, the true felicity.

Active, consists in agreeable motion; it is not happiness, but the means to produce it. Thus the absence of hunger is an article of felicity; eating the means to obtain it.

The *summum bonum* is to be not pained in body, nor troubled in mind. i.e., Indolence of body, tranquility of mind.

To procure tranquility of mind we must avoid desire and fear, the two principal diseases of the mind.

Man is a free agent.

Virtue consists in 1. Prudence. 2. Temperance. 3. Fortitude. 4. Justice.

To which are opposed, 1. Folly. 2. Desire. 3. Fear. 4. Deceit.[17]

When Jefferson makes happiness the aim of life, and proceeds to iden-tify the chief good, i.e., the chief happiness of man as indolence of body and tranquility of mind, he is saying essentially that felicity is an entirely private affair, and politics, insofar as it is an activity, at best a means to the achievement of bodily indolence and mental tranquility. In short, Jef-ferson holds that the basic and final aim of human existence is at least a-political. Since Epicurus understands political life essentially to be the practice of compulsion, and since compulsion is unpleasant,[18] political

17. For comparison, a succinct statement of the Epicurean (including Lucretian) philosophy is to be found in Strauss, *Natural Right and History*, 109–15.

18. Cf. ibid., 111.

life is essentially unpleasant. In several places, Epicurus says the greatest happiness essentially involves detachment from affairs. The greatest happiness is not only a-political, but anti-political.

In large part, Jefferson's understanding of Epicurean philosophy came through the filter of Pierre Gassendi, whose philosophical work was essentially an attempt to synthesize certain precepts of moral or social living extrapolated from traditional Christian thought, with the Epicurean philosophy.[19] The extent to which Jefferson understood Gassendi's project is uncertain. In any case, it is not necessary to ascertain the extent and/or accuracy of Jefferson's understanding of Gassendi. What is both certain and immediately pertinent to the present argument is that Jefferson considered the Epicurean philosophy to be politically deficient, as his letter to Short testifies: "Epicurus and Epictetus give laws for governing ourselves, Jesus a supplement of the duties and charities we owe to others."[20]

As we shall shortly see, Epicureanism's lack of what we might call a social doctrine provided no real ground on which to stake a claim against its completeness. In any case, Jefferson held the Epicurean philosophy to be perfectly sufficient and conducive to true human happiness. Jefferson was an Epicurean through-and-through. Jefferson was a man who loved society, by which we mean the company of other persons. For all his protestations of *horror politicae*, his spirits flagged and his faculties faltered whenever he found himself disengaged from national affairs.[21] On first glance, this could go to show that Jefferson really did not believe what he so consistently protested: that he never liked, and eventually hated politics.[22] To be sure, a psychological investigation of Jefferson would have to take a keen and penetrating look at evidence of this kind. We have another, two-fold purpose: to establish with at least a degree of prob-

19. Koch, *Philosophy of Thomas Jefferson*; see also Boorstin, *Lost World of Thomas Jefferson*.

20. Jefferson to William Short, Oct. 31, 1819, in Merrill, *Thomas Jefferson*, 1431.

21. Cf. McCullough, *John Adams*, 450–51. Page references to the Paperback edition. There, McCullough quotes at some length from a letter Jefferson wrote to his daughter, Polly, in which he confesses his uneasiness when necessarily engaged in society during the period of his retirement from public affairs from 1793 to 1797. Jefferson continued to write that withdrawal from the world, "[L]ed to anti-social and misanthropic state of mind."

22. Cf. Letter from TJ to JA, February 28th, 1796 in *WJA*, 8:517. For other correspondence between Adams and Jefferson from this period, *v.* Cappon, *Adams Jefferson Letters*, 253 *et passim*. Cf. also McCullough, *John Adams*, 449–41, 687nn.

ability the extent to which the principal draftsman of the Declaration was influenced by Epicureanism; to establish the presence of Epicureanism in the intellectual milieu that gave its form to the *mens* of the founding generation of Americans.

Epicurean Conventionalism in America

In order to accomplish this task, we need to explore another, further aspect of classical Epicureanism, namely its understanding of the role of convention in the life of human beings. "Convention" Englishes the Latin *conventio*, itself a substantive derived from the composite verb, *convenire*. Convention therefore names a coming together, in this case, the coming together of human beings in society. The Epicurean understanding of convention runs roughly in the following way:[23] the good is the pleasant, and the pleasant is the good. The sum of pleasure, the perfect pleasure that is unmixed with pain and pleasant beyond all other things that please, is accessible only through philosophy. Here, philosophy names the pursuit of that which is good before all reasoning, calculation, restraint and compulsion; this good is what we recognize and pursue as infants, i.e., pleasure. Human beings from the very beginning of their lives, feel immediately only pleasure, or sensibly perceive the attraction to pleasure, only. This pleasure, further, is bodily pleasure; for the Epicurean, this is sufficient proof that the human being naturally seeks his own good. Convention, i.e., society, constrains and compels, so that social living is antithetical to philosophical living, since philosophical living is precisely the systematic and perfect avoidance of society's constraints and compulsions. Philosophy requires education, which is instruction in how systematically and perfectly to avoid the constraints and compulsions of society. There is, however, a catch: while genuine pleasure in the Epicurean sense does require that the seeker of it successfully avoid the constraints and compulsions of society, it is nevertheless impossible to achieve genuine Epicurean pleasure in isolation from *societas*, i.e., other people. A closer examination of the threefold division of Epicurean goods will bring this point into better focus.

In the absence of civilized society, it is impossible to meet the conditions of that pleasure to which the Epicurean philosopher aspires. Such

---

23. The discussion of convention follows Leo Strauss's presentation of philosophical conventionalisms in his *Natural Right and History*, 110–17.

pleasure, we have seen, is indolence of body and tranquility of mind. To achieve the sum of pleasure, the human being must learn to distinguish among classes of things: first, there are those things that are pleasant, though mixed with an element or at least the possibility of pain (wine, for example, leads to elevation and also to suffering and illness if taken in excess); next, there are things that are not pleasant in themselves, though conducive to pleasure (this is the class of useful things); finally, there is that class of things, which is neither pleasant in itself, nor conducive to genuine pleasure. This class of things is called the class of the noble.

Noble things are pleasing only to the extent that they are admired or desired by the multitude. Noble things are good only to the extent that people say they are good, which is to say that they are good by convention. The first class of things may be pursued to the extent that experience of them is conducive to appreciation of the Epicurean *summum bonum*. This is true of the final class as well. The virtues of prudence, justice, fortitude and temperance fall into the second class, the class of the useful.

The Peculiarity of Justice

While prudence, fortitude and temperance issue immediately in either pleasure or the avoidance of pain (prudence leads a man to abey his hunger with wholesome food, thus repairing the body; temperance leads him to a proper general care of body and mind; fortitude leads a man to overcome his insalubrious attractions and aversions[24]), justice is different. Justice is pleasant only to the extent people believe one to have it. Injustice is unpleasant only when people detect it, or generally suspect it[25]; even then, it is not strictly injustice itself that is unpleasant, but only the consequences of its detection or suspicion. Leo Strauss illustrates the point by a comparison of justice to the good of friendship:

> Both justice and friendship originate in calculation, but friendship comes to be intrinsically pleasant or desirable for its own sake. Friendship comes to be at any rate incompatible with compulsion. But justice and the association that is concerned with

24. These examples are given independently of Strauss's discussion of Epicurean thought, on which this section also and otherwise heavily relies.

25. The people who come to recognize injustice must be able to influence public opinion in order to make it painful for the unjust one. General suspicion is, on the Epicurean reading, painful only when it is, so to speak, enforceable.

justice—the city—stand or fall by compulsion. And compulsion is unpleasant.[26]

The philosopher will exploit the means made available through civilized society in order to live at its fringes, and to be entirely free of sincere devotion to the city.

In light of this, it is possible to see how Jefferson's insistent deprecation of politics, as well as the suffering he experienced when withdrawn from society, were perfectly in line with Epicurean philosophical conventionalism. For the Epicurean, freedom from the constraints and compulsions of society—from social convention—is not a matter of breaking convention in secret; it is entirely a matter of cultivating *indifference* to convention as such, while preserving conventions in their usefulness.[27] Conventional philosophical justice is, on this reading, precisely the cultivated disregard for those aspects of social life, which are necessary to the good, though no part of it. Justice, the characteristic of life in the city, is intrinsically meaningless to philosophy. Its essence is worthless to the Epicurean philosopher.

A Peculiarity of the American Political Conversation

On the one hand, we have Adams, in whose discussion of education in America as a project ordered to the preservation and furtherance of the knowledge that is necessary to the health of a republic, we detected a commitment to a real and substantial common good. On the other, we have Jefferson, who makes all activity, including politics, to be ancillary to the cultivation of a basic human good that is at least a-political. The

26. Strauss, *Natural Right and History*, 111.

27. There is an Epicurean explanation for Jefferson's persistent refusal to free his slaves, even as he deplored the institution of slavery: keeping men in bondage favored bodily indolence and mental tranquility, while deploring slavery as an abomination made Jefferson a champion of conventional mores. There are also Epicurean explanations for other paradoxes in Jefferson's private and public behavior, such as his constant profession of esteem for the yeoman farmer when considered next to his profligate spending; his refusal to give his assent to the creation of a national bank, and his constitutionally dubious exercise of federal executive power, which trebled the size of U.S. holdings with the stroke of a pen. For an Epicurean conventionalist, there is not only nothing in the least contradictory in Jefferson's behavior; there is every reason for him to have acted precisely as he did; Jefferson used his much cultivated reputation as the sage of Monticello, in order the better to confirm precisely those conventions which were to his estimation most conducive to the furtherance of his philosophical idiocy.

peculiarity of the American political conversation is that the Adamsian and Jeffersonian ideas are both constitutively present in it. On the one hand, tradition is the mode of understanding, and the condition of inquiry into the American. On the other, everything constitutive of the tradition is seen as merely conventional. It is not really to be taken seriously, though the semblance of participation in it, or at least the pretence of acquiescence to it, will be necessary to anyone who would pursue the Epicurean ideal. As we shall see presently, the difference between the two is precisely the difference between the understanding of science as principled knowledge and the idea of science as the domination of nature.

The Semantic Ambiguity of Science

A 1956 UNESCO report[28] on political science in the United States claims that "The most consistent and significant trend in American political science for more than two generations has been toward 'science',"[29] when, "by 'science' is meant what are understood by students of politics to be the conceptions and techniques of the physical and biological sciences."[30] No less a figure than Bernard Crick[31] cited that report approvingly in a book he brought out to explain how it came to be that the United States has the most well-trained and best-equipped "professional political theorists"[32] of any nation ever. "The study of politics in the United States today," Crick asserts, "is something in size, content and method unique in Western intellectual history."[33] This was at the end of the 1950s, the decade that saw among other events the publication of Voegelin's *New Science of Politics*, which expressed the need for a recovery of the science of order, and the first three volumes of *Order and History*, which proposed to address the need expressed in the earlier work. In the same decade, indeed, in the published version of a series of Walgreen lectures given one year after Voegelin's own, Pulitzer prize-winning historian Daniel

28. Waldo et al., *On Political Science in the United States of America*.

29. Ibid., 20.

30. Ibid.

31. Sir Bernard Crick (1929–2008) was a leading figure in and historian of the academic discipline known as political science. He wrote or edited more than 20 books, including a life of Eric Arthur Blair (George Orwell), for which he is probably best known outside the academy.

32. Waldo et al., *On Political Science in the United States of America*, 20.

33. Crick, *American Science of Politics*, xi.

Boorstin asserted, "No nation has ever been less interested in political philosophy or produced less in the way of theory.[34]"

It seems that Crick and Boorstin are in naked and diametric disagreement regarding the state of political science in the United States. Crick hails the U.S. as the glory of political science, while Boorstin suggests that the United States in 1950 could not care less for it, or at least for something called "political theory," of which Crick's professional political theorists are the presumptive practitioners. Boorstin was himself a leading figure in the American academy. We cannot therefore suppose that he was unaware of the growth of political science as an academic discipline.

When Boorstin talks about "political theory," his point is simply that, at the time he wrote his essay, most citizens of the United States did not require abstract systems of thought to justify their way of living. Boorstin notes that, when Abraham Lincoln said "Four score and seven years ago, our fathers brought forth on this continent a new nation, conceived in liberty and dedicated to the proposition that all men are created equal," he was not saying "the words of a political theory," but, "affirm[ing] that an adequate theory already existed in the first epoch of national life." In other words, "America" adequately expresses the experience of nationhood; it seems reasonable, that is, to suppose that Boorstin's discovery of what he calls, "an adequate theory" is the discovery of the fact that, "in the first epoch of national life," the symbolism of American order was transparent to those who lived under the power structures designed to protect it. What was the thing to which Americans were indifferent, and why did the growth of political science in the American academy not count for him as "political theory"? Is it still the case that America is indifferent to it, and if so, why, and to what extent? Most importantly, whence this American indifference?

34. Boorstin, *Genius of American Politics*, 8. Boorstin's best known work is his trilogy, *The Americans*, the volumes of which are *The Colonial Experience*, *The National Experience* and *The Democratic Experience*. For this last, published in 1973, Boorstin won the Pulitzer Prize for historical writing. A lawyer, university professor, and author of over 20 books, Boorstin served as Librarian of Congress from 1975 to 1987. He died in 2004.

An Original Agreement: The Practice
of Science at the Founding

There is another, indeed prior point in Boorstin and Crick's discussions, on which we find the two in substantial agreement. Crick says that the founding generation did not need to pursue what he understands "political science" to be, because the Americans of the founding generation felt that political science was possessed and practiced by their political leaders. "In America," Crick writes, "political science was felt to exist already in the conduct of her own statesmen, not in the books of the professors."[35] The reason Boorstin gives for Americans' lack of concern for "political theory" is that, while Americans are largely uninterested in the academic discipline of political science, "No nation has ever believed more firmly that its political life was based on a perfect theory."

The point of agreement, therefore, is in both authors' placement of America's traditional self-interpretation in the way of an older tradition, though neither invokes it explicitly, nor even gives any sign of their being aware of it. If Crick is correct in saying that Americans did not develop political science as a separate academic discipline because they believed it to be practiced by their statesmen, and if Boorstin is correct in identifying a general acceptance of American political life as being conducted according to a "perfect theory," then the American self-understanding is one according to which Plato's vision in the *7th Letter*[36] has been, or is at least on its way to being achieved. If at first glance this sounds improbable, or even outrageous, then remember that the claim is not that Americans had, in fact, achieved such a state of affairs. Nor is it to say that Americans were closet Platonists. Rather, the claim is that Americans understood happiness in political life to depend on the presence of wise wielders of political power, and that their own modes and orders of government were, by this standard, at least tolerable. Taken all together, this places America in a tradition of thinking that is rather older than that of seventeenth century liberalism.

---

35. Crick, *American Science of Politics*, 5. There Crick cites this as a fact that sets the fundamental difference between the French and American revolutions in relief. That the two revolutions are in fact different revolutionary types is an open question, as it was in the founding period, itself.

36. 326b1–3. "[T]he ills of the human race would never end until either those who are sincerely lovers of wisdom come into political power, or the rulers of our cities, by the grace of God, learn true philosophy."

In order further to place the American tradition, Boorstin recognizes the paradox involved in simultaneously affirming both America's disdain for, and commitment to what he calls theory. Boorstin believes that a key to understanding much of that, which he judges to be good in American institutions lies in its resolution. "[T]he two sides of the paradox explain each other," argues Boorstin, and the account he gives of their explanation turns on a concept he calls "givenness". Givenness, in its turn, has three fundamental aspects.[37] There is the givenness of the American past, i.e., the belief that the very first Americans, or the Founding Fathers bequeathed to posterity a political theory that is perfectly adequate to any and all possible present and future needs.[38] The second aspect is the givenness of the present, i.e., the belief that, "'The American way of life' harbors an 'American way of thought' which can do us for a political theory, even if we never make it explicit and even if we are never able to confront ourselves with it."[39] This, continues Boorstin, "is the idea that to Americans political theory never appears in its nakedness but always clothed in the American experience."[40] Givenness, finally, is "the quality of our experience which makes us see our national past as an uninterrupted continuum of similar events, so that our past merges indistinguishably into our present."[41]

Boorstin's phenomenology of "givenness" allows that Americans might understand their presence in a national experience as an uninterrupted continuum. If, on the other hand, faith in the wisdom of political leaders should fail, and if the continuity of American experience should be broken, or our view of it darkened, one possible outcome would be the semblance of opportunity for something very like what Crick understands as "political science" to gain currency. The academic discipline we know today by the name of political science was a long time coming in the United States, notwithstanding Crick's estimation that:

> RIGHT FROM the founding of the new Republic there were good reasons why the study of politics should grow into a distinct, large and powerful academic discipline, something very

37. Boorstin, *Genius of American Politics*, 9.
38. Ibid.
39. Ibid.
40. Ibid.
41. Ibid.

different in both content and size from almost anything, then or now, in European education.[42]

This is to say: the rise of political science in the American academy, with its turn toward the positive method of the natural sciences, could be a sign of the erosion of that ordering force, which Boorstin called, "givenness." Put another way: there is more than one understanding of America, and more than one understanding of science, and those who subscribe to, let us say, underwrite one America or another, one science or another are in competition for control of the elements of representation, whether these be found in school boards, university faculties or seats on the Supreme Court. Some have characterized this state of affairs as a culture war. Cavell has called it his quarrel with the profession of philosophy. Let the present serve to place the quarrel further (in the past, and also in the future), in America, by placing America in the way of philosophy.

Cavell and the Experience of the Ordinary

If and when a society becomes conscious of itself as the ordered existence of human beings, each of which is a special locus of the truth of existence and therefore a participant in the truth of order, then the society will begin to live the search for order as a being in quest of the ordinary. Being in quest of the ordinary is being involved in the search for that which brings order to quotidian existence. It is a search for those things in and through which the good of being in society becomes intelligible. It is, then the search for those common experiences of society in which the good of society itself is manifest. In short, the quest for the ordinary is the quest for the common good.

Experience: the Clothing of American Thought

When Boorstin said the political theory of America presents itself, "in the clothing of the American experience," he was talking about Americans' education in their peculiar way of thinking through participation in expressions of belonging.[43] The American experience, argues Boorstin, is essentially the experience of belonging to the continued actuation of

42. Crick, *American Science of Politics*, 3.
43. Cf. Boorstin, *Genius of American Politics*, 13 *et passim*.

the national vision, whether at the poll, in church or around the dinner table. We further recall Voegelin's constantly calling us back to the experiences of transcendence that are constitutive of society, which is to say that experience of society is the intimation of transcendence. Voegelin was calling us back to the experiences of transcendence in and through society as the proper field of theoretical investigation, so that America is philosophically fertile ground. Boorstin's recognition of the "theory" of politics in America as being "clothed" in Americans' experience of nationhood will mean that philosophy in America has always been there, and only requires uncovering. This uncovering might be an undressing, or even a despoiling, of the facts of America's history. We cannot know in advance, which it will be. We have to assume the risk.

In any case, Cavell has heard the call to something like the work we are proposing in a text of Emerson:

> The process of discovering and announcing a fact is something Emerson (in "The American Scholar") calls thinking and describes in a way philosophers of our time will have difficulty recognizing as part of the work they are obliged to do: Emerson writes of a process "by which experience is converted into thought," which is a way of making the meaning of a fact public.[44]

44. Cavell, *Cities of Words*, 29. Cavell is quoting from the following passage:

The preamble of thought, the transition through which it passes from the unconscious to the conscious, is action. Only so much do I know, as I have lived. Instantly we know whose words are loaded with life, and whose not. The world, – this shadow of the soul, or other me, – lies wide around. Its attractions are the keys which unlock my thoughts and make me acquainted with myself. I run eagerly into this resounding tumult. I grasp the hands of those next me, and take my place in the ring to suffer and to work, taught by an instinct that so shall the dumb abyss be vocal with speech. I pierce its order; I dissipate its fear; I dispose of it within the circuit of my expanding life. So much only of life as I know by experience, so much of the wilderness have I vanquished and planted, or so far have I extended my being, my dominion. I do not see how any man can afford, for the sake of his nerves and his nap, to spare any action in which he can partake. It is pearls and rubies to his discourse. Drudgery, calamity, exasperation, want, are instructors in eloquence and wisdom. The true scholar grudges every opportunity of action past by, as a loss of power. It is the raw material out of which the intellect moulds her splendid products. A strange process too, this by which experience is converted into thought, as a mulberry leaf is converted into satin. The manufacture goes forward at all hours.

The full text may be found in Carpenter, *Ralph Waldo Emerson*, 59–60.

First and foremost, there is the alarming appearance of "conversion," which is a word that had great power in the ears and minds of Emerson's audience. *Conversio* is a kind of turning. The issue might be made to turn on an indirection. In one short and powerful paragraph of a short and powerful book exploring the literary (in Cavell's parlance therefore epistemological and metaphysical) conditions of America and America's discovery, Cavell follows Emerson's calling of America, "New, yet unapproachable," because America is always before us and always behind us. If America is unapproachable by local motion, and if America is nevertheless discovered, then perhaps America's discovery involves turning in place, turning into and out of oneself, i.e., in conversion—but where does it all begin? Cavell, following Emerson, says the American scholar is essentially involved in turning experience into thought, which, he says, is a way of making the meaning of a fact public. To make the meaning of a fact public is nothing, if it is not a declaration.

More to this, Cavell, discussing two sentences[45] from Thoreau's *Walden* in "The Philosopher in American Life," notes:

> Reading is a variation of writing, where they meet in meditation and achieve accounts of their opportunities; and writing is a variation of reading, since to write is to cast words together that you did not make, so as to give or take readings. Since these accounts are of what Thoreau calls economy, which is his philosophical life,[46] it follows that his economics, resulting from the

45. "This car-load of torn sails is more legible and interesting now than if they should be wrought into paper and printed books. Who can write so graphically the history of the storms they have weathered as these rents have done?" From "Sounds" in Harding, *Variorum Walden*, 111.

46. From *Walden*, "Economy":

Which would have advanced the most at the end of a month, – the boy who had made his own jackknife from the ore which he had dug and smelted, reading as much as would be necessary for this, – or the boy who had attended the lectures on metallurgy at the Institute in the mean while, and had received a Rogers' penknife from his father? Which would be most likely to cut his fingers? . . . To my astonishment I was informed on leaving college that I had studied navigation! why, if I had taken one turn down the harbor I should have known more about it. Even the poor student studies and is taught only political economy, while that economy of living which is synonymous with philosophy is not even sincerely professed in our colleges. The consequence is, that while he is reading Adam Smith, Ricardo, and Say, he runs his father in debt irretrievably.

In Harding, *Variorum Walden*, 60. I will not for the moment insist upon finding

interplay of writing and reading, is what he claims as philosophy. An implication of this line of interpretation is that while philosophizing is a product of reading, the reading in question is not especially of books, especially not of what we think of as books of philosophy. The reading is of whatever is before you.[47]

To read whatever is before us is to take stock of the concrete conditions in which we are, in which we say that we find ourselves. Cavell sees the thrust of Thoreau's argument to be that philosophical life is an economy, a rule of the house, and that this rule emerges from our domestic activity; that is, we can speak of economics precisely because we have houses and (must) keep them. Cavell, through Thoreau, is criticizing economics, generally, so Cavell's and Thoreau's general criticism of economic theory must apply itself to something that we may call the "economic theory of capitalism." This is not to say that Cavell (or Thoreau, for that matter), rejects capital ownership. He means to say that we can have an idea of ownership only and to the extent that we really do own things. This is the sense of his observation, "Either we are able to rethink a thought that comes our way, to own and assess it as it occurs, or we must let it pass, it is not ours."[48] This, in its turn, is roughly Cavell's way of saying that the American way of being together is not theoretical. In saying this, however, he is not denying the possibility of a theory of America, but pointing us to the necessary starting point of America's theorization. A key to this is in the title of the chapter of Cavell's work in which the remark appears: "The Philosopher in American Life." In recalling us to the rule of the house, the economy from which we must learn the theory of economics, Cavell is pointing us to the national life of the people of the United States as the place in which to find America.[49]

We shall shortly consider in more detail the use of economic terms in Thoreau's writing. For our present purposes, let us recall John Adams's description of rulers as, "attorneys, agents, and trustees, for the people."

---

oblique reference to Plato's statement of the good life in the Republic (at 372a1–c1), though I do point to it as a possibility, and reserve, so to speak, the right to re-direct.

47. Cavell, *Quest*, 18.

48. Ibid., 19.

49. Remember that Voegelin's theoretical *point de depart* is political reality, so that there is at least plausibly a point at which Voegelin and Cavell meet, and if their meeting is one of agreement regarding the basic object of theoretical inquiry, then it is at the least possible to claim that they participate in what MacIntyre calls a tradition of inquiry.

These are names for activities that exist in the daily economic life of citizens. Adams further discussed the conditions of rulership as these were understood in America, saying, "If the cause, the interest and trust, is insidiously betrayed, or wantonly trifled away, the people have a right to revoke the authority that they themselves have deputed, and to constitute abler and better agents, attorneys, and trustees."[50] Once again, this is not to suggest the opportunity of an "economic" interpretation of American political life, when economic refers to the modern study of systems of production and exchange according to mathematical and statistical models. It stands to indicate the existence of a specific American political vocabulary, which authors from at least the time of Adams (and we have seen that Adams got it from somewhere) have employed. This is what is before us. Our project, and Thoreau's, and possibly Emerson's and certainly Adams's, is that of reading whatever is before us.

The Circumstances of Writing and the Reading of Circumstances

That Cavell believes in such a project, that he considers himself to be involved in it somehow, is witnessed by Cavell himself when he says of a passage in Thoreau's *Walden*[51] in which Thoreau advances the claim to be writing the first book of philosophy, and announces the need to inherit philosophy:

> Thoreau's invocation of the oldest Egyptian and Hindoo [*sic*] philosophers should itself secure the fact [that Thoreau, in

50. Diggins, *Portable John Adams*, 218–19.

51. Cavell is discussing the opening lines of the third chapter of *Walden*, which is entitled, "Reading". The passage reads, in pertinent part:

> WITH a little more deliberation in the choice of their pursuits, all men would perhaps become essentially students and observers, for certainly their nature and destiny are interesting to all alike. In accumulating property for ourselves or our posterity, in founding a family or a state, or acquiring fame even, we are mortal; but in dealing with truth we are immortal, and need fear no change nor accident. The oldest Egyptian or Hindoo philosopher raised a corner of the veil from the statue of the divinity; and still the trembling robe remains raised, and I gaze upon as fresh a glory as he did, since it was I in him that was then so bold, and it is he in me that now reviews the vision. No dust has settled on that robe; no time has elapsed since that divinity was revealed. That time which we really improve, or which is improvable, is neither past, present, nor future.

Harding, *Variorum Walden*, 96.

claiming to write the first book of philosophy, is not claiming priority with respect to other philosophers, but that he is, as Cavell says, "co-eval" with them], along with its implication that America must inherit philosophy not—or not alone, not primarily?—from Europe, but also from where Europe inherited it, from wherever Plato inherited it (which only philosophy will know). Here is just another version of *Walden*'s mythical brag to philosophy, specifically announcing, in all modesty, that to inherit philosophy you have already to be in the way of philosophy.[52]

Among other things, Cavell is here saying that the condition of America's being amenable to theorization, is that America be already an expression of an experience of order. Cavell understands, and would have his readers understand that, as Aristotle learned from his teacher, the experience of order is the wondrous beginning of all philosophy. On this reading, a theory of America will need to say what is specific, what is peculiar to the experience of order that is in America; American philosophy, whatever form it might take, in order to be philosophy, must be a critical reflection on the thaumazeic experience as it occurs in America.

More to this, as in order further to place America in the way of philosophy: wonder—an experience possible only in community—the experience of the community of the divine and the human, is the condition and the constitutive of the experience of order. Socrates' interpretation of the Delphic oracle is a challenge to the city (one that cannot be known not to be a mortal threat, at least not prior to examination). Thoreau would have America take up Socrates' challenge to the city—to embrace, rather than indict Socrates' commitment to philosophy. This is to say, Thoreau would make America to stand or fall on her ability to make good on Socrates' commitment. Thoreau's claim to be contemporary with the most ancient philosophers ought to be read in this light. Consider now the following from Emerson's essay, "Nature":

> Give me health and a day, and I will make the pomp of emperors ridiculous. The dawn is my Assyria; the sunset and moonrise my Paphos, and unimaginable realms of faerie; broad noon shall be my England of the senses and the understanding; the night shall be my Germany of mystic philosophy and dreams.[53]

52. Cavell, *Quest*, 19–20.
53. Carpenter, *Ralph Waldo Emerson: Representative Selections*, 17.

Emerson, the American scholar, here claims that the whole history of civilization, and all philosophy is contained in one American day. This claim, in its turn, establishes the question of America's relation to philosophy, as one, not of negation, but of assumption. To the extent that there is an America to speak of, it will have in it the whole project of civilization—and in a way that leaves open the question whether America depends on that project, or whether that project depends upon the success of America, and finally, whether these are really alternatives, i.e., really mutually exclusive.

This latest reflection does not establish that there is wonder in America, but only that an American has said (in some sense or other of the word) a wondrous thing. Returning now to Thoreau's brag, his claim to have written the first book of philosophy, it is necessary to consider that to write the first book of philosophy need not entail denying that other books of philosophy have been written. It may be a claim to excellence, for example; or it may be a claim to give philosophical expression to the new order of the ages in America. Anyway, there is still the matter of civilization's and philosophy's recapitulation in America. Cavell says it happens quite ordinarily, through undistracted reading of what he calls, following Emerson, the common, the near, the familiar and the low:

> I ask not for the great, the remote, the romantic; what is doing in Italy or Arabia; what is Greek art, or Provençal minstrelsy; I embrace the common, I explore and sit at the feet of the familiar, the low. Give me in-sight into to-day, and you may have the antique and future worlds. What would we really know the meaning of? The meal in the firkin; the milk in the pan; the ballad in the street; the news of the boat; the glance of the eye; the form and the gait of the body; — show me the ultimate reason of these matters; show me the sublime presence of the highest spiritual cause lurking, as always it does lurk, in these suburbs and extremities of nature; let me see every trifle bristling with the polarity that ranges it instantly on an eternal law; and the shop, the plough and the ledger referred to the like cause by which light undulates and poets sing;—and the world lies no longer a dull miscellany and lumber-room, but has form and order; there is no trifle, there is no puzzle, but one design unites and animates the farthest pinnacle and the lowest trench.[54]

54. Ibid., 68.

With due respect for the mountainous scholarship treating this and similar passages of Emerson's writing as so many transcendentalist manifestos, the text quoted above nevertheless contains an explicit call for classical metaphysics, precisely in Emerson's demand for the ultimate reason of things. Emerson, moreover, asks to see the ultimate reason of things in what he calls the suburbs and extremities of nature, and this is a sign of the enduring presence of a more ancient way of viewing the world and our way of knowing it—or at least of the desire for such a way. Let Emerson's employment of the word, "suburbs" be a pointed reference— by inversion—to the understanding of the city as *cosmion*—by implication—to the idea that *cosmos* is *megalopoliteia*. Emerson's continuation of the discussion, in which he asks to see a single law (he says "a like cause") tie together such artifacts of civilization as a shop, a plough and a ledger, with natural phenomena (the undulation of light) and cultural expression (the song of poets), is a call for a recovery of the classical understanding of order, in which modes of human living were not seen as disconnected from the movements of the larger world, but as threads in an intricate weave running through all that is. Whatever Emerson's position, whatever his status and his stature within the American tradition of inquiry and nationhood, his expression of desire for understanding in such a direction means that a theory of politics rooted in the critical clarification of the American experience of order must range more widely and sound more deeply than any mere inventory of seventeenth and eighteenth-century liberal ideas, however well and thoroughly prepared. This is, by the way, another, further point on which Cavell and Voegelin find themselves in agreement. Each, in his own way, rejects the catalogue, even critically composed, of ideas as the proper work of philosophy. We are searching for what Voegelin called, "The unfolding of the typical in meaningful concreteness,[55]" which is beginning to sound very much like what we may now hear Cavell call "the ordinary".

Order and the Ordinary

The final essay of Cavell's work *In Quest of the Ordinary* is called "The Uncanniness of the Ordinary". That essay is Cavell's attempt to express some philosophical concerns regarding what he calls, the ordinariness

---

55. Voegelin, *NSP*, 89.

or everydayness of language.[56] Primarily (and as the title of the essay suggests), Cavell is concerned with what he calls the uncanniness of the ordinary:

> The uncanniness of the ordinary is epitomized by the possibility or threat of what philosophy has called skepticism, understood (as in my studies of Austin and of the later Wittgenstein I have come to understand it) as the capacity, even desire, of ordinary language to repudiate itself, specifically to repudiate its power to word the world, to apply to the things we have in common, or to pass them by. (By "the desire of ordinary language to repudiate itself" I mean—doesn't it go without saying?—a desire on the part of speakers of a native or mastered tongue who desire to assert themselves, and despair of it.)[57]

Let us begin with the words, "uncanny" and "ordinary." That which is uncanny is unsettling. The American Heritage Dictionary gives "eerie" as a synonym; it says that the uncanny intimates something of a supernatural origin or source. As a second definition, American Heritage gives, "So keen and perceptive as to seem preternatural."[58] "Ordinary," on the other hand, is normal, common, the kind of thing one might see and hear most every day. Ordinary also describes the kind of role one has in an institution, e.g., as ordinary professor. Most interestingly, ordinary names the constitutive element of a group, as in the *ordinarius loci*. Now, to be normal is to be that which corresponds to the norm, but it is also that which sets the standard, as in the *ecole normale des hautes etudes*.

The ordinary in quest of which Cavell has gone and calls us to go, is at once that which is normal in each sense we have discussed, and so

---

56. Cf. Cavell, *Quest*, 153–54. Everydayness is the standard English translation of one of Heidegger's central terms, and the phrase, "extraordinariness of the ordinary" does appear in Heidegger's essay on "The Origin of a Work of Art", in *Poetry, Language, Thought*, 143–62. Cavell does not consider himself as using the word in the same way Heidegger does. At 154 of *Quest*, Cavell recognizes the pertinence of Heidegger's phrase, but continues to say, "[M]y intuition of the ordinariness of human life, and of human life's avoidance of the ordinary, is not Heidegger's. For him, the extraordinariness of the ordinary has to do with forces in play that constitute our common habitual world; it is a constitution he describes as part of his account of the technological, of which what we accept as the ordinary is as it were one consequence; it is thus to be seen as a symptom of what Nietzsche prophesied, or diagnosed, in declaring that for us 'the wasteland grows,' a phrase Heidegger recurrently invokes in *What is Called Thinking?*"

57. Cavell, *Quest*, 154.

58. Pickett et al., *American Heritage Dictionary of the English Language*, s.v. "ordinary" and "uncanny."

contemporaneously bears all the ways of being ordinary. The ordinary constitutes after the manner of an *ordinarius loci*, and sets the norm even as it expresses and conforms to it. Said shortly, the ordinary is simultaneously that which brings order and that which is ordered;[59] hence, the uncanniness of the ordinary. The uncanniness of the ordinary is precisely the tendency of the ordinary to present itself at once as ordered and as ordering. To see both constantly without eschewing the question which is which, is philosophy. Aristotle knew this when he wrote his *Categories*. His teacher, Plato, knew that living in the best city requires such thought.[60]

The Search for Order in America from Emerson to Plato

In 2004, Cavell published a book called *Cities of Words*, a title that will be familiar enough to readers of Plato, and likely require no further elucidation.[61] Cavell's concern with the American author, Ralph Waldo Emerson, emerges once again from the pages of that effort and presses upon us Cavell's perception of Plato's nearness to America, and America's familiarity with Plato:

> When [Emerson] says in "Fate," "Ideas are in the air," can we doubt that he is invoking Plato's theory of forms at the same time that he is speaking, in 1850, of the absorbing issue of slavery, as if inquiring as to our participation in, call it our stance toward, these ideas? He goes on to follow out the literal consequence that something essential to our lives, the air we breathe, would be fatal to us but for the fact that our lungs are already filled with this air, allowing us to withstand the weight and pressure of air from above by the counterpressure of that air from within ourselves. This becomes, I take it, a parable whose moral is that the issue of slavery is a matter of life and death, for the nation and for the nation's breath, its speech, its power to understand

59. The bibliography of the philosophical treatment of the *ordo ordinans* and the *ordo ordinatum*, would on its own run to the length of a doctoral dissertation. Let these remarks further serve to place the suggestion that there is an intimate connection between the classical tradition of inquiry, carried forward and perfected in the Christian era, and the present investigation.

60. Cf. Plato, *Republic*, 368e2.

61. I will not insist on reading the book's sub-title, *Pedagogical Letters on a Register of the Moral Life*, as a précis of Plato's *Republic*.

itself, and therewith for philosophy, whose demand for freedom is incompatible with slavery.[62]

If we are careful to read Cavell as he would be read (which is to say, if we read Cavell as Cavell himself reads), then of course we must say, "Yes, we can doubt that Emerson is discussing either Plato or slavery in that passage." It would be a mistake, however, to consider that Cavell is looking for an escape from doubt, or from the tendency to doubt. In Cavell's essay titled, "The Philosopher in American Life," which is the opening essay *In Quest of the Ordinary*, Cavell articulates the idea that Emerson and Thoreau, in developing a sense of the ordinary that Cavell discovers in their treatment of the common, the familiar, the near and the low, somehow "underwrite" the sense of the ordinary that he derives from Wittgenstein's later philosophical practice, and from the philosophical practice of John L. Austin, who was Cavell's teacher. Cavell says that this notion of his, while persistent, is "[A]ll but inexplicit." We are left to understand that the only explication of the most persistent thought in his opening lecture in quest of the ordinary consists in Cavell's calling that thought, "all but inexplicit." Leave aside the fact that being, "all but inexplicit" is like being "a little bit pregnant". In any case, the passage from Cavell that we began to consider a few moments ago gives us a few other clues regarding the way in which he hopes we will read him. The first clue is in the word, "underwrite." Cavell is preoccupied with economic terms. Actually, it is more accurate to say that Cavell is preoccupied with Thoreau's preoccupation with economic terms, which preoccupation he expresses in several places throughout his many works.[63] This preoccupation is a lifelong one for Cavell, and one that informs much of his thought, but that we needs must trace out of the specific discussion of this particular economic term (for reasons of economy).

To underwrite is to agree to pay a sum *in casu*, or to act as guarantor of something (a promise to pay a sum or to deliver goods). To underwrite is to assume the risk, in whole or in part, of a promise to pay in case of a valid claim. Emerson and Thoreau, then, assume the risk of Wittgenstein and Austin's philosophical practice. We wonder how two American authors, who flourished more than a half century before either Wittgenstein or Austin were born, could possibly underwrite the philosophical practice of the two philosophers. The answer to this paradox is to be had in

---

62. Cavell, *Cities of Words*, 7.

63. Cf. ibid., 19 *et passim*.

the way Cavell understands reading and writing; what they are, and how we ought to do the one and the other.

Toward a Reading of the Declaration

Cavell pays attention to words; we suspect he would like us to pay attention to him paying attention to them. The corollary to Cavell's understanding of reading is, then, the requirement he places on writing:

> [in writing] one must give over control of one's appropriations, as if to learn what they are. [64]

In order to grasp fully the significance of this statement, the reader needs to know that Cavell asks early on in his essay whether there can be any speaking that is not quoting. If there is not, then all speech will be basically quotation, so it will be useless to quote, insofar as there is no original to be quoted.[65] The metaphysical implications of this line of questioning are manifold. One need only think of St. Thomas, who found the newness of the world to be a question un-decidable by reason, alone.[66] If God's saying, "Let there be light!" etc., is God's giving sound to His breath and speaking the being of the world, then the whole world is a divine quotation, and the human capacity for language is on this reading an ability to speak of the divine, and a lack of attention to this fact of language, when understood as this ability, could make all speech blasphemy.

This line of thinking involves America, the founding document of which explicitly invokes the question, when it deploys the language of creation in order to justify its claim to independence. The implications of this line of questioning for America will come even more clearly into view as we begin a direct discussion of the Declaration. When Americans claim, "We hold these truths to be self-evident: that all men are created equal; that they are endowed by their Creator with certain unalienable rights, etc.," they are making a specific claim for America, i.e., that America is the place in which the truth of Man's equal creation is plain for all to see. When the blight of slavery, an institution incompatible with liberty and therefore inhuman, was about to be eradicated from American life, Lincoln prayed that, "[T]his nation, under God, shall have a new birth

---

64. Cavell, *Quest*, 25.

65. Cf. ibid., 24

66. Cf. Aquinas, *ST* I Q.46 a.2

of freedom." In light of these reflections, we see that Lincoln's prayer is no mere flight of rhetorical fancy, but is made in earnest. In light of the American experience, Lincoln says, either "We the People" are "One nation under God," or we are no nation at all[67] (and substantiating such claims for America and for philosophy will depend in large part on our ability to read the documents of national foundation, which requires first that we have learned to read).

Quoting and Misquoting

The point is that Cavell is apt to teach us something about how we ought to read those documents. Cavell called the idea that Emerson and Thoreau underwrite the philosophical practice of J. L. Austin and the later Wittgenstein, "[P]erhaps the most pervasive, and yet all but inexplicit[68]" thought in the series of lectures he was then presenting. These lines immediately followed:

> I see both developments—ordinary language philosophy and American transcendentalism —as responses to skepticism, to that anxiety about our human capacities as knowers that can be taken to open modern philosophy in Descartes, interpreted by that philosophy as our human subjection to doubt.[69]

Cavell went on to trace his conviction that philosophy responds to skepticism by preserving the skeptical argument[70], "As though the philosophical

---

67. It were pertinent to note a peculiarity of the diction, "Under God": readers of this diction in the twenty-first century are wont to understand it as an indication of ontological stature, or status, especially when the diction appears as part of a phrase like, "One nation, under God, etc." While this reading is not wrong, as far as it goes, it nevertheless does not go far enough. In Lincoln's mouth, or from his pen, the words, "under God," do not indicate ontological status, only. They also, and even primarily, refer to God's providence. This is illustrated by the following, which comes from an address Lincoln made to the participants in a Sanitary Fair in Philadelphia, on June 16th, 1864: "We accepted this war for an object, a worthy object, and the war will end when that object is attained. Under God, I hope it never will end until that time." Quoted in Basler, *Abraham Lincoln: His Speeches and Writings*, 752. Here, the expression refers broadly to the Divine providential governance of human affairs. The nineteenth-century audience was arguably attuned to the contemporaneous presence of multiple and complementary connotations in the expression.

68. Cavell, *Quest*, 4.

69. Ibid.

70. Ibid., 5.

profit of the argument would be to show not how it might end but why it must begin and why it must have no end, at least none within philosophy, or what we think of as philosophy." To preserve the skeptical argument is to remain in conversation with it, to refuse disengagement.

Philosophy exists in the openness to the skeptical crisis, i.e., in the willingness and ability to embrace entirely the constant, often annoying and possibly discouraging question, "How do you know (that you are a man, slave)?" and the assertion, "I deny (that you are my equal, for you are a negro)," and the challenge/dismissal, "I do not believe you (when you claim through your mere humanity, an equal right to the inheritance of liberty in America)," without succumbing to anger when one is annoyed, without giving in to the temptation to discouragement, without ever, ever, ever losing heart, no matter what.[71]

The Implications of (Mis)Quotation

As it is, the precise quotation of Emerson's essay would be, "Certain ideas are in the air." Having by now seen a considerable amount of Cavell's reading and writing, it is reasonable to presume that Cavell the author would not expect a reader to pass over his omission without a second thought; indeed, his omission may very well be designed to set the word, "certain," in relief, and hence the notion of certainty, hence the experience of being certain, and thence what it means to say that there are certain ideas in the air. We know that Cavell finds Emerson's claim to philosophy, or at least Emerson's call for philosophy (and how the one is the other is something we cannot here fail to note, even as we must postpone investigation for a little while, yet), in Emerson's constant misquotation of texts in the philosophical canon. Cavell is also an author whose insistence on taking absolute responsibility for his words makes it impossible for us to dismiss his omission as a mistake.

One possible explanation is that Cavell is calling our attention to Emerson's claim of certainty for the ideas that are in the air, i.e., his claim that there are ideas in the air and that they are certain. There is, however, another way, one that neither privileges nor prejudices the foregoing possibility; it is a way that has the character of proven usefulness in Cavell's

---

71. At least one tradition of philosophy, epitomized by the story in *Republic VIII*, takes the fearless descent into unknowing, the beginnings of the therapeutic of philosophy, as its highest aspiration. The philosopher returns to the cave.

work: the juxtaposition of disjointed sentences. Take the following from Emerson:

> Man is timid and apologetic; he is no longer upright; he dares
> not say "I think," "I am," but quotes some saint or sage.[72]

Here, Emerson is quite unmistakably alluding to a philosopher. Catching this, Cavell asks whether this fact might stand to indicate that Emerson is confessing an inability to speak, i.e., that the best he can do is make use of others' words. Cavell pushes the issue so far as to say that language is, that words are, an inheritance; it is, and they are commonly before us; we must come into ownership of them.[73] Without disputing Cavell's reading, there is nevertheless something further to see and to say. Emerson's thought as it is expressed may be philosophical precisely to the extent that Emerson does not quote Descartes exactly. Suppose there is a claim to philosophy in the very fact that Emerson is not exactly quoting Descartes. Cavell might then be claiming philosophy for himself, in so precisely misquoting Emerson. This might have consequences for any attempt to discern an answer to the present question, especially if (it could be established that) Cavell's misquoting is the result of his having quoted from memory. In such a case, Cavell's claim for philosophy might be that philosophy depends on misquoting, which would be a kind of imperfect recollection. If quoting is reproducing an image of something, at its most basic level a word, and if the starting point of our approach to philosophy must be the imperfect quotation of some word, then the suggestion might be that misquoting a word or words is precisely a deliberate attempt to make us think the Platonic metaphysics. In other words, Cavell may well be asking whether philosophy begins in the imperfect representation of a *logos* (the reader will remember that imperfect, in the sense of the word that is nearest to its Latin root, does not mean faulty, but unfinished or incomplete). There is, arguably, no more Platonic a thought.

With all this in mind, consider now that to word the world is another way of turning an experience into thought; to word the world is precisely to make its meaning public (add to this that there is an open question in philosophy whether the world is a fact, that is, whether the world is made). Wording the world is precisely what God does when He creates it. God gives humanity the power of *logos* so that mankind might have, under Him, lordship over creation. The *logos* becomes flesh and

72. Carpenter, ed. *Ralph Waldo Emerson: Representative Selections*, 101.

73. Cf. Cavell, *Quest*, 106–14.

dwells among us, and gives us words to say that do things: *hoc est enim corpus meum*. In that story, words open doors between the worlds. The structure of the world in which we live may change when the right person says the right things in the right circumstances; for example, political bonds among distinct peoples may be dissolved by declaring their dissolution. The last chapter considered the circumstances of the American case. The question has now become: who is to say the words?

Cavell and the Authority to Declare (in) America

To ask "who is to say?" is to ask by what authority a speaker speaks. Think of the Founders' claim for the new constitution that "We the People," ordain and establish it. Consider now Patrick Henry's question, "What right had they to say, 'We the People'?"[74] Henry's right to pose the question is established (we may presume) by the fact that Henry was an early advocate of separation from the British Empire and a signer of the Declaration of Independence, which contains the words:

> We hold these truths to be self-evident, that all men are created equal, that they are endowed by their Creator with certain unalienable Rights, that among these are Life, Liberty and the pursuit of Happiness. —That to secure these rights, Governments are instituted among Men, deriving their just powers from the consent of the governed, —That whenever any Form of Government becomes destructive of these ends, it is the Right of the People to alter or to abolish it, and to institute new Government, laying its foundation on such principles and organizing its powers in such form, as to them shall seem most likely to effect their Safety and Happiness.

To the truth of the claims advanced in the whole document, we say in surety whereof, the congressmen memorably pledged their lives, their fortunes, their sacred honor. We note this last fact, i.e., the signatories' pledge, which was in the name of the United States, in Congress assembled, because a half-dozen generations of scholars in the United States have attempted with varying degrees of success to reduce the ideas of the Declaration to a minimally modified mimickery of John Locke's famous axiom, and the revolution it proclaimed to justify to a mere exercise in

---

74. Patrick Henry to Virginia Ratifying Convention, June 4th, 1788 in Bailyn, *Debate*, 596.

Lockean political theory. The similarities between the Declaration's formula and Locke's own are undeniable. Nevertheless, the desire to explain the justification of American independence in terms of Lockean or otherwise liberal political theory is ultimately paradoxical.

John Adams, who sat on the Declaration's drafting committee and all but single-handedly carried the day for independence, spoke of the independence of America and the American Revolution in the following terms:

> Who was the author...of American Independence [?] . . . We might as well inquire who were the Inventors of Agriculture, Horticulture, Architecture, Musick [sic]. . . [The] only true answer must be the first emigrants. The Revolution was [therefore] effected before the war commenced. The Revolution was in the minds and hearts of the people; a change in their religious sentiments of their duties and obligations.[75]

We may understand the question, "Who was the author of American independence?" to be asking, "In whom does American independence have authority?"[76] Adams's reply, that the only true answer must be the first emigrants, would find authority in their experience of exodus, for he describes them as emigrants, and not as immigrants. They came out of the Old World; their coming into the New, where they established a way of life, eventually allowed their descendants to say with probity, "this is good," in describing the way of life that they had inherited, and so without reference to the king of Great Britain. The first emigrants were involved with each other in constructing what Cavell has called, "The conversation of justice."[77] The first emigrants were also, therefore, immigrants, for they came into conversation with one another. Their words eventually wrought

---

75. Adams to James Madison, July 25th, 1818; Adams to James Tudor, Nov. 7th, 1816; Adams to Hezekiah Niles, Feb. 13th, 1818, quoted in Ellis, *Passionate Sage*, 103–5.

76. The English word, "authority" is derived from the Latin noun, *auctoritas*. The Latin suffix, -*itas* is used to indicate a state or condition; *auctor-itas* is therefore the state or condition of being *auctor*. *Auctor*, in its turn, is one who brings into being, who takes the initiative. The *auctor* is one who does the action of the verb *augere*, i.e., one who gives birth to something else from within himself and nourishes it. Those who speak *cum auctoritate* are those whose speech in some fundamental way alters the world, changes fundamentally the structure of reality. For the etymology of *auctor-itas* and *augeo, ere*, see Benveniste, *Le vocabulaire des institutions indo-européennes*, 396–7.

77. Cf. Cavell, *Cities of Words*, 172. Cavell is following and answering John Rawls, i.e., providing his own account of what Rawls calls the conversation of justice.

momentous changes in the world. An important moment in the history of that conversation, is the Declaration of Independence, which we have seen Jefferson describe as a document that aimed neither at originality of principle or sentiment, but that was not copied from any particular previous writing; the intention of the Declaration was to express the American mind in a tone and spirit proper to the occasion.[78]

Whatever else this means, it tells us that the American mind does not express itself in others' terms; the words it speaks are its own, though deliberately, they are not novel. America does not speak first, but is called upon to speak, and expresses itself in a way that is appropriate to the call to which it speaks:

> When in the course of human events it becomes necessary for one people to dissolve the political bands which have connected them with another. . .a decent respect for the opinions of mankind requires that they should declare the causes which impel them to the separation.

It might be useful at this point to visit a pertinent practical example of this way of thinking, specifically, one that occurs in Cavell's *Cities of Words*, precisely in his chapter on Locke:

> I recall . . . Emerson's accusation and confession that we no longer speak or think for ourselves, no longer say "I think," "I am," but "quote some saint or sage." . . . [I]t follows from this loss of capacity to outface a doubt of our existence, that we in effect declare that we haunt our existence. The implications for the body politic are immediate, since if I have no voice of my own in which to express my thoughts, I cannot give my consent to be governed and our condition is that we haunt our society. It cannot hear us.
>
> But here, could we express Emerson's longing for America to discover itself by imagining him to declare, "Man is timid, he is afraid to say, 'I think,' 'I consent,' but instead quotes, for example, Locke?"[79]

The Declaration is not exactly quoting Locke. The words of that document, which we have given above, are similar enough to Locke's language; they are similar enough to let us note and possibly —so we might understand the Founders to be requiring of us— to know the difference. The document does not say, "Mr. Locke tells us that all men are created

78. Cf. Bergh et al., *Writings of Thomas Jefferson*, 16:118.

79. Cavell, *Cities of Words*, 69.

equal, and everybody knows how smart Mr. Locke is, how important he is, how right he is." The *Declaration* says, "We hold these truths to be self-evident:" so that the thirteen political societies are united in claiming these truths each for its own in America; what is more, the thirteen States of America, through their representatives to Congress, are claiming that "these truths" are immediately apparent to the reason as true in America and for Americans. Simply stated, the truths of the Declaration are visibly present as ordering forces in American life, if only one will come and see for oneself. There is no argument in the Declaration because self-evidence cannot, as such, be argued.

By 1826, Adams had recognized the importance that the commemoration of the first public promulgation of the Declaration had gained for the national community. He considers, however, that it is only a point of relief in a much larger conversation, one begun by generations of men and women already long since passed in 1800.

The Declaration, on its own, would confirm Adams, who essentially claimed that America is a place in which a man discovers that he is free, which is to say that he is a man; as we have seen through Cavell's Platonizing discussion of Emerson (and Thoreau), this discovery is (the same as) a call to philosophy, or rather, one possible response to the call from philosophy. Again, there is everything quite the opposite of arcane in this language. If Cavell is right to claim for philosophy that it is essentially a responsiveness, which must not shun the possibility of skepticism but must preserve skepticism as a possibility in order freely to choose self-subjection to intelligibility,[80] then we may say that America must preserve the possibility of merely mouthing Locke in answer to the question of the authorship of American independence (which is another way of posing the question of authority—we assume that the issue is not who held the pen) in order to respond with its own authority, in order to say, "We the People." Put another way: if what we have discussed with Cavell has produced a tenable thesis regarding America, and if our way of reading with Cavell is even minimally fruitful, then we may wonder that so many who take the name, "American," and even pretend to glory in that name, are so eager to assert America's debt to Locke.

If Cavell's claim for America (made through Emerson) can hold (or be made to hold), i.e., that Emerson finds philosophy for America (which is more-or-less a matter of opinion), by finding philosophy in America

80. Cf. Cavell, *Quest*, 4–7 et passim.

(that philosophy is to be found in America is a matter of fact, one that will be established in the finding of philosophy in America), then what might be described, what indeed has been described as America's(ns') rejection of philosophy may very well be in some cases a well-founded accusation. This would be, this is America's desiring to make itself intelligible, and despairing of it. This would be, this is Americans' repudiation of language as something learned in, as something imparted by, America, and so of America and Americans as people with whom to speak. We read the resolution of the 2nd Continental Congress, which, on the 2nd of July, 1776, voted in favor of Richard Henry Lee's June 7th motion:

> RESOLVED: That these United Colonies are, and of right ought to be, free and independent States, that they are absolved from all allegiance to the British Crown, and that all connection between them and the State of Great Britain is, and ought to be, totally dissolved.[81]

The work thus far advanced has aimed at recovering two things: the first is the urgency of asking upon what basis Congress' claim of right rests; the second is the question whether anyone may be satisfied with an answer like, "Because we are Americans." As to the first, consider that in so resolving, the members of Congress were signing their own death warrants, and committing the states they represented (and so the peoples, whose states those were, which the members represented) to war, and all the immense expense in life and treasure that is the price of war. To say that they did so in order to test a parlor theory of the origin of politics, is not to praise the worth of philosophy; it is to indict the founders as moral imbeciles, at best; at worst, they would be rabid, bloodthirsty ideologues.

As for the second, allow for a moment that Thomas Jefferson had an important role in the Declaration's authorship, without further essaying to establish what, exactly, his role might have been, and recall Jefferson's description of the Declaration as an expression of the American mind, along with his placement of all its authority in the felicity of its expression.[82] Though Locke is clearly present as one contributor to the sentiments of the day, the authority of the Declaration rests on its harmonizing of those sentiments, which, as Jefferson himself has just attested, is

---

81. Ford, *Journals of the Continental Congress*, 5:425.

82. Cf. "Jefferson to Henry Lee, May 8th, 1825," in Bergh et al., *Writings of Thomas Jefferson*, 16:118–19.

an expression of the American mind. This is not Lockean. This is something different.

Directions of Convers(at)ion

Thus far, two distinct and distinctively American vocabularies have emerged. One is economic. The other embraces terms of direction, movement and orientation. It is with this second vocabulary that the work is presently concerned. When Emerson discusses America as new, yet unapproachable, it is because America is always before us and always behind us, so that discovering America is a matter of turning into it, and we called this turning a conversion, which involved turning experience into thought and making the meaning of a fact public. John Adams locates the authorship of American independence in the "first emigrants", so that the authority of America is always in its being brought out; Thomas Jefferson says the authority of America's Declaration rests on its harmonizing of the sentiments of the day, wherever and however these be found and expressed. America is either approachable, or it is not. As Cavell puts it in *This New Yet Unapproachable America*, "I cannot approach it alone; the eventual human community is between us, or it is nowhere."[83]

If we take ourselves as somewhere, whether here or there, nevertheless always with something before us and behind us, then we are always quite literally, in between. This observation brings into view a thematic affinity between Voegelin and Cavell (and eventually among all three principal interlocutors). Voegelin characterizes the political space, the conceptual space of human existence as *metaxy*, the space between the beginning and the beyond.[84] It will not be a stretch to hear this as being between what is before us and what is behind us. Coming into America will then be a matter of emigration from ourselves, as we are, and a coming into something that will be like a received mode of speech, a discovery of ourselves as participants in a conversation that we did not start and cannot finish, a conversation regarding precisely the question of who we are and where we find ourselves. This is at once *conversio* and *conversatio*, where this last is an outpouring of self into community of sense.

83. Cavell, *This New Yet Unapproachable America*, 108.

84. Cf. Voegelin, *OH* 4:50 *et passim* in *CW* 17. Cf. also Voegelin, *OH* 5:43 *et passim* in *CW* 18. The introductory essays to each volume, by Michael Franz and Ellis Sandoz, respectively, are extremely useful and even essential tools for those readers not already well-versed in Voegelin's work.

CHAPTER 3

Constituting (Knowledge of) a Nation

ANYONE WHO ENGAGES CONTEMPORARY questions of U.S. Constitutional interpretation enters upon what Alasdair MacIntyre has called a field of radical conflict, at the heart of which is a disagreement about the kind of people Americans are, i.e., about the constitution of the people of the United States. As in MacIntyre's discussion of what Cavell has called the "headline moral issues of the day (e.g. the question whether protecting the right to and practice of procured abortion is a fundamental duty of government or state-sanctioned murder, or perhaps both)," so it is in the discussion of the Constitution's interpretation, generally: each position, each camp involved pretends to have the right method of interpretation, and therefore to be the authentic interpreter of the meaning of American nationhood.

At the same time, they conduct the debate, such as it is, in isolated abstraction, as though the question of interpreting the Constitution properly were a question of choosing and applying the right analytical concepts to a series of abstract "theoretical" conundra.

In point of fact, the Constitution is a form of government, i.e., a plan for the construction of representative elements for a society of human beings. The hashing-out at Philadelphia of the proposal for a form of government famously involved soaringly erudite engagement of the age-old philosophical question as to the best form of government. Those seemingly abstract discussions, however, were conducted with a view to the American genius for government. Determination, in the abstract, of the powers and principles most necessary to the construction of plausible

99

representative elements, was part and parcel of the search for those powers and principles in their American incarnations. As Forrest McDonald
has noted, the Framers were politically polyglot:

> They could speak the language of Bolingbroke, Montesquieu,
> Locke, the classical republicans, Hume, and many others.[1]

McDonald goes on to say that the Framers would choose to employ one
language or another, according to what he calls the political languages'
relative rhetorical appropriateness to a given argument.[2] What seems to
escape McDonald, though through no fault of his own, is the difficulty,
even the impossibility of translating the political language of, say, the
classical republicans, into the language of Locke or Hume. The point is
that the list McDonald gives, if taken as a list of abstract political theories,
is a list of theories, the respective presuppositions and subsequent problems of which are largely antithetical and often irreconcilable.

In other words, discussion of the proper form to give the elements
of representation in America produced fluid transition from one political language to another, and this is telling; specifically, it tells something
important about the American experience of political life. In light of the
consideration that the proposed draft law was submitted to a citizenry
whose decision to ratify would be based upon their estimation of the
proposed elements' aptness to provide effective existential representation, the fact becomes particularly significant.

The significance is in the mental and spiritual aptitude required
to move so easily from one political vocabulary to another, and back
again—essentially, to be simultaneously at home in what MacIntyre
calls different traditions of inquiry. MacIntyre's example *par excellence*
of the thinker at home in multiple traditions of inquiry is St. Thomas
Aquinas, who simultaneously inhabited the Augustinian and Aristotelian traditions. Indeed, on MacIntyre's reading, the mode of St. Thomas'
simultaneous inhabitation of the traditions was synthesis. Thomas' great
intellectual achievement was that of synthesizing the Augustinian and
Aristotelian traditions, which had until his synthesis appeared as a pair

---

1. McDonald, *NOS*, 235.

2. The American incarnations of political principles, no less than Americans'
education in the history of political thinking, were a matter of history, or, if you will,
experience. When John Dickinson remarked, "Experience must be our only guide.
Reason may mislead us," he was addressing a specific question during a specific debate
on a specific day. The question was where to lodge the power to originate money bills.
Cf. Farrand, *Records of the Federal Convention of 1787*, 2:278. Henceforth *Records*.

of rival and incompatible traditions. Thomas' responsibility for an intellectual accomplishment that permanently changed the world is so great that the tradition he established bears his name.

The argument of this thesis is that America is the name of another synthesis of apparently rival and incompatible traditions. Who is responsible, and how and to what extent, are questions to be explored only after establishing that the conditions for such a synthesis obtained. As Voegelin put it at the end of the *New Science of Politics*:

> The American Revolution, though its debate was already strongly affected by the psychology of enlightenment, also had the good fortune of coming to its close within the institutional and Christian climate of the ancien régime.[3]

Said shortly, America is what Voegelin sees in the contemporaneous presence of the psychological pressure of the Enlightenment and the consolidation of civilizational tradition. The present project is therefore about establishing the following: that America is a living synthesis of notions, both ancient and modern; that the synthesis takes place in the national life of the American people; that the synthesis is an attempt to reply to problems of modernity and provide a way to overcome those problems. The task of the present chapter is to show how the thesis, as the work up to this point has made it possible to understand and articulate it, is arguable.

The first step in the direction of completing that task, is to show that Voegelin's understanding of the circumstances of the conclusion of the American Revolution is at least defensible. The next step will be to show how those circumstances were concretely felt in the spiritual, intellectual and moral life of the nation.

Exploring the Circumstances of Conclusion

The significance of what Voegelin called the conclusion of the American Revolution within the institutional and Christian climate of the ancien régime is epitomized in John Adams's marginal rejoinder to Mary Wollstonecraft's *Defence of the French Revolution*:

> If the Empire of superstition and hypocrisy should be overthrown, happy indeed will it be for the world; but if all religion

3. Voegelin, *NSP*, 241.

and all morality should be over-thrown with it, what advantage will be gained? The doctrine of human equality is founded entirely in the Christian doctrine that we are all children of the same Father, all accountable to Him for our conduct to one another, all equally bound to respect each other's self-love.[4]

At the same time, we must account for what Voegelin calls the gnostic forces present in America, forces that are most clearly manifest in the tendency of modernity to destroy history and so to render tradition quite literally unthinkable. Unchecked, these would force America into the apotheosis of modernity, which is popularly known as post-modernity.

The eminent Harvard historian, Arthur Schlesinger Jr. (perhaps unintentionally) diagnosed this part of America when, in the 1995-edition of his book on *The Disuniting of America*, he epitomized Thomas Paine's understanding of the American Revolution by saying, "The unstated national motto was 'Never look back,'"[5] a chilling observation, and all the more so for its coming from the pen of an historian. Cavell has followed Emerson in describing America as new yet unapproachable, because it is always before us and always behind us. At a certain point in "Experience" Emerson asks, "Where do we find ourselves?" and answers, "In a series of which we do not know the extremes," and "We wake and find ourselves on a stair," which, Cavell notes, is a step:

> Only it takes the lasting of the essay to realize that this *is* an answer. The most renowned phrase for what I was calling the power of passiveness—a power to demand the change of the world as a whole, Emerson sometimes calls it revolution, sometimes conversion—is what Thoreau will call civil disobedience.[6]

I would like to take Cavell's reading a step further, and note that stairs bring us from storey to storey. A century and a half ago, George Bancroft wrote:

> Our land is not more a recipient of the men of all countries than of their ideas. Annihilate the past of any one leading nation of the world, and our destiny would be changed . . . Our country stands, therefore, more than any other, as the unity of the race.[7]

4. Haraszti, *John Adams and the Prophets of Progress*, as cited in McCullough, *John Adams*, 619.

5. Schlesinger, *Disuniting of America*, 29.

6. Cavell, *This New Yet Unapproachable America*, 115

7. Bancroft, *Literary and Historical Miscellanies*, 355–56.

The story of America is one in which anyone and everyone is invited to participate, because to participate in the American story is to tell one's own, albeit in the language, let us say, the words of America. The Constitution is the words of America, *par excellence*. The role those words play in the telling of the story of America is unknowable apart from the place they have in the American story. Think, once again, of Lincoln's Independence Day speech in 1858:[8] to the extent that the Constitution provides elements of representation that adequately represent the existence of such men as Lincoln described, the Constitution represents the story of America. To lose contact with the historical situation of the Constitution's creation or crafting, is to lose contact with the story that makes the Constitution meaningful. It is to take oneself out of the story, so that one can neither hear it nor tell it.

How do we know the story is meaningful in the first place? To ask this is to ask whether there really is political community. Another thinker who has spent much time in conversation with Cavell has put the matter this way:

> We come to language as something that is already there before us in the practices of our elders. The criteria for calling something what it is are there in practice before we are, and we cannot come to thought and linguistic practice without them . . . Public words and the criteria for their use are there before us, and they are the only things we have to go on.[9]

In his essay on philosophy's recounting of the ordinary in Cavell, Stephen Mulhall puts the matter this way:

> The claims of the philosopher to speak for others when stating what is said when may be rebuffed in particular cases, but the claim to be speaking on someone's behalf is a condition for speech per se, in its absence, one would not be speaking privately (speaking a private language)—one would not be speaking at all. In this respect, Cavell's interpretation of contractarian politics comes to a conclusion which is parallel to his interpretation of morality; for in the latter case too, despite the fact that we may find our moral universe to be unshared by our interlocutor, our being open to moral debate and confrontation—our capacity to

8. V.s., 19, 19n.30.

9. Eldridge, ed., *Stanley Cavell*, 3–4.

elaborate our actions—is not just a condition for moral agency
but a condition for agency tout court.[10]

The upshot of all this is that we have no way of knowing, say, of assessing
the meaningfulness of the American (or any other conversation) outside
the conduct of it. We are free to take—indeed many of the founding
generation did take—the words of the proposed Constitution to be representative of the designs of a grasping, interested cabal, intent on rap-
ing the land and the populace, on preserving their despotic rule over an
enslaved race and achieving endless self-aggrandizement at the expense
of the larger portion of the continent's humanity, a humanity duped by
high-sounding words hiding base blandishments addressed to their own
acquisitiveness, the actuation of which was presumably prevented by the
systemic industrial imbecility of the vast portion of mankind. To think
this way is not to think that America is this; it is to think there is no
America. America does not refuse anyone the right to think this way,
even and especially to think so publicly. The First Amendment to the
Constitution provides for absolute freedom of speech in matters touching the common weal. This is America's announcement of its willingness
endlessly to listen, and endlessly to respond. America does not give in to
the temptation to exclude from itself, from the conversation that constitutes it, the possibility, the right of anyone existing under her representative institutions, to express doubt, even radical doubt, irreducible doubt,
of America's existence. Endless responsiveness is, as we have seen, the
condition of philosophy and the characteristic of at least one tradition
of inquiry.

Embodying America: The Challenge of Representation

Writing in 1952, Voegelin could claim that America's institutions best
represented the truth of the soul. America's institutions, however, embody
America, and America depends on what the American people are, just as
much as the American people are such, i.e., are the *American* people precisely to the extent that they are prepared to recognize themselves and each
other as the present bearers of the American story, i.e., the story of the world
as told in the American tongue, with American words. As late as 1963, a
representative of America could stand in the symbolic shadow of Abraham

10. Mulhall, *Stanley Cavell: Philosophy's Recounting of the Ordinary*, 67.

Lincoln and claim equal rights under American institutions of representation as a consequence, not of notional assent to abstract principle, but by real participation through consent to the story told by "[T]he magnificent words of the Constitution and the Declaration of Independence," words written by, "the architects of *our* Republic." Call this the American tradition of inquiry that is the American tradition of nationhood.

This would make the current crisis of Constitutional interpretation a profound spiritual crisis in America, the adjudication of which will in large part depend on our ability to understand what the Framers did in constructing the institutions that have played so important a part and for so long in the proper representation of the truth of the soul. This will eventually necessitate a recovery of the Founding Fathers' understanding of the truth of the soul, but we already knew that; it is what we have been after all along. Since the founding generation's decision to adopt the Constitution was, whatever else it was and before it was anything else, precisely the decision to recognize publicly, i.e., declare and constitute themselves a people of a certain kind, it is reasonable to think that a recovery of the terms of that original debate will aid in finding a way toward resolution of the current crisis. In other words, the debate over ratification of the proposed Constitution in 1787–1788 was in large part a debate over whether to have an American people. In order to recover the significance of the ratification debate, we need briefly to go a little further back in time, to July, 1776.

Reading above the Lines: The Declaration and Nationhood in America

The Declaration of Independence makes public an American conviction to the effect that:

> When in the course of human events, it becomes necessary for one People to dissolve the political bands which have connected them with another, and to assume among the powers of the earth, the separate and equal station to which the Laws of Nature and of Nature's God entitle them, a decent respect to the opinions of mankind requires that they should declare the causes which impel them to the separation.

Most of us reading these words reflexively, almost automatically understand the people of the United States of America and the people of Great

Britain to be the referents. This is not the case, for two related reasons. Firstly, as Stephen E. Lucas has noted,[11] the phrase sets the tone of the whole document. The whole document, and the first sentence especially, is a general statement of principle, in which the specific moral legitimacy of the revolution is grounded. Since it is a general statement of principle, the immediate referent cannot be the two "peoples" aforementioned. At best, the British people and the American people could provide an instance of the general principle the Declaration invokes, though per the second reason, not even this is actually the case. The second reason is tied to the first, and rather more pedestrian: (*pace* Lucas[12]) no such political animal as the "People of the United States" existed at the time, and even if it did, it was not party to the Declaration of Independence.

In point of fact, the United States of America did not come into existence until the States had ratified the Articles of Confederation in 1781, the year in which major hostilities with the forces of the British Empire ended.[13] The signers of the Declaration left their autographs in their capacities as agents of the States that had sent them to Congress. Each of the thirteen States of America asserted the right to dissolve the bands of political union with Britain. By the time American representatives working with their British counterparts in Paris had reached a peace treaty and communicated its contents to the competent authorities, a quorum in Congress was so hard to come by that the peace treaty could not be ratified for some time.[14] By the end of 1785, the Continental Congress (by then styled the Congress of the Confederation) had effectively ceased to exist as a governing body.[15] The struggle for independence had brought about the existence of thirteen independent states, tied together in a nominal confederation. In short, the existence of anything to call an American people, in the sense of a political society unified under a representative and so in form for action in history, most certainly did not exist. Between 1776 and 1789, then, the people in America became one

11. Lucas, "Justifying America," 75.

12. Cf. ibid., 75–77.

13. During the period between the drafting of the Articles in 1776, their revision and adoption by the Continental Congress in 1777, and the 1781 ratification, the Continental Congress *de facto* conducted the war in the name of the States.

14. Congress eventually did ratify the Treaty of Paris, in January of 1784, more than two months after its officers received it.

15. For the what is still the best history of the Congress, see Burnett, *The Continental Congress.*

American people. The questions before us now regard what happened, and how, and why.

Full Faith and Credit:
Toward the Constitutional Convention

Two major issues showed the confederation, such as it was, to be unworkable.[16] There was a financial crisis over the unpaid debts, both public and private, carrying back to the Revolutionary War and before; then there was an uprising in Massachusetts, led by Capt. Daniel Shays, lately of the Continental Army, from whom the uprising takes its name, Shays' rebellion. The uprising was neither large, nor terribly violent. The participants in the insurrection were pardoned within a year of its suppression, with the exception of Shays, himself, who received his pardon in the summer of 1788.

Henry Knox depicted the rebellion as having consisted of more than 10,000 men, armed and disciplined, ready to carry the rebellion from New England, southward, in order to redistribute property, generally.[17] The rebellion was nowhere near so large as Knox would have had it; nor was its design of any sort approaching the ambition ascribed to it by Knox. Knox's epistolary description of the rebellion and its designs was, however, made known throughout the colonies, as newspaper publications of his account abounded, causing general fervor.[18]

A Crisis of Faith

The domestic tranquility had been disturbed. Serious questions pressed themselves on the founding generation. Grudgingly at first, though steadily nevertheless, people began to recognize that there was not enough public virtue to sustain a republic—at least not one conceived along classical or traditional lines.[19]

16. Cf. McDonald, *E Pluribus Unum*, 27–70, 227–57; cf. also McDonald, *NOS*, 143–83.

17. A recent and readable history of Shays's Rebellion is Richards, *Shays's Rebellion: the American Revolution's Final Battle*. Still worthy, however, is Szatmary, *Shays' Rebellion: The Making of an Agrarian Insurrection*.

18. Cf. McDonald, *NOS*, 177, 177n62.

19. Ibid., 178–79.

In short, there was a crisis of faith in America. Faith, here, recalls the classical Roman juridical term, *fides*. *Fides* is, in contemporary language, something akin to "fair play" or "fair dealing"; still, these do not render the idea adequately. The Latin, *æquitas*, would be rendered adequately by these last. For the Roman, *fides* is that state created when a man gives due respect and reasonably expects to have his due from his fellows, the reasonable expectation of which is a consequence of one's own decorous conduct and the habit of receiving decorous treatment and observing decorous conduct in one's fellows. In reasonably current English, we might render *fides* as, "good faith." Still, this last does not entirely explain the strength of the Latin, *fides*. The etymologist, Émile Benveniste, notes that *fides mihi est apud aliquem*;[20] to have faith in someone else is not to place something of one's own in someone else, but to have something of that other placed in oneself. *Fides*, then, is something akin to "credit[21]" in reasonably contemporary English. One has credit with another to the extent that the other gives him credit; one gives credit to the extent that the credited party keeps faith. The relation, then, if it is to exist at all as a relationship of faith, must be reciprocal.

The events of 1783–1787 had revealed to the founding generation the fact that life as a people could not continue without the establishment of faith among the citizenry. The question remained as to the exact nature and structure of the faith that was to be kept, if there was to be an American people, at all. Questions about who was to keep faith with whom, and who would be the arbiters of faith, and by what means and modes and orders, remained as well. Ultimately, the two questions would resolve themselves into a single, overriding question: how to keep faith in America.

Federalists and Fœderalists

Several were the possible responses to this crisis of faith, manifest as an acknowledgment of the lack of virtue among the citizenry; these were variously (re)presented by the men of myriad means, dispositions and tempers present at the Philadelphia convention. Many were totally disillusioned with republicanism, considering the enterprise a failure. These advocated the adoption of a more authoritarian form of government, one

20. Lit. "Faith is for me in someone else."
21. Remembering that "Credit" is the third person singular form of *credo, ere*.

tending toward monarchy, even if its proponents never explicitly named it as such. Others, still enamored of republicanism in the classical sense, would advocate the education of the public in classical virtue, by providing example and incentive to be virtuous. Still others considered that the time was ripe for a radical re-thinking of republican government, and so would suggest wholly new principles, generally those of selfish pursuit of private interest bent to the public good. Some were present at the convention who advocated one or more of these positions.[22]

Generally, the delegates to the convention fell into camps espousing one of two basic outlooks: national and fœderal. This, however, can be confusing to the casual reader, since it was the nationalist party that eventually appropriated the term, "fœderal", in its modern permutation, "federal." This appropriation, or rather, its more-or-less complete consolidation took place only after the work of the convention was concluded. The famous trio of apologists for the proposed constitution, Alexander Hamilton, James Madison and John Jay, effectively carried out the appropriation of the term in their *Federalist* papers. Supporters of the proposed constitution eventually came to be known as, "federalists," and their opponents, "anti-federalists." Anti-federalism, however, is something of a misnomer, since the people falling under that rubric were almost uniformly in favor of maintaining a "fœderal" union, i.e., a con-federation of states, in which the states would remain supreme. In other words, calling the nationalists by the name of federalists is justified, since these eventually adopted that name for themselves, and are commonly known by that name and under that spelling; the supporters of a con-federal union of states are often styled "anti-federalists," though for present purposes the term, "fœderalists" seems rather more apt to preserve the sense of the debate in which they were engaged, and the spirit of their involvement in it—for the "fœderalists" were neither simply nor primarily opposed to the "federalists."[23]

Someone might object to this terminology as anachronistic. While it is true that the delegates, themselves used the various orthographies somewhat irregularly, it is also true that this itself tells something about the nature of the debate underway at the Convention; federal and fœderal both are derived from the Latin *fides*, though fœderal perhaps more

22. For a detailed breakdown of the delegates and their positions, cf. McDonald, *NOS*, 179, 185–219.

23. The preceding discussion is heavily indebted to that, which appears in McDonald, *NOS*, 185–219, 225–60.

readily recalls the archaic *fœdus*. This is pertinent, since the classically erudite men of the founding generation were well aware of the fact that a *fœdus* was a juridical term indicating an agreement among free states for aid and assistance. The *fœdus*—to which Rome was always the superior party, notwithstanding that *fœdera* might have been either æquua or *iniquua*, was between Rome and another state or city or tribe; it required assistance upon demand in exchange for continuing to allow local princes at least nominally to control the internal affairs of their princedoms. The *fœdus æquum* established specific parity of rights and duties as these were determined in the *fœdus*. Most importantly, *fœdera* neither expressed nor implied, and in fact neither extended nor exchanged the rights of citizenship to those living under the federate states.[24]

The states were, according to the fœderalists, atomic political units. They represented the political societies by which they were constituted. The states, further, were the only adequate representatives of their citizens, insofar as the citizens were citizens of the states, and did not derive their citizenship rights from the central authority, nor could they be made to derive their citizenship rights from the central authority without destroying the states as representatives of political societies directed by citizens. The question underlying the entire convention, to which the Constitution was the response, was that of the nature of the trust (*fides*) that existed among the people in America, and how that trust ought to inform and be informed by the new government, i.e., what kind of *foedus* to make, what the terms of agreement among the States should be—and before all else, who should establish them.

24. There has been scholarly debate over the critical usefulness of the terms in recent years and decades. Beginning with Ernst Badian's study of the legal instruments of Roman diplomacy and foreign policy, and running through a generation and more of scholarship, scholars tended to deny that the terms were really part of the Roman technical vocabulary. Cf. Badian, *Foreign Clientelae, 264–70 B.C,* 25–27. Following Badian, Erich Gruen argued in the early 1980s that the qualifiers *æquum* and *iniquum*, were not technical terms in antiquity, and so ought not to be used as criteria by which to distinguish among the various types of bilateral agreements into which Rome entered during her long history. Cf. Gruen, *Hellenistic World and the Coming of Rome,* 14–16. More recent works, however, have employed the categories unproblematically. The scholarly debate is interesting, though largely beyond the scope of the present investigation, which is interested in recovering the *forma mentis* of the American founders. For this purpose, it is pertinent to note that the Romans had the concepts of equality and inequality in making agreements with foreign powers. Cf. Bederman, *International Law in Antiquity,* 189–206. The founders were sensible of and sensitive to the conceptual distinctions, and had much of their understanding of them from the Roman sources directly.

The Question: The Framers' Proposal and the Debate of the People

The Constitution begins with the words, "We, the People of the United States." When the delegates to the Philadelphia convention chose to make "We, the People" the competent enactor of the proposed Constitution— when they included an explicit assertion of popular authorship in the text of the proposed Constitution— they were arguably breaking with the understanding of the work they had been assigned to do, an understanding they shared with their constituents at the outset:

> Almost all the delegates who attended the Constitutional Convention . . . believed it necessary to reorganize and strengthen the central authority . . . Few Delegates, however, thought of themselves as representing America or the American people. The [vast majority of delegates] thought of themselves as representing the people of the several states severally—or to put it differently, they were there as representatives of separate political societies.[25]

That each State's delegation, no matter how large, had a single vote in Convention, attests to this conviction; indeed, the voting scheme was a consequence of it. So it was no mean pluck that brought the Framers so to draft the Preamble. They were not, however, necessarily breaking entirely with the express purpose of the Convention. The need to strengthen the central government was rooted in a prior concern: preservation of the states, and of peace and good will among the states. Assuming the Framers considered themselves as having conscientiously pursued the end for which they had been sent to Philadelphia, we must conclude that the Framers themselves considered the practical matter of preserving the states to be entirely dependent upon the recognition and action of a people of America.

---

25. McDonald, *NOS*, 185, 185n1. In a vote at the beginning of the Convention, only 3 of the 55 delegates voted against the idea of working to strengthen the central government. Two of the three were eventually brought around, and the one who remained stubborn in his refusal of the project shortly abandoned the Convention. See also Farrand, *Records*, May 30, 1:35.

The States in Question:
Three Exemplary Cases

It was not in the least clear to every Framer, let alone the delegates of the several ratifying conventions, that "the People" was an agent competent to "Ordain" and "Establish" the Constitution. Assuming *causa argumenti* that the people[26] were competent, the consequences of their competence and their eventual ordination and establishment of the proposed Constitution were not the objects of general approval, applause and admiration.

George Mason and the Claim
to Con-Federacy

George Mason of Virginia couched the issue in terms of the kind of government the draft instrument proposed to create. He argued that, despite some appearance to the contrary, the proposed constitution would essentially destroy the states. He made his case in remarks to his state's ratifying convention on June 4th, 1788:

> Mr. Chairman—Whether the Constitution be good or bad, the present [Preambulary] clause clearly discovers, that it is a National Government, and no longer a confederation. I mean that clause which gives the first hint of the General Government laying direct taxes.[27] The assumption of this power of laying direct taxes, does of itself, entirely change the confederation of the States into one consolidated Government. This power being at discretion, unconfined, and without any kind of controul, must carry every thing before it. The very idea of converting what was formerly a confederation, to a consolidated Government, is totally subversive of every principle which has hitherto governed us. This power is calculated to annihilate totally the State Governments.[28]

26. The eighteenth-century practice of capitalizing "People" when employing it to name a political society, while significant, since it indicates an understanding of a people as a proper noun, i.e., a personal subject, is nevertheless awkward in 21st century usage, and on this ground is generally not followed in the body text of the present work.

27. Cf. Constitution of the United States, Article 1§2c3. This is the clause that also contains the notorious "three-fifths compromise" by which 60 percent of a state's slave population would be counted toward the apportionment of seats in the House of Representatives.

28. Bailyn, ed., *The Debate on the Constitution*, 2:605. Henceforth *Debate*.

The American understanding of the power to tax was so deeply and firmly and pervasively rooted, that it justified resistance to the Crown in the mind of the colonists, and eventually united the states in the cause of independence. The palpable revulsion in Mason's discussion is therefore understandable. If the power to tax is a power that inheres in the people and their representatives, then the power to levy direct taxes implies that the ultimate representative of the people in America is central government. Mason perceives that to give the central government power to tax is effectively to transfer representation of the people to the central government, thus effectively removing the States' representative quality; to remove that is to destroy the States, even if they continue to exist in name.

If the Framers eventually recognized the practical necessity of speaking to and through the "People of the United States," it was because they came to understand during their discussions and debates that there was a set of problems common to all those who participated in political life in America. What they proposed was a common way of dealing with, say, thinking publicly about, those problems. The former order of confederation was inadequate, not because its ordering of relations among the States was defective, but because the Articles of Confederation were based on an hypothesis, i.e., that there was no common political life in America beyond that of the States in their relations with one another, which had proven to be false. In order adequately to represent the common political life of Americans, it was necessary properly to identify the subject of that life. Thus, in proposing the people as the enactor of the new Constitution, the Framers were inviting the political societies in America to declare themselves one people.

The Case Against an American People: Patrick Henry

Not every person in each political society even agreed that such a people existed. In Virginia, once again, we had the example of Patrick Henry. He spoke the following on the floor of the Virginia Convention, also on June 4th, 1788:

> That this is a consolidated Government is demonstrably clear, and the danger of such a Government, is, to my mind, very striking. I have the highest veneration of those Gentlemen, -but Sir, give me leave to demand, what right had they to say, *We, the People.* My political curiosity, exclusive of my anxious solicitude for the

public welfare, leads me to ask who authorised them to speak the language of, *We, the People,* instead of *We, the States?* States are the characteristics, and the soul of a confederation. If the States be not the agents of this compact, it must be one great consolidated National Government of the people of all the States. [29]

The question is one of authority. Henry desires to know who the author of the proposed form of government shall be. After he notes that, "States are the soul of a confederation," and that, "if the states be not the agents of the compact," then "the proposed government must be 'one' and 'National,'" Henry roundly rejects the whole plan of union on the grounds that then the proposed Constitution's pretense to be con-federal is absurd. Henry's question —What right had they to say, "We, the people"?—is also an inquiry after the identity of the authorizer of the Philadelphia delegates. It is in this that the question reveals its theoretical moment: since the States themselves authorized the delegates to act in their names, it shall be of the essence to know whether the States invested the delegates they sent to Philadelphia with the authority to undo the very organs they represented there, organs from which the delegates' very legitimacy as representative actors flowed.

There is a sense in which Henry's argument is correct, and his objections just. Under the Articles, and according to one line of republican thought in the United States under them, the States are indeed the soul of a confederation. The States, however, are themselves en-souled, i.e., possessed of a vital principle not reducible to the machinery of government. The soul of a State is the people that has chosen to erect the machinery of its government.

The States were political societies, i.e., groups of human beings organized under a representative for action in history. The States accepted the proposed Constitution in Congress. The States submitted the proposed Constitution to their citizenries. The Citizenry of each State was represented by delegates to a ratifying convention. The question to which the citizenries needed to give answer through their delegates, then, was that of whether their thirteen political societies were constituted by thirteen

29. In Bailyn, *Debate,* 2:596–597. The best treatment of the Anti-Federalist case and the best presentation of the anti-Federalist materials is still Herbert J. Storing's *Complete anti-Federalist.* Originally published in 1981 in seven volumes, it is as of 2007 available in a three-volume edition. The new edition is divided according to the original scheme and contains the original table of contents. At the time of this writing, however, I have not seen the newer edition.

separate peoples, or whether there was one people articulated in thirteen distinct political societies. In other words, the ratifying conventions were really attempting to answer the question whether there was an American people. If the former, then Henry is correct. If the latter, then the one people requires a representative in order to act in history as a people, and the proposed Constitution then could be at once the symbol of the truth of the people and the instrument by which the people determines its existential representation, and through which the people defines and circumscribes the competences and the powers of its existential representatives. A vote to ratify the Constitution, therefore, was a vote at once to affirm one American people, to establish the people's representative, and to consent to the proposed mode of achieving the people's representation.

An Ambiguity Exposed:
Fisher Ames in Massachusetts

Every convention addressed itself to the question regarding the nature of the government proposed, i.e., whether it is federal or consolidated. Under this form, the question reveals with equal readiness the concern of the delegates to the ratifying conventions for the right discernment of the font and end of governing power under the proposed Constitution. Fisher Ames' intervention in the Massachusetts convention helps bring this further into view:

> Much has been said about the people divesting themselves of power, when they delegate it to representatives; and that all representation is to their disadvantage, because it is but an image, a copy, fainter and more imperfect than the original, the people, in whom the light of power is primary and unborrowed, which is only reflected by their delegates. I cannot agree to either of these opinions. The representation of the people is something more than the people. I know, sir, but one purpose which the people can effect without delegation, and that is to destroy a government. That they cannot erect a government, is evinced by our being thus assembled on their behalf.[30]

In this speech, Ames is attempting to refute the thesis according to which political power resides properly only in "the people" understood as a mere conglomerate. Ames takes no pains to elucidate, and may well have

---

30. Bailyn, *Debate*, 2:892.

been less than perfectly conscious of the fact that he was using the term, "the people," in two distinct and discrete senses. The first instance of "the people" refers to a mere conglomeration of individuals. The second, if Ames' discourse is to be coherent, must refer to the people in its represented (and therefore represent-able) character. In order to attenuate the confusion, it is useful to substitute Cicero's language for Ames' own. This exercise shall also set in high relief the extent to which Americans' minds were rooted in and indebted to the *forma mentis* of classical antiquity.[31] Imagine Ames had said, "The representation of the *multitude* is something more than the multitude, simply considered." Even better:

> Much has been said about *the masses* divesting themselves of power, when they delegate it to representatives; and that all representation is to their disadvantage, because it is but an image, a copy, fainter and more imperfect than the original, *the masses*, in whom the light of power is primary and unborrowed, which is only reflected by their delegates.

The masses here refers to a group of individuals sharing only physical proximity. In order to choose delegates, the masses (the multitude) must reach an accord as to what things are to direct them in their choice of representatives, and to those things that shall circumscribe their representatives. In order to reach such an accord at all, the conglomerate mass of individuals must already have more than physical proximity in common: they must be conscious of their sharing certain interests; they must, that is, have the experience of community. Their choice of representatives, then, is an explication of their understanding of those experiences as having revealed the good of being bound together in them. It is in this sense that Ames considers "The representation of the people" to be "something more than the people." At the very least, Ames' assertion would require that the "something more" be understood in a way that is other than strictly and simply numerical, i.e., that it stands to indicate something qualitatively different from and superior to an undifferentiated mass of humanity. In the same speech, Ames offers the following clarification:

> I know, sir, that the people talk about the liberty of nature, and assert that we divest ourselves of a portion of it when we enter into society. This is declamation against matter of fact. We

---

31. In performing this exercise, we ought to take care to note that the English preposition, "of" can have the strength of the Latin, *de* (Eng. "on" or "about", or sometimes "down from") or of the Latin (possessive) genitive.

cannot live without society; and as to liberty, how can I be said to enjoy that which another may take from me when he pleases? The liberty of one depends not so much on the removal of all restraint from him, as on the due restraint upon the liberties of others. Without such restraint, there can be no liberty. Liberty is so far from being endangered or destroyed by this, that it is extended and secured. For I said that we do not enjoy that which another may take from us. But civil liberty cannot be taken from us, when any one may please to invade it; for we have the strength of the society on our side.[32]

Liberty is natural to human being, then, to the extent that society is natural, this last being the seat of the exercise of liberty. Liberty has need of society, for it is in society that the limits on individuals' license, to which last Ames refers with the language of "due restraint upon the liberties of others," are placed with justice. Each individual is other to everyone else in society, though in society all are fellows together. In society, then, each individual member is limited in his exercise of personal license, and so to the same extent as all others who are his fellows. The determination of what is due to each, however, on Ames' view, ought not to be made by the people largely considered; indeed, such determination ought not be made by the people largely considered because it cannot be made by the people largely considered. This is the perfect synthesis of the ancient maxim, *ubi societas ibi ius*, with the Ciceronian discussion of the origin and scope of civil councils.[33]

Ames' discussion, moreover, is exemplary of the American understanding of the question at issue, namely the question whether there is there an American people. Ultimately, the conventions ratified the Constitution, so the people did "Ordain and establish this Constitution for the United States of America." The proper understanding of the States' decisions severally to ratify the Constitution, therefore, is that the persons participating in the political lives of the States were thereby deciding to accept the Framer's proposal, i.e., that there is a people of the United States, because the States are united "of America" and America is the idea that lives in the people. America is the name of the place, physical and conceptual, in which they live.

32. Bailyn, *Debate*, 2:893.
33. Cf. Cicero, *DRP* I.xxv.39, xxvi.41.

Reading the Lines:
The Meaning of the Preamble

"We, the People of the United States . . . Ordain and Establish the Constitution for the United States of America." This is the simple act carried out by the people, in and through the States, by means of ratification. The "People of the United States," however, "Ordain and Establish" the Constitution:

> In Order to form a more perfect Union, establish Justice, insure domestic Tranquility, provide for the common defence, promote the general Welfare, and secure the Blessings of Liberty to ourselves and our Posterity.

If the decision to ratify was a decision to have a people, it was also a decision to have a people of a certain kind, dedicated to certain propositions. The preamble states the reasons for their decision to be a people, and the ends for which they decided so to constitute themselves. The Preamble presents the Constitution as the definitive statement of the people of the United States regarding their decision to be a people governed according to the precepts of the document thus announced.

The Constitution is ordained and established by the people directly, "in Order to Form a more Perfect Union." The term, "Perfect," in 1787, had not the same meaning that it has for us, today. Better stated, it did not immediately suggest to the reader the same thing that it tends to suggest today. We tend immediately to understand perfect in the sense of "unblemished," or "complete." In 1787, "Perfect," meant something rather more close to its Latin root, in the sense of, "finished," or, "mature." Thus, the people, through the Constitution, assume directly the responsibility for strengthening, i.e., completing and bringing into maturity the Union of existing political societies. The people continues to be in several political societies, though they no longer accept the delegation to the State governments of responsibility for the tutelage of union among themselves. The responsibility for the tutelage of the Union is assumed by the people of the United States, directly. Just as there is a people of the United States insofar as the States are united, so the Union of the States is the responsibility of the people; the people is responsible for the Union because the Union is a consequence, an act of the people.

We can understand the end of establishing justice by a similar reading. The people directly delegate to the Federal government the responsibility for creating and maintaining such institutions as are charged with ensuring that faith be kept among the States and among the people in the States.[34] The preservation of the common defense and promotion of general welfare are delegated by the people, directly, to the Federal government. The, "Common Defense," is, then, the defense of the people of the United States, in each State; the general welfare is the welfare of the States, generally, to be sure, and so of the people of the United States as the people is in each State and in the States, severally. The correctness of this reading is to be found in the final element in the Preamble's catalogue of ends in ordaining and establishing the Constitution.

"To Secure the blessings of Liberty to ourselves and our posterity," is the final stated aim of the Constitution in its Preamble. We are wont, at the dawn of the twenty-first century, to think that the Framers, with this language, were asserting that liberty was to be understood as its own blessing; on this reading all goods of free society would to flow directly from liberty as water from the source of a river. This was not the understanding of the Framers.

Liberty, in the minimal sense of freedom from external coercion, may be had by any group sufficiently numerous, motivated, talented and well-armed. The same group that had so lately won liberty may and in fact does often deny with utmost celerity the liberty of some other faction. This occurs when human beings are not properly instructed in the right conduct of liberty. The Constitutional Convention, itself, owed its existence to Americans' intimate experience with this appalling fact. The requisites of successful liberty are, to paraphrase Sallust, private frugality and public liberality, a free spirit in counsel, the reasonable expectation that virtue would be rewarded with honor, and the confidence that wickedness cannot go unpunished. The blessings of liberty are, in short, the general flourishing of fully human life. As John Adams noted in his *Thoughts on Government*:

> The foundation of every government is some principle or passion in the minds of the people. The noblest principles and most generous affections in our nature then, have the fairest chance to support the noblest and most generous models of government. . . . A Constitution, founded on these principles, introduces knowledge among the People, and inspires them with a conscious dignity, becoming Freemen. A general emulation takes place, which causes good humour, sociability, good manners,

34. Constitution of the United States of America Art. III §2.

and good morals to be general. That elevation of sentiment, inspired by such a government, makes the common people brave
and enterprizing. That ambition which is inspired by it makes
them sober, industrious and frugal. You will find among them
some elegance, perhaps, but more solidity; a little pleasure, but
a great deal of business—some politeness, but more civility. If
you compare such a country with the regions of domination,
whether Monarchial or Aristocratical, you will fancy yourself in
Arcadia or Elisium [sic].[35]

Adams is accurate in portraying the common conviction of the Founding
Fathers that, without the blessings of liberty no republic can long remain
in existence. The stated purpose of government according to the Declaration of Independence is, among other things, the protection of liberty. If
liberty improperly exercised will decay into anarchy and then despotism,
then government must be interested in and therefore rendered capable
of regulating conduct, at least to such an extent as will allow government
to protect society against the worst effects of liberty poorly exercised—in
other words: to proscribe some behavior, to set conditions on other behavior, and to prescribe still other behavior, while either encouraging or
discouraging certain other kinds of behavior—and thus to secure that the
balance of liberty would bring blessings. Republican government under
the Articles of Confederation tended to give way to the forces in human
nature that were directly inimical to liberty, i.e., the opposites of her
blessings. The Framers recognized that the States, alone, could not secure
the blessings of liberty, because the states by themselves could neither
inculcate the virtues necessary to secure the blessings of liberty, i.e., to
make liberty attractive for the right reasons, nor could a purely national
government, howsoever constituted, protect liberty in America, because
liberty in America was lived by individuals in societies constructed of
numberless small communities, the needs and circumstances of which
were as various and disparate as the communities themselves.

There was more to this, however. If Adams was correct, or at least
accurate in portraying a general conviction of the Founders, in saying
that the foundation of every government is some principle or passion
in the minds of the people, then the decision to ratify the Constitution
ought also be understood as an expression of the American people's self-
understanding at the time of ratification. If the Constitution depends
on the people's attachment to the noblest principles and most generous

35. Adams, WJA, 4:194, 199–200.

affections of our nature, then the success of the attempt at governance will depend upon the people's ability to live up to their estimation of themselves, that is, to prove their professed attachment. This is what Adams meant when he said that a government founded on the noblest sentiments and most generous affections of our nature will introduce knowledge among the people and inspire them with a conscious dignity. Adams is most emphatically not saying that a republican form of government automatically does these things.[36] He is saying that no government that fails to introduce knowledge, inspire the people with conscious dignity, etc., can hope to ensure what the Preamble to the Constitution called, "The Blessings of Liberty."

There is a further point, one that involves the relation of virtue to morality, and that is a basic problem in politics, the theoretical treatment of which can be traced at least as far back as 4th century Athens. We pick up the trail, so to speak, in the waning days of Rome's Empire, whence we shall trace it backward and forward. In his essay to establish the aptness of Christian religion to inform and perfect human beings for Roman citizenship, St. Augustine of Hippo found himself asking what the *mores* of the Romans were, that God should have deigned to help them in the expansion of their rule.[37] In short, the *mores* of a society are those things that the members of society love or desire in general. The difficulty is, however, that good *mores* are only necessary, and not sufficient, to good social order. In order for society to thrive, in order for the blessings of liberty to be preserved and protected in society, society's members must actually, and not only apparently possess the characteristics generally esteemed as good and worthy.

The political haggling over the charter of the Bank of The United States is apt to illustrate the principle. In 1790, the financial position of

36. The text cited above does admit of some ambiguity on the point. If we look to Adams's copy of Rousseau's essay on *The Social Contract*, however, we find written in the marginalia a response to Rousseau's observation to the effect that in the end, men are what their governments make them. Adams replied, "The government ought to be what the people make it." Cf. McCullough, *John Adams*, 619.

37. Cf. Augustine, *De civitate Dei* V.xii.1. *Mores* is the plural of *mos, moris* 3f., which may be rendered as characteristic, or trait, but that is more effectively rendered as a standard or object commonly accepted as worthy of pursuing. Thus, inquiry into the *mores* of the Romans was inquiry into the objects that Romans generally considered worthy of pursuit, and standards they generally considered as proper guides to practice. Citations of Augustine's *De civitate Dei* are to the book, chapter, and section numbers as given in Trapè, ed., *La città di Dio*.

the United States was anything but rosy. Alexander Hamilton concocted a scheme that, if enacted, would have been the salvation of the infant republic's solvency and the foundation of the republic's economic future. Congress was persuaded of its expedience and passed Hamilton's proposal in the House and Senate. Only the President's signature was outstanding, and in those days, Presidents would refuse to sign a bill only if they could not positively ascertain the proposal's pursuance to the Constitution. The question therefore remained as to the constitutionality of Hamilton's plan. The new Constitution vested in the Congress of the United States with power:

> To make all Laws which shall be necessary and proper for carrying into Execution the foregoing Powers, and all other Powers vested by this Constitution in the Government of the United States, or in any Department or Officer thereof.[38]

The President of the United States, George Washington, asked his Secretary of State, Thomas Jefferson, to share his opinion of the constitutionality of Hamilton's plan. Jefferson responded in a letter, which based itself on the text of the Constitution, as above. In that letter, Jefferson refused to reduce the sense of the Constitutional term, "necessary" to synonymy with "expedience." Congress had not power to erect a bank (the cornerstone of Hamilton's proposal), because the Constitution did not grant that power explicitly to Congress, and a Bank was not, strictly speaking, necessary.[39] The President also required an explanation from Hamilton, who was his Secretary of the Treasury. Hamilton responded:

> Every power vested in a Government is in its nature *sovereign*, and includes *by force of the term*, a right to employ all the *means* requisite, and fairly *applicable* to the attainment of the ends of such power.[40]

The limits of sovereign power are only that the action countenanced by a legislature be, ". . . not immoral, nor contrary to the essential ends of political power."[41]

38. Constitution of the United States, Article 1 §8 c18.

39. This section is heavily indebted to the discussion in McDonald, *States' Rights and the Union*, 28–33.

40. Freeman, *Hamilton: Writings*, 613; cf. also McDonald, *States' Rights and the Union*, 31n9.

41. Ibid. McDonald also notes that express Constitutional exclusion of a given power were also a limit, though it were hardly necessary to mention such a thing in the text of the present discussion.

Jefferson, whose fame as an advocate of "limited government" is nigh on universal, recognizes no limit to the power of government other than the textual or structural limits of its constitution. In practice, Jefferson would have made the whole financial future of the United States to depend on his opinion of the meaning of a word. Hamilton, on the other hand, who is popularly reputed (if at all he is known) as a conniving, wrangling, haggling Machiavel, with neither moral sense, nor the restraint that ought to accompany it, argues that no government will serve the good, unless the people for whom the government is given love good and hate evil. Hamilton in essence argued that. only when no one to whom some aspect of a government is charged, could dare to do evil in the light of day, for fear of public outrage, and only when public officials are terrified of public wrath in the event that they should fail publicly to prosecute and punish evil-doers according to the law, can government function. The shared notion of right and wrong, and not the constitutional structure of a government, is the last bulwark against tyranny. Without good government, order in social life will decay, for there is "[A] degree of depravity in human nature"[42] which government must check. By the same token, if depravity is general and dominant, then the best government can hope to do is to keep people from "destroying and devouring one another."[43]

Let the blessings of liberty be something called happiness, or the good life. The good life requires liberty, and liberty, if it is to guarantee and not destroy the good life, requires virtue, and virtue does not come easy. Some forms of government tend to subvert it, though no government can provide it. All good government requires it, and republican government requires more of it, and in more members of society, than any other form of government. The idea that the Framers' Constitution would be apt to preserve the blessings of liberty could seem plausible only to men who had a certain understanding of human nature. The actual aptitude will always depend on the people's ability to live up to the best angels of their nature. So, what was the Founders' understanding of human nature, that the Constitution seemed apt adequately to represent and preserve it?

42. *Federalist #55*, 273.
43. Ibid.

Interlude

The Claim of Difference

AMERICA IS THE NAME given to the physical place, extended in space and enduring over time, in which human beings come to live together in such a way as to make the truth of the claims advanced by the Declaration plain for all to see who come to live there. It is, therefore, the name the Founders give to the conceptual space in which they come to recognize each other as participating in the truths claimed for their lives by their representatives through the Declaration. Of course, the claim that the truth of America is plain for all to see who come there to live will depend entirely on the way of life adopted by those who are there and imparted to those who arrive, whether by birth or by boat.

The Declaration has become a symbol of truth in and for America and Americans. This has not meant an end to the struggle for existential representation in America, however. Indeed, the greatest advancements in the differentiation of American truth have been achieved in ongoing struggles for existential representation under the symbol of America. Among those struggles, the civil rights movement of the 1950s and '60s is exemplary. The exemplar of the civil rights movement as a struggle for existential representation under the symbol, America, is surely Martin Luther King Jr.

The American King

King was an American representative, precisely because he sought with his mind and his body to show, not how the elements of power erected for the preservation of American society were in need of fundamental change, but how they were being employed in a manner systematically and diametrically repugnant to the truth they were designed to realize. King was arrested several times during the course of his work. Most famously, he was arrested on 12 April, 1963, on the charge of parading without a permit. King, with Ralph Abernathy and other leaders of the nationwide agitation for civil rights, had come to Birmingham, in Alabama. King had called on Birmingham in order to lead a non-violent[1] citizens' manifestation, the purpose of which was to protest the injustice of laws that segregated white persons from black persons in Birmingham, the capital, and Alabama, and the whole south of the country and the whole country, generally.

King set out his reasons for pursuing non-violent action in a letter dated April 16th, 1963, in which he responded to a series of concerns expressed by fellow clergymen regarding the conduct of civil rights agitation in Alabama. Three points of the letter interest us at present. The first of these is King's close analysis of the nature of law:

> You express a great deal of anxiety over our willingness to
> break laws. This is certainly a legitimate concern. Since we so
> diligently urge people to obey the Supreme Court's decision of
> 1954 outlawing segregation in the public schools, at first glance
> it may seem rather paradoxical for us consciously to break laws.
> One may ask: "How can you advocate breaking some laws and
> obeying others?" The answer lies in the fact that there are two
> types of laws: just and unjust.[2]

---

1. N.B. this is a technical term. Mohandas K. Ghandi elaborated non-violence as an integral motive force, and not simply tactical implementation, of his agitation for Indian national liberty. Dr. King synthesizes its main points in the Letter: "In any nonviolent campaign there are four basic steps: collection of the facts to determine whether injustices exist; negotiation; self- purification; and direct action."

2. The King Papers Project at Stanford University has already published six of a projected fourteen volumes in their critical edition of the papers of Dr. Martin Luther King Jr., covering the years 1929–1963. King's "Letter from a Birmingham Jail" and "I Have a Dream" speech, however, are so widely known and published, in hardcopy and electronically, that I have not cited specific editions.

It is not only necessary, but right and good to obey the law. This means that the edicts of constituted authorities must enjoy habitual obedience, and so precisely insofar as they come from the constituted authorities. The order of society would disintegrate without obedience to constituted authority. The need for a constituted authority is clear, and the nervous tension in the minds of the nine religious leaders who wrote to King is perfectly understandable and even laudable, as King himself is at pains to recognize in the Letter. King's argument appeals to what we might call the *idem sentire*, the "common sense" of American society. Having thus presented his problematic in terms as favorable to his inter-locutors as possible, King enlarges:

> How does one determine whether a law is just or unjust? A just law is a man-made code that squares with the moral law or the law of God. An unjust law is a code that is out of harmony with the moral law. To put it in the terms of St. Thomas Aquinas: An unjust law is a human law that is not rooted in eternal law and natural law. Any law that uplifts human personality is just. Any law that degrades human personality is unjust. All segrega-tion statutes are unjust because segregation distorts the soul and damages the personality. It gives the segregator a false sense of superiority and the segregated a false sense of inferiority. Segre-gation, to use the terminology of the Jewish philosopher Martin Buber, substitutes an "I-it" relationship for an "I-thou" rela-tionship and ends up relegating persons to the status of things. Hence segregation is not only politically, economically and sociologically unsound; it is morally wrong and awful. Paul Til-lich said that sin is separation. Is not segregation an existential expression of man's tragic separation, his awful estrangement, his terrible sinfulness? Thus it is that I can urge men to obey the 1954 decision of the Supreme Court, for it is morally right; and I can urge them to disobey segregation ordinances, for they are morally wrong.

The second and third principle points of interest emerge from this para-graph. The second point is that the law, in order to be just, i.e., to conform to the good of the people and the constitution of society, must edify hu-man personality. This is to say that the law presupposes an idea of man, of which it is a reflection. Basically, we may say that the structure of any given society reflects the way its members conceive human nature, so that a society with a warped vision of human nature will have bad laws and will suffer under the effect of them. It would be, then, the duty of those within society who recognize the evil effects of a warped understanding of human nature, to correct the mistaken understanding; one of the ways in which to effect the correction, indeed the best way, is to secure habitual acceptance of edicts that are in conformity with the proper understanding of human nature.

The third point of note is that King, in citing Socrates, Martin Buber and St. Thomas Aquinas, is not involving himself in an isolated, ivory tower meditation, abstracted from social reality.[3] He is making explicit the historical instances of thought in which truths active in the formation of an idea of man that we may call, "American", received theoretical articulation; King accomplishes his explication, precisely by recalling certain thinkers who articulated the ideas constitutive of that history. Simply put, "America" is an expression of certain ideas that inform and illuminate society in the United States. Thus, the States are united "of America". America unifies the States. America also, and indeed in the first, unites Americans, for it is Americans who make the union of States. For this reason, and to the extent that this is true, could King write in reply to the clergy's objection to his presence as an 'outside agitator', "Anyone who lives inside the United States can never be considered an outsider[4] anywhere within its bounds."

King gives several persons in example of his understanding of the when and how of civil disobedience's justification:

> Of course, there is nothing new about this kind of civil disobedience. It was evidenced sublimely in the refusal of Shadrach, Meshach and Abednego to obey the laws of Nebuchadnezzar, on the ground that a higher moral law was at stake. It was practiced superbly by the early Christians, who were willing to face hungry lions and the excruciating pain of chopping blocks rather than submit to certain unjust laws of the Roman Empire. To a

3. N.B. St. Augustine is the favorite Church Father among American Protestants who cite sources other than Sacred Scripture and Protestant commentaries thereupon. Augustine was the paternal inspiration of the Puritan founders of the New England States. Augustine was also widely respected by Anglicans and their Episcopalian cousins. Martin Buber's fame and influence in the 1960s is too well known to comment; St. Thomas Aquinas' stature among the Catholic intelligentsia explains itself. In sum, Dr. King is appealing to the three religious traditions that converge in America, the Protestant, the Catholic, the Jewish. See Herberg, *Protestant, Catholic, Jew*, 1983.

4. N.B. "Outsider" translates literally the Greek *xenos*, who is outside the sphere of the *xynon*, "the common." This is but one among many examples of King's idiom drawing on classical concepts of critical science and classical symbols of polity in a way that we can call ordinary.

degree, academic freedom is a reality today because Socrates
practiced civil disobedience.

The Jewish faithful disobey Nebuchadnezzar because they participate in
the direct experience of Divine transcendent order. The three take part in
that order by virtue of their having been born into the race of men that is
representative of humanity under the direction of the Divine. The three
are directly under the Divine and are his representatives in history; no
human being has authority over them. The importance of Hebrew history
for the American *forma mentis* is recognized virtually universally.[5]

Noteworthy then, is that our discussion of Dr. King's rhetoric to
this point at the very least suggests the following: that King is not citing the faithful three simply because certain rabbis were cosignatories
of the open letter that occasioned his response. Instead, we may say with
a degree of plausibility that King is responding to his interlocutors as
an American addressing Americans. It is in this context that we must
understand King's invocation of the story from the Hebrew Scriptures.
Thus, the American expression of order is traceable to the emergence
of Hebrew order in its explosion of one-to-one cosmic analogy in social
structure beginning with Pharaoh-Ra, and proceeding to Israel's encounter with the Babylonian order of empire epitomized by Nebuchadnezzar).

Socrates discovered the human-divine orientation by giving attention to the voice of a god. The inscription above the entrance to the Delphic Oracle, "Know thyself!", was generally understood to mean, "Know
that you are not a god," which is to say, "Think human thoughts.[6]"
Socrates recognized that, if the inscription meant what Athenians took
it to mean, then every human attempt to obey the dictum would be in
contravention of it, for the human person who heeds the command is
heeding the words of a god, which is precisely the activity proscribed by
the construction, which Athenian society had put on the command. In
so doing, Socrates is challenging the Athenian understanding of what a

5. Recently, Michael Novak has argued that the Founders were animated by commitment to what he calls a Hebrew metaphysics. My insistence on limiting our claims
here to Hebrew history ought not in any way to be taken as implying a position regarding Novak's thesis, consideration of which were beyond the scope of this essay. See
Novak, *On Two Wings*.

6. This idea has its echoes and resonances in America, e.g., in the poetry of Wallace Stevens. See "Chocorua to Its Neighbor" in Kermode and Richardson, *Stevens*,
263–68. For a discussion of the poem's relation to Cavell's thematic of the human
voice, see Colapietro, "Striving to Speak in a Human Voice: A Peircean Contribution
to Metaphysical Discourse."

human being is; by issuing such a challenge, which is a new claim regarding human nature, Socrates is setting himself up against the authority of Athens as interpreted by Socrates' Athenian contemporaries. That King is able to call on Socrates to witness the justice of King's own act of civil disobedience in America, i.e., King's claim to the effect that America in some way requires his act of civil disobedience, or that King's own act of civil disobedience is American and that the American is steeped in the tradition to which Socrates' act in some wise belongs (which is to say that America has benefited from Socrates' act—and this is King's almost explicit claim—thereby incurring a debt that America must pay and pay in kind), suggests that America is (has paid its debt by becoming?) a conceptual space in which the apparently intractable enmity of Athens for Socrates has been overcome. Would this not mean, in its turn, that America, i.e., the conceptual space in which that union of persons is formed and nurtured, which forges the union of States and gives sense to the name, "United States of America", is essentially the conception of a philosophical mission? Is this not the answer to the political problem proposed by Plato in another famous letter? Would it not explain the strange, even uncanny fact that, while the Athenian crisis of order produced Socrates and Plato, and the Roman crisis of the late fourth and early fifth centuries issued forth in St. Augustine, and the internecine wars of Europe in the aftermath of Christendom's disintegration gave Hegel to the warring German principates; the United States, through all its many crises, has never had a philosopher, but never failed to have a statesman?

The Examples of King:
Athens and Jerusalem in America

As we have begun to see, another question that King's "Letter" presses upon us is that of Athens and Jerusalem. A certain author, whose works and whose teaching have achieved national prominence of late in both the universities and the public discourse of the American nation, has argued that Athens, the representative of philosophy, is locked in eternal and irreducible opposition to Jerusalem, the city founded by faith.[7] Assuming

7. Cf. Strauss, *Natural Right and History*, esp. 74. While a certain amount of scholarly work has in very recent years allowed some tentative revision of Strauss's understanding of the alternative, "Athens or Jerusalem" as basic and unavoidable—see Zank, *Leo Strauss*—the fact remains that Strauss confirmed the basic tenets of his most clear and absolute statement on the subject in the preface to the 7th impression of *Natural Right and History*, which he wrote in 1970, only three years before his death.

for the sake of argument that there is or can be such an opposition, and admitting the possibility of that opposition's being eternal and irreducible, is not America as King presents it to us in his use of it an overcoming of the opposition of Athens and Jerusalem? Does America overcome the enmity of Athens and Jerusalem? Is it rather true that America is possible because the opposition of Athens and Jerusalem has been overcome?

King says that the first Christians deliberately disobey "certain unjust laws of the Roman Empire." What laws were they, and on what grounds does King presume to call them unjust? Generally, Christians would face execution because they committed treason by refusing to swear by the god Augustus or by the reigning Emperor. In the Roman order of empire as it existed in pagan antiquity, the State was the supreme religious authority, originally in the Senate and, from the time of Augustus, the Emperor, who assumed the presidency of the college of augurs and the high priesthood of Rome. The reason for this was that the State was still understood to be the direct and unique mediator between the earth-bound human and the divine transcendent. The advent of Christianity is a direct political challenge to the power of the Caesars: when Christ says to Caesar (through Caesar's representative), "Yes [I am a king], though my kingdom is not of this Earth,[8]" Christ is claiming two things: His kingdom could never be conquered by Caesar, even though Caesar should conquer and rule over every square inch of the planet; He, as the earthly representative of an other-worldly realm, is mediator between God and man. When Christianity is accepted by a sufficient number of citizens, the imperial order itself will be threatened; the State will no longer be divine mediator for the Roman people. A Roman who accepts Christianity, however, does not thereby cease to be a Roman, just as a Platonist does not cease to use his reason in his embrace of Christianity.

It is for precisely this reason that the Roman order of empire required a rethinking; for precisely this reason, St. Augustine responds to the Roman crisis of order in the 5th century by arguing that Christianity is not the bane of Roman imperial order, but its completion and perfection, or rather that Christianity represents the chance for Rome to keep faith with its best angels.[9] *Fides* (faith), after all, is a technical term of Roman jurisprudence.[10] It is in precisely Augustine's understanding of the Roman

8. See John 18:28–40.

9. Cf. Augustine, *De civitate Dei* II.xxi.3.

10. In other words, a civil order founded by persons professing Christian faith will not claim for itself the role of mediator. That role is played by the Church, which

sense that America is founded on faith, for the American decision to have a people emerges from the debate over what kind of *foedus* to make among persons whose depravity requires a certain degree of circumspection and distrust, but whose other qualities justify a certain portion of esteem and confidence.[11] The American choice for a republic is an expression of assent to an understanding of human being as naturally capable of faith, for republican government presupposes the presence in human nature of precisely those qualities, which justify esteem and confidence in a higher degree than any other form.[12] Is this not reasonable? The Founding Fathers believed that it is; believing its reasonability, they acted.

Our claim for America is that America is the expression of an experience that makes a difference. The American tradition, in which King lives and for fellows in which he writes, is itself steeped in the tradition we have just discussed. In order to understand the expression of America, i.e., in order to grasp that of which America is an expression, we must turn to the human experience of order on the continent called North America. A way toward that task, as it were, may be found in King's own public and representative use of America.

King and America

Later in 1963, from the steps of the Lincoln Memorial, King gave a speech to the quarter part of one million Americans, gathered on the National Mall. That speech, known the world over as the "I Have a Dream" speech, illustrates the presence of a particular American idiom, the origins of which we saw in the writing of the critical period, so that the presence of

---

dispenses Divine grace and represents the truth of the soul by providing the wherewithal properly to order the soul, i.e., by exercising its *munus docendi* and its *munus sanctificandi*. A civil order founded by Christians will order its organs of power to the tutelage of each individual's personal conversation with the Divine transcendent. There is a case to be made, indeed there is being made a case, in the paragraphs above, for which the inherent and inalienable dignity of each and every human being is unthinkable without Christianity, though it does not require that one assent to Christianity in every doctrinal particular, nor even that one be conscious of the Christian, and by implication Hebrew and Greek philosophical traditions, of the American vision of man; the very Christianity of the idea, further, requires that government provide protection for the integrity each and every person's conversation with the Divine.

11 Cf. *Federalist* #55, 273.

12. Cf. Ibid.

the idiom as a part of or a sign of the ordering power of the conceptual space called America was assured as lately as 1963.

In that speech, King employs the words, "America" and "American" a total of nine times. The oblique references to America, such as "the nation", and "our republic" are myriad. More important than "the nation", and prior both chronologically and conceptually in the speech, is Dr. King's use of the first person plural possessive article, "our", in describing the "nation." Dr. King opens his speech by claiming, "I am happy to join with you today in what will go down in history as the greatest demonstration for freedom in the history of our nation." From the very beginning, then, Dr. King presents his case as a full member of the American nation, and the importance of this cannot be overstated, for it was precisely this that was at stake.

In speaking as an American, King is making himself a representative of America. The logic of King's speech, further, is such that America is an idea that is, that must be, embodied—its existence outside the American nation is a sort of half-life, and its flourishing depends on the right ordering of the body politic that knows itself as America. Those who embody America are responsible to America, and so to each and every one of their fellows. We see this logic at work when King says:

> When the architects of our republic wrote the magnificent words of the Constitution and the Declaration of Independence, they were signing a promissory note to which every American was to fall heir. This note was a promise that all men, yes, black men as well as white men, would be guaranteed the unalienable rights of life, liberty, and the pursuit of happiness. It is obvious today that America has defaulted on this promissory note, insofar as her citizens of color are concerned. Instead of honoring this sacred obligation, America has given the Negro people a bad check, a check which has come back marked "insufficient funds."
>
> But we refuse to believe that the bank of justice is bankrupt. We refuse to believe that there are insufficient funds in the great vaults of opportunity of this nation. And so we have come to cash this check, a check that will give us upon demand the riches of freedom and the security of justice.

In the first place, King assumes the inclusion of "black men as well as white men" in the promises of the Declaration. The second thing to emerge is the affinity, to the point of interchangeability and, in this particular idiom, synonymy of the terms, America and Justice, American and Just. The riches of freedom and the security of justice are stored, says King, in the vaults of America. As the economic language suggests, however, King, was not inventing an idiom; however deft his use; he was only using the language of public discourse in the United States, as he had inherited it.

Through all the turmoil of the second half of the last century, the citizenry of the United States constantly asked themselves, in deliberating any question important to the common good, what the "American" thing to do might be. Racial segregation was decried as un-American. Communism was un-American. This last, interestingly, produced a backlash of fear and suspicion that led to the formation of the House Un-American Affairs Committee (HUAC), which eventually became the object of most vitriolic condemnation as being itself essentially un-American.

In the minds of U.S. citizens, America was synonymous with goodness, American with the good, and un-American with evil. If to ask, "What is the American thing to do?" was to ask, "what is the right thing to do?" then to ask, "What is America?" was to ask, "What is the good?" The U.S. citizenry was concerned with discovering the good, and convinced that it must be directed by the object of that search in its national life. At the same time—and this is the genius of King's employment of the American idiom—the citizens of the United States recognize themselves as Americans. In its turn, this claim to be Americans, is to recognize that there is good in the order of society in the United States. There is a grave danger in this: properly ordered, America will be informed by the right apprehension of the good; there is, however, no guarantee that some, and so perhaps even a majority, or at least a number sufficient to subvert the order of society, would pervert the order of understanding, whether by inversion, or replacement. This is the unavoidable risk involved in founding a nation in view of the good.

In other words, America is not an empty concept. It is not that, in the words of one historian, "The Jeffersonian [i.e., American rhetoric as guided and established by the Declaration] magic works because we permit it to function in a rarefied rhetorical region where real-world choices do not have to be made.[13]" Quite the contrary, American rhetoric "works" precisely to the extent that citizens of the United States can and do inform and perfect their citizenship by sharing in common experiences of the good, to which they give the name, America, and from which

13 Ellis, *American Sphinx*, 10.

they receive the name, Americans. This is what King saw, and this is the reason for which he was able to say:

> [M]any of our white brothers, as evidenced by their presence here today, have come to realize that their destiny is tied up with our destiny. . .their freedom is inextricably bound to our freedom. We cannot walk alone.

Many thousands of the participants in the manifestation at which King delivered his remarks had, quite literally, marched on Washington, walking to the capital from hundreds of miles away, as in a pilgrimage. King's language is symbolic, to be sure; it is a symbolic extension of U.S. citizens' concrete act of coming to the head of the United States, by which act Americans came together in the living heart of America.

Concluding his speech, King says, "[I]f America is to be a great nation, this [dream of mine] must become true." Far from operating at a rarefied level, King's dream is, "deeply rooted in the 'American Dream,'" so that the American Dream is fertile soil, and not rare atmosphere. Fertile soil, however, is made of the detritus of years past, which nurture the new growth, the roots of which keep both the organism and the soil that nurtures it, in place. This is another way of saying that the American people is constituted. The question is how.

CHAPTER 4

American Anthropology

THE UNDERSTANDING OF HUMAN nature that is constitutive of the conceptual space called America has disparate sources, all of which are present with varying degrees of explicitness and, from moment to historical moment, varying degrees of ordering force within America, itself. Eventually, we shall have to trace in broad strokes the development of the American anthropological conversation from its historical beginnings to the time of ratification; in order to prove the presence of the conception of the human in that conversation at the time of ratification, we shall have to move forward thematically in the history of the American people. Such a project, however, would on its own be a mere history of ideas.

It could be an intellectual history of America, even a very good one. It could never, as such, be philosophy, that is, a clarification of concepts that penetrates to the principles of order emerging from critical reflection on the form, contents and conduct of society in America. A properly philosophical project will require that we locate America in the larger discussion of order that is political science, or philosophy. Our work has been about such a project from the outset.

In the first phase of our work, we saw with Eric Voegelin that the basic problem of political science is the problem of representation, and that America, insofar as it emerges in history as a contest over representation, is an especially apt field for study of the basic problem. In a second moment, we saw how the ordering forces at work in America originated in social and theoretical contexts that pre-dated the historical emergence of America, so that the American way of interpreting existence through the generation of America and the symbols that represent the truth and existence of America (e.g. the Declaration of Independence and the Constitution), including representative institutions for American society, taken together, were constitutive of a tradition of inquiry, and at the same time, possibly, of nationhood. We saw how, in this tradition of nationhood, the search for order was, in the founding moment of America, conducted as a quest for the ordinary, and this established the American tradition as one at once of inquiry and nationhood. The work of this chapter aims at examining the ordinary in America, with a view to recovery of the principles of order in American society.

The work of this chapter therefore constitutes the conceptual nucleus of the whole project, in which the order of society in America that has begun to emerge through the earlier chapters in a manner amenable to theorization, will actually begin to be theorized. A larger discussion of the project of philosophy as the science of order can no longer be postponed, if our work is to achieve, as it has set out to achieve, the beginnings of America's theoretical articulation.

At the same time, it shall be necessary to keep the authors who serve as the argument's principal interlocutors in conversation with one another. Otherwise, we will risk making them appear external to the central theoretical question at issue, and therefore merely secondary or even ancillary contributors to the theoretical articulation of America that has become our present work. We begin with Voegelin, for it is Voegelin who, among the three, not only provides the most robust theoretical framework in which to operate, but, as we have seen, also declares the work of constructing that framework to be directly and intrinsically pertinent to the problem of America.

Toward the Origin of American Order

From about the middle of his intellectual career, Voegelin's theorizing came to be centered on the question of "Gnosticism" and "Modernity." Gnosticism names doctrinal and religious movement that started in late Antiquity after the advent of Christianity, and continued in underground rivulets through the centuries of Christian expansion and European consolidation under the symbol of Christendom. It may seem odd to begin the crucial chapter in a work that aims at giving the beginnings of a theoretical articulation of America, with a discussion of such a movement. It will appear less so if we recall that no less a thinker than the Yale literary critic Harold Bloom has identified in gnosticism the true American religion, over and against the professed Protestantism of a majority of Americans, even ostensibly pious ones.[1] Thus, for both Bloom and Voegelin, gnosticism is a type of intellectual and religious attitude toward the world. The essay to follow will (as a matter of course, and not intent) correct Bloom's understanding of the American gnostic, so as to confirm the basic tenet of his thesis, insofar as this admits of the following re-diction: If American religion is understood as the worship, the cult of America, then America's worship (the cult of America) is a gnostic cult. To be in America is therefore to be in some sense religious. Being religious in America does not, however, necessarily imply the practice of American religion when this last is gnosticism. An understanding of gnosticism is crucial to the understanding of America for reasons connected to both the preceding discussion of religion and the discussion of evidence we previously entertained. The exact nature of the connections will emerge during the course of this chapter's work. For now, it is possible to give an inkling of them, found in an observation Cavell makes at the beginning of his essay on "The Philosopher in American Life":

> The sense of the ordinary that my work derives from the practice of the later Wittgenstein and from J.L. Austin, in their attention to the language of ordinary or everyday life, is underwritten by Emerson and Thoreau in their devotion to the thing they call the common, the familiar, the near, the low. The connection means that I see both developments—ordinary language philosophy and American Transcendentalism—as responses to skepticism, to that anxiety about our human capacities as knowers that can be taken to open modern philosophy in Descartes, interpreted by that philosophy as our human subjection to doubt.[2]

Before proceeding with discussion of the passage, it is necessary to note, for reasons that shall present themselves shortly, that "knowers" names those who have *gnosis*. Now, Cavell has argued that Emerson and Thoreau are writers who somehow figure in what we have been calling the American tradition of inquiry, a tradition that is also one of nationhood.

---

1. There is a discernibly gnostic strain in Bloom's writings from a very early date, though this is not the place to argue the point. For more, see Fite, *Rhetoric of Romantic Vision*, 4, 64–90; For Bloom's developed understanding of religion in America, see Bloom, *American Religion*.

2. Cavell, *Quest*, 4.

Further, when Cavell names skepticism as that to which (certain elements, at least, of) the American tradition responds, he is naming the pathological state into which the human person inevitably falls, who gives in to the desire to escape the condition of the world, which is ignorance—and this is, as we shall see, the beginning and the heart of gnosticism—so that the presence of a response to it in America is the presence of a response to gnosticism. Finally, the Cartesian attempt to found knowledge on the evidence of clear and distinct ideas, which figured so prominently in our earlier discussion of the proper way to read the Declaration of Independence, insofar as it may be taken to open modern philosophy, opens precisely that way of thinking, which the understanding of America that we are attempting to recover by drawing on America's founders, contests.

Voegelin's Understanding of Gnosticism in Brief

Voegelin observes that as a spiritual phenomenon, gnosticism is not limited to the movement begun in the second century A.D., but is one of the responses to the disintegration of ordering institutions in various societies at the origin of what he calls the age of ecumenic empire.[3] Traceable as far back as the seventh century B.C.[4] Mediterranean resistance to the expansionist aims of Persia, the emergence of ecumenical empire eventually resulted in the disintegration of Hellenic society organized through the *polis*, and gave rise to the sweeping ecumenical effort of the ambitious Macedonian prince-ling, Alexander.[5]

The rise of Rome further reduced the earlier civilizational cohesion of Hellenic societies, while the earlier rise of new imperial orders further in the East, brought about the expiration of the order of being experienced in society through, e.g., the Egyptian, Babylonian and Assyrian empires.[6] The result was a spiritual vacuum, in which the old expressions of order, insofar as they no longer ordered society effectively, were no longer adequate expressions of participation in the *cosmos*.[7]

---

3. Cf. Voegelin, *OH* 4:13 *et passim*.

4. Cf. Voegelin, *SPG*, 254; cf. also *OH* 4:167.

5. Cf. *OH* 4:170.

6. Cf. ibid., 126–28, 142–48, 160–66.

7. Cf. ibid., 174–88, 189.

Among the various responses to this forlorn spiritual state (to borrow Voegelin's phrase), brought on by the disintegration of social order, there was gnosticism. The essential characteristic of gnosticism is its conception of the world as an evil, benighted place into which human being has been thrown by some obscure power, and with which human being has become entangled. Entanglement with the world is experienced as incorporation, so the gnostic drive toward the destruction of the evil world is experienced as a search for a way to escape from the matter that holds human being in its alien captivity:

> For [the gnostic] the world has become a prison from which he wants to escape: "The wretched soul has strayed into a labyrinth of torment and wanders around without a way out. . . . It seeks to escape from the bitter chaos, but knows not how to get out."[8]

In short, through the rejection of corporality gnosticism represents also a rejection of philosophy, if philosophy is what Voegelin recognizes in the Socratic, and by extension Platonic and Aristotelian, tradition: the openness of the soul to the transcendent ground of the order of being, which means the vision or *theoria* in the corporeal order of things of a ground or *arche* experienced as loveable, i.e., beautiful, true and good.

The range of expression that the gnostic experience had in antiquity was so wide as to make the identification of it as such extremely difficult.[9] The proper interpretative key is teleological. Gnosticism, however expressed (whether through, e.g., moral laxity to the point of libertinism, or the cult of mystery, or ascetic remove), always experiences the world as irrational, and life in it as life in a prison of ignorance (*agnoia*):[10]

> The world is no longer the well-ordered, the cosmos, in which Hellenic man felt at home; nor is it the Judaeo-Christian world that God created and found good. Gnostic man no longer wishes to perceive in admiration the intrinsic order of the cosmos.[11]

Gnosticism therefore seeks to escape the world—to escape the condition of the world—by escaping ignorance, that is, through knowledge (*gnosis*). The knowledge of the gnostic, however, is not the philosopher's object of

8. Voegelin, *SPG*, 254–55.

9. Cf. ibid., 251–56. The critical usefulness of the term has been challenged. For a statement of the argument against the critical usefulness of gnosticism as an analytical and interpretative category, see Williams, *Rethinking "Gnosticism."*

10. Cf. Voegelin, *SPG*, 256.

11. Ibid., 254.

loving pursuit. It is always brought, as a gift of salvation, from a source that is alien to the world and its conditions, the world's enemy.[12]

The effects of the gnostic penetration into the symbology through which society's elemental, existential and transcendental representation is given, are inevitably corrosive.[13] For good or for ill, the world is inescapable, and attempts to escape the world will inevitably not only fail, but bring social disorder in proportion to the depth and breadth of the gnostic penetration into society.[14] In antiquity, the power of gnosticism was checked by other civilizational forces, most importantly Christianity.[15]

The Christian differentiation of the *saeculum* in which Church and State (Pope and Emperor) were articulated as the existential and transcendental representatives within the distinct spiritual and temporal spheres of order,[16] provided the robust institutional structure necessary to suppress gnosticism and its corrosive influence on order. More to this, and more importantly, Christianity was not merely a check on the disintegration of social order. Nor was it essentially a restoration:

> The gnostic's flight from a truly dreadful, confusing, and oppressive state of the world is understandable. But the order of the ancient world was renewed by that movement that strove through loving action to revive the practice of the "serious play" (to use Plato's expression)—that is, by Christianity.[17]

Christianity transformed the order of society, bringing with it a new social reality and opening new possibilities for social life. Christianity did not, however, because on its own premises it could not break the power of gnosticism in history. Since Christianity cannot force anyone to see that the world is good, but can only show it through lives of sanctity, in the midst of institutions designed for all men, noble but fallen creatures awaiting the final fulfilment of their redemption: St. Paul describes them as people who see now through a glass darkly, capable of recognizing the goodness of the world only through premonitions; St. Augustine in book after book of the *City of God* presents them as pilgrims in a foreign city. In the explicitly Christian scientific vocabulary, this state or condition

12. Voegelin, *SPG*, 254.
13. Cf. ibid., 256.
14. Cf. ibid.
15. Cf. Voegelin, *NSP*, 149–74
16. Cf. ibid., 178.
17. Voegelin., *SPG*, 256.

is characterized as eschatological tension. The term, however, refers to a universal human experience of the world as good, and at the same time not yet good enough—not yet as good as it should be. The allure of speculative *gnosis* would (and does) still hold sway over those incapable of enduring such a tension of existence in history, before the final oncoming of goodness in the world, which Christians call *parousia*.[18]

The Structure of Gnosticism: Gnosticism as Skepticism

At this point, employment of a slightly modified Cavellian technique will serve at once to elucidate the point and ground the claim to its pertinence for America. The pure technique consists in juxtaposing texts that appear at some remove from one another within a given work, in order to illustrate the presence of a theme or idea under consideration. Cavell calls the technique an "exemplary yoking of sentences,"[19] which he undertakes, "in order to force us to stop over them."[20] Our yoking will be not of a pair, but of a pentad of texts, taken from the works of our three principal interlocutors. The purpose of the exercise is to show at once through our interlocutors how philosophy's particular kind of interest in the common represents a concern with gnosticism, specifically the concern with contesting gnosticism's disclaimer of the world's basic goodness: the world is evil because it is unintelligible. First, we revisit some further lines of Cavell:

> (1) I understand [philosophy] as a willingness not to think about something other than what ordinary human beings think about, but rather to learn to think undistractedly about things that ordinary human beings cannot help thinking about, or anyway cannot help having occur to them. . .such things, for example, as whether we can know the world as it is in itself, or whether others really know the nature of one's own experiences, or whether good and bad are relative, or whether we might not now be dreaming that we are awake, or whether modern tyrannies and weapons and spaces and speeds and art are continuous with the past of the human race, and hence whether the learning of the human race is not irrelevant to the problems it has brought before itself. Such thoughts are instances of that characteristic

18. Cf. Voegelin, *NSP*, 187–88; cf. also Voegelin, *SPG*, 309–10.
19. Cavell, *Cities of Words*, 22.
20. Ibid., 21.

human willingness to allow questions for itself which it cannot answer with satisfaction.[21]

What Cavell calls philosophy and discusses as undistracted thinking about ordinary human occurrences, is what Voegelin calls political science. As we shall see, the terms are interchangeable:

> (2) [T]he subject matter [of political science]. . . is nothing esoteric; rather, it lies not far from the questions of the day and is concerned with the truth of things that everyone talks about. What is happiness? How should a man live in order to be happy? What is virtue? What, especially, is the virtue of justice? How large a territory and a population are best for a society? What kind of education is best? What professions, and what form of government? All of these questions arise from the conditions of the existence of man in society. And the philosopher is a man like any other: As far as the order of society is concerned, he has no other questions to ask than those of his fellow citizens.[22]

Beyond the explicit disavowal of extraordinary questions and a location of the impetus to science in the conditions of social life, there is a common point in the writing of the two thinkers, one that will come into view if we carefully consider Cavell's employment of "the ordinary." The key is to see that the "ordinary" in Cavell's passage has the possible meaning of average, or everyday. Cavell alludes to the possibility of reading "ordinary" as a term synonymous with "everyday", among other places, in his essay on the Philosopher in American life.[23] There, Cavell also alludes to the danger in not recognizing that the uncritical acceptance of "ordinary" as a synonym for "everyday" is dangerous, i.e., in not recognizing that the words are in fact subject to equivocation.[24] Cavell calls the ordering power of the ordinary its "uncanniness."[25] We note, however, in light of our own investigations, that the uncanniness of the ordinary is a sense that arises only when the ordering power of the things that happen every day, say, ordinarily, is not so much consciously and explicitly rejected, as (pre-)supposed not to exist; and this is a particularly advanced state or acute symptom of the social foundering that gives rise to both philosophy

---

21. Cavell, *Themes out of School*, 9.

22. Voegelin, *SPG*, 257–58.

23. Cavell, *Quest*, 6.

24. Cf. Cavell, *Quest*, 3–26.

25. Ibid., 153–78.

and gnostic speculation (that may give rise to either). The senselessness of existence, the experience of existence as senseless, is the basic tenet of gnosticism. On this reading of "ordinary" then, to think about something other than what ordinary human beings think about is the end, the goal, the purpose of gnostic spirituality. In light of this, we begin to see that Cavell's willingness not to think about something other than what ordinary human beings think about is precisely a willingness not to engage in gnostic speculation. This would seem to be at odds with at least some of the questions that Cavell adduces as examples of ordinary human mental occurrences. Surely, one may ask doubtfully whether other minds exist, that is, other minds capable of sharing the experience of others in an understanding way. "We" may not ask such a question, because "we" supposes the sharing of experience, and if experience is being shared, then it is intelligible. So the question really is whether there is a "we" to speak of, a "we" of which each of us is a part; say, we, the people. The raising of the question is, however, a human possibility, perhaps even an inevitability, humanly speaking. It is not, therefore, in the refusal of the question, but in its raising and embrace, that we find ourselves, and finding ourselves is the task of philosophy. This brings us to the second text from Cavell:

> (3) I came to the idea that philosophy's task was not so much to defeat the skeptical argument as to preserve it, as though the philosophical profit of the argument would be to show not how it might end, but why it must begin and why it must have no end, at least none within philosophy, or what we think of as philosophy.[26]

One could insist, and press the question, such as it is: "But how do we know? How do we know that we are really in conversation with one another? How do we know that our words mean anything at all?" The fact is that there is no way, apart from or outside a community of sense, to know that the conversations, which take place among the members, are meaningful. This does not mean that one cannot recognize conversations taking place, e.g., in a language one does not understand. It does mean, however, that one cannot ever recognize community of meaning if one posits a proof external to the conversations of the community itself, that people talking in the strange language are in fact making sense to, and of, each other, as a condition of granting recognition. Said simply, if one doubts the possibility of meaningfulness, as such (as do both the gnostic

26. Cavell, *Quest* 5.

and the skeptic), then one will never be convinced that this or that word, or sentence, or paragraph, etc., on to society as a whole, is meaningful.

In the chapter of his work *After Virtue*, titled, "Virtues, Unity of Life and Concept of a Tradition" MacIntyre writes:

> (4) The most familiar type of context in and by reference to which speech acts and purposes are rendered intelligible is the conversation. . . [C]onversation, understood widely enough, is the form of human transactions in general. Conversational behaviour is not a special sort or aspect of human behaviour, even though the forms of language-using and of human life are such that the deeds of others speak for them as much as do their words. For that is possible only because they are the deeds of those who have words.[27]

We recall that MacIntyre describes the human condition as essentially worded. Human beings' discovery of themselves as worded, let us say Hellenic-ally, as logical beings, does not occur in a vacuum. We know we have words only to the extent that we share them. If someone were to say to me, "Your house is on fire!" and if I were to respond, "Well, how do I know that what you are saying is meaningful? Before I call the Fire Department, I am going to ask you to prove that what you just said makes sense," my erstwhile interlocutor will not be able to answer me (of course, he might point to the smoke billowing from the kitchen window, at which point I could require he prove the meaningfulness of his gesticulation, and so on, and so forth). The point is that we have words because and to the extent that we have words for conversations, and in conversations; we have conversations about things, subjects, topics, events, etc., in sum, about the world in which we, through our words, through the exercise of our being logical, find ourselves. Finally, it is worthwhile once again to recall that to have words means, in English, to engage in verbal controversy; America is an attempt to have words between the worlds.

Wording America

The words of the Declaration, "We hold these truths to be self evident," and the words that follow, are words in the American conversation. To require external proof, say, by way of demonstration in formal abstraction, of the internal coherence of the idea of self-evidence, when this is

27. MacIntyre, *After Virtue*, 210–11.

ripped from the experiential context in which the claim to it occurs, is to refuse to recognize America's claim to give intelligible expression to its experience of the world, precisely because it is a refusal to recognize the world as intelligible, logical. It is a refusal to recognize the human power to word the world. Once again, Cavell calls this refusal of recognition "skepticism". Skepticism, however, in light of our present discussion, is beginning to show itself as gnosticism's twin sister:

> (5) [F]or me, the uncanniness of the ordinary is epitomized by the possibility or the threat of what philosophy has called skepticism, understood as the capacity, even desire, of ordinary language to repudiate itself, specifically to repudiate its power to word the world, to apply to the things we have in common, or to pass them by. (By, "the desire of ordinary language to repudiate itself" I mean—doesn't it go without saying?—a desire on the part of speakers of a native or mastered tongue who desire to assert themselves, and despair of it.). . . My idea is that what in philosophy is known as skepticism (for example, as in Descartes and Hume and Kant) is a relation to the world, and to others, and to myself, and to language, that is known to what you might call literature, or anyway responded to in literature, in uncounted other guises—in Shakespeare's tragic heroes, in Emerson's and Thoreau's "silent melancholy" and "quiet desperation," in Wordsworth's perception of us as without "interest," in Poe's perverseness."[28]

The three American authors quoted as literary exemplars of engagement with skepticism, i.e., Emerson, Thoreau and Poe, each offer terms for what Cavell calls skepticism, the opposites of which lead at once to philosophy and to the oft-forgotten literary genre known as declaration. The opposite of "silent melancholy" is vital verbosity; the opposite of "quiet desperation" is restless hope, and the opposite of "perverseness" is conversion. The vital verbosity of the Declaration is found, first and foremost, in the Signers' pledge of their lives, fortunes and sacred honor to the words of it. Restless hope was the impetus for America's first settlement. Conversion is another name for the Christian's pilgrimage in the world, by which the Christian learns to know the goodness of this world in view of the next. As we shall see, the possibility of America turns on this last.

There is no proof, external to conversation, that can prove the meaningfulness of conversation as such. To require such proof is nothing

---

28. Cavell, *Quest*, 154–55.

short of madness. To deny the self-evidence of the truth declared in the Declaration, on the basis of formal incoherence exposed by a rarefied consideration of the logical form of the claim, is to refuse to treat the claim as one about the truth of America, made to a candid world, by and for American society; but to treat the claim of the Declaration in this way, insofar as it wilfully removes the claim from the conversational context in which it occurs and in which it makes sense (or not), is precisely to seek escape from the world's condition.

Voegelin has noted that what he calls "the enlightened form of philosophizing"—by which he essentially means a form that has been thoroughly penetrated by gnosticism—depends, indeed is entirely rooted in the expectation of such external proof, if being external to a community of sense or meaning can be taken as roughly equivalent to being external to the experiences, the sharing of which constitutes the community:

> [The enlightened] thinker operates on symbols that have been developed by mystic-philosophers for the expression of experiences of transcendence. He proceeds by ignoring the experiential basis, separates the symbols from this basis as if they had a meaning independent of the experience which they express, and with brilliant logic shows, what every philosopher knows, that they will lead to contradictions if they are misunderstood as propositions about objects in world-immanent experience.[29]

Gnosticism, like its sister, skepticism, denies the intelligibility of experience. The former does so on the basis of a basic presupposition, i.e., that the condition of the world is *agnoia*. Skepticism internalizes the condition of the world, making it, and therefore its order, essentially unknowable; but this is the same as saying its condition is unknowing.

Gnosticism: The Nature of Modernity in Voegelin

The fact that the re-emergence of gnosticism in the West took place within the strong framework of a culturally and institutionally Christian society made sure that its early articulations would appropriate the existing Christian symbology and bend it to its purposes. If we take Augustine as the principal intellectual architect of Christian society in the West, then the first thinker to break with his building plan was a thirteenth century Calabrese monk, Joachim of Fiore (Flora):[30]

29. Cf. Voegelin, *OH* 2, 349.

30. See West and Zimdars-Swartz, *Joachim of Fiore*.

Joachim broke with the Augustinian conception of a Christian society when he applied the symbol of the Trinity to the course of history. In his speculation the history of mankind had three periods corresponding to the three persons of the Trinity. The first period of the world was the age of the Father; with the appearance of Christ began the age of the Son. But the age of the Son will not be the last one; it will be followed by a third age, of the Spirit. The three ages were characterized as intelligible increases of spiritual fulfilment.[31]

That this speculative break happened at all is an early sign of the opacity of order that would culminate in the disintegration of the *res publica Christiana*; crucially, the use of the pre-eminent Christian symbol of the Divine in its loving transcendent relation to itself and the world of creation in order to explain the movements of mundane history accomplishes, in principle, the construction of an *eidos* of history: the total immanentization of the *eschaton*, meaning the closing of what is ultimate in men's understanding of themselves and of the world within the bounds of the world itself. The temporal order differentiated by Augustine as the *saeculum senescens* is replaced by a new paradigm, in which the movement of history is ordered toward an end to be achieved within the temporal boundaries of historical existence:

> The attempt at immanentizing the meaning of existence is fundamentally an attempt at bringing our knowledge of transcendence into a firmer grip than the *cognitio fidei*, the cognition of faith, will afford; and gnostic experiences offer this firmer grip in so far as they are an expansion of the soul to the point where God is drawn into the existence of man.[32]

Voegelin also explains that, and how, Joachim's speculation creates four new classes of symbols, which govern the internal interpretation of politics down to the present.[33] First, there is the conception of history as the sequence of three ages, culminating in a final realm; second, there is the symbol of the leader, who emerges to inaugurate each stage of history; third, there is the prophet of the new age, a figure often blended or blurred into the second; finally, there is the brotherhood of autonomous persons. At this point, the crucial importance for America of the gnostic symbology in its modern acception comes more fully into view.

31. Voegelin, *NSP*, 178.

32. Voegelin, *NSP*, 189.

33. Ibid., 179.

Two symbols, especially, have aspects directly pertinent to America and our discussion of it. The first of these is the symbol of the succession of stages in history, which, in the case of the encyclopaedic movement,[34] articulated history into the ancient, medieval and modern periods.[35] The prevailing cultural tendency at present continues to be that of thinking of modernity as an historical period. With Voegelin, however, we have been able to trace the origins of modernity back to the gnostic movement that began in antiquity, and found modernity to be the manifestation of gnosticism's re-emergence as a social and intellectual force acting on Western civilization from within. Modernity, in other words, is not a period in the history of Western civilization, but a growth within it, a phenomenon that has given rise to movements, some of which have competed—and continue to compete—on a mass scale for existential control of the societies that participate in the Western civilizational project:

> Gnostic experiences determine a structure of political reality that is *sui generis*. A line of gradual transformation connects medieval with contemporary gnosticism. And the transformation is so gradual, indeed, that it would be difficult to decide whether contemporary phenomena should be classified as Christian because they are intelligibly an outgrowth of Christian heresies of the Middle Ages or whether medieval phenomena should be classified as anti-Christian because they are intelligibly the origin of modern anti-Christian-ism. The best course will be to drop such questions and to recognize the essence of modernity as the growth of gnosticism.[36]

America is a reply to and an attempt to overcome the problems of modernity thusly understood.

In the last century, the gnostic mass movements of Communism and Nazism-Fascism were successfully countered by the strength of the so-called "free institutions," i.e., the institutions founded by societies with a self-understanding originally resistant to gnosticism. The struggle was carried out at the institutional level, and was of such moment that nothing less than the continued existence of the societies that had erected the free institutions for themselves was at stake: the struggle against the mass movements masked a creeping gnostic corrosion within the very

---

34. Cf. MacIntyre, *Three Rival Versions of Moral Enquiry*, 9–31, 127–48, 170–236; see also Barzun, *From Dawn to Decadence*.

35. Cf. Voegelin, *SPG*, 300–304.

36. Voegelin, *NSP*, 190.

societies that had free institutions, most especially within American society. That corrosion has continued, so that the illumination of America
from within by an American story has now been darkened, giving rise to
a new, full-blown civilizational crisis occasioning the very work of recovery in which we are engaged.

The second symbol of direct and immediate concern to our present
project is the brotherhood of autonomous persons. Voegelin adduces the
Puritan community of the Elect as one of the various historical expressions of the symbol, and it is worthwhile to see the context in which he
places the example:

> In the third age the church [sic] will cease to exist because the
> charismatic gifts that are necessary for the perfect life will reach
> men without administration of sacraments. While Joachim
> himself conceived the new age concretely as an order of monks,
> the idea of a community of the spiritually perfect who can live
> together without institutional authority was formulated on prin-
> ciple. The idea was capable of infinite variations. It can be traced
> in various degrees of purity in medieval and Renaissance sects,
> as well as in the Puritan churches of the saints; in its secularized
> form it has become a formidable component in the contempo-
> rary democratic creed; and it is the dynamic core in the Marx-
> ian mysticism of the realm of freedom and the withering-away
> of the state.[37]

Elsewhere, Voegelin discusses August Comte's early 19th century varia-
tion of the brotherhood of autonomous persons based on altruism,
which, he notes, is the secular-immanent force that, substituting love in
the Christian sense, allows humanity to conceive itself as a brotherhood
without a father.[38] If we recall John Adams's marginal rejoinder to Mary
Wollstonecraft's *Defence of the French Revolution*, to the effect that the
notion of equality is entirely rooted in the Christian notion that we are all
children of the same father, then the need to continue in the work of recovery becomes clear: either the democratic order of society is based on
an understanding of human nature as essentially un-fathered, in which
case we are either gods, or bastards—worse—we may be the children of
a state that has undergone apotheosis; or it is based on some other principle, or understanding of ourselves.

37. Voegelin, *NSP*, 180.
38. Cf. Voegelin, *SPG*, 296.

The line we have taken from Adams comes from the end of America's founding generation. It will eventually serve as the beginning of an epilogue to the founding moment. Insofar as the work in which we are engaged is a work of recovery, we must begin at the beginning of America, with the first settlers. Here, we encounter an interesting particular: the first European settlers of America were Puritans, and therefore, gnostics. If, therefore, we are to understand how the order in history that is America came to be a reply to and an attempt to overcome modernity, we shall need to look to the history of order in America.

Calvinism, Puritanism, and the Gnostic Beginnings of America

In the main, the religious doctrine of the early colonists was Calvinistic,[39] and the attempts to organize religion in the colonies were carried out according to variations of Calvinist ecclesiology. According to the previously given characterization of gnosticism, we can now argue that this was essentially gnostic. Discussing in fact Original Sin and the effects of it in the *Institutes of Christian Religion*, Calvin describes human nature as vile and depraved,[40] without qualification, saying of human beings, that "their whole nature is, as it were, a seed-bed of sin, and therefore cannot but be odious and abominable to God."[41] More importantly, in New England especially, though not only there,[42] and to the extent they were doctrinaire Calvinists, the settlers were also "Puritan," a name that originated in the third century and was brought out of mothballs to denigrate those who sought to "purify" Christian worship and social organization more or less along the lines of Calvin's *Institutes*, which call for the creation of

39. In Virginia, the Church of England was established early on, and there were many non-Calvinist communities, especially in the western regions and the middle colonies. By numbers, however, and by importance in terms of influence on the development of American culture, the most significant theology and ecclesiology was Calvinist.

40. Calvin, *Institutes of the Christian Religion* II.i.4–7. Book, Chapter and Section references are to Calvin's final Latin edition, as given in Norton, ed., *Institutes of the Christian Religion*, 1599. The Norton edition is available in electronic format through the Center for Reformed Theology and Apologetics; cf. Kerr, ed., *A Compend of the Institutes of the Christian Religion*, 42–43.

41. Calvin, *Institutes*, II.i.8–9; cf. Calvin, *Compend*, 44.

42. Cf. Bonomi, *Under the Cope of Heaven*, 16.

communities of "the elect" to stamp out unrighteousness and, by their sinless, shining example, prove their election and give glory to God.[43]

The "purification" the Puritans proposed, however, was neither cleansing, nor in the usual sense, a corruption. Following Richard Hooker,[44] Voegelin remarks that Puritanism was:

> [N]ot based on Scripture but was a "cause" of a vastly different origin. It would use Scripture when passages torn out of context would support the cause, and for the rest it would blandly ignore Scripture as well as the traditions and rules of interpretation that had been developed by fifteen centuries of Christianity. In the early phases of the gnostic revolution this camouflage was necessary—neither could an openly anti-Christian movement have been socially successful, nor had gnosticism in fact moved so far away from Christianity that its carriers were conscious of the direction in which they were moving.[45]

What makes the revolution "gnostic" is the drastic opposition between an old world, utterly currupt, and a new world in which corruption is definitely eliminated. This breaks the tension in which goodness can be discerned in the world, even as something always to be realized, that is, the tension involved in experiencing the world as at one and the same time good, and not good enough, not as good as it should be. This was first differentiated for Western civilization in the classical philosophical tradition, by the recognition in the world of an *eidos* or archetype, traces or intimations of the divine transcendent in imperfect representations of true being in mundane reality; Christian inheritance of that tradition carried forward the process of differentiation, which produced the eschatological symbolism analyzed by Voegelin. The gnostic revolution, refuting the classical and Christian inheritance, brings the tension to a breaking point, either by collapse or by explosion. In the specific, and for Voegelin paradigmatic case of the Puritan revolution in England, the tendency was decidedly toward collapse of the tension:

43. For a recent presentation of Calvin's political thought, see Stevenson, *Sovereign Grace*. Stevenson's presentation is thorough, if sympathetic. The "Christian freedom" of the book's sub-title, and throughout the book, is actually Stevenson's (very good) take on Calvin's own understanding of Christian freedom.

44. For Voegelin's discussion of Hooker's *Laws of Ecclesiastical Polity*, see *NSP*, 197–205. The *Laws* have been published as part of Hill, ed., *The Folger Library Edition of the Works of Richard Hooker*. See also Voegelin, *History of Political Ideas*, vol. V, *Religion and the Rise of Modernity* in *CW* 23:70–107.

45. Voegelin, *NSP*, 200.

> On the basis of this [immanentizing] fallacy, gnostic thinkers,
> leaders, and their followers interpret a concrete society and its
> order as an eschaton; and, in so far as they apply their fallacious
> construction to concrete social problems, they misrepresent the
> structure of immanent reality.[46]

The presence of this kind of thinking about America, in America, is certain[47]. The "City on a Hill" that lived as a symbol of America as lately as Ronald Reagan's 1989 Farewell Address to the nation[48], is no other than the city on a hill roughly 30 miles East of the Mediterranean coast and 8 miles due West of the northern tip of the Dead Sea. It is Jerusalem, and more importantly, the New Jerusalem in which the elect will live forever in eternal happiness and glory with God:

> Without ever becoming more than half-conscious of their mo-
> tives, the New England divines turned to the logic of the federal
> theology for an escape from the logic of time. Once more they
> were striving to extricate themselves from the round of neces-
> sity, from the dead level of material and implacable fact, and to
> assure themselves and their people that not only was Christian
> history coming to its foreordained climax in their Jerusalem,
> but that theirs would be an exception to all the cities that ever
> before had been set upon a hill, and would resist degeneration
> with the sustaining help of the Covenant of Grace.[49]

The key to this is recognizing the conflation of "the federal theology" with the order of society. While Puritans maintained the distinction between the government of the Church and civil government, to be a member of the Church was for Puritans to be a member of society. There was, in Catholic Europe, a long tradition of conditioning participation in public life on the basis of Church membership. While this condition did exclude non-Church-members, the exclusion was generally established by civil statute or civil approval of and support for long-standing practice. In other words, neither the identification of the Church with society, nor the exclusion of the non-baptized, was a matter of principle. They were prudential safeguards on or for the order of society, but not an intrinsic

46. Voegelin, *NSP*, 223.

47. See Emerson, *Puritanism in America, 1620–1750*.

48. Ritter and Henry, *Ronald Reagan: The Great Communicator*, 179–85. For a critical appraisal of Reagan's public speeches, see Houck and Kiewe, *Actor, Ideologue, Politician: The Public Speeches of Ronald Reagan*, esp. 265–67.

49. Miller, *New England Mind*, 464.

part of the social order. It was precisely the erection of such a prudential arrangement into a principle of social organization that distinguished the Puritan social project.

To the extent that its beginnings were Puritan, America's beginnings were therefore also gnostic, for the search for an escape from "material and implacable fact" is precisely the promise of gnosticism. New England sermons from the period are not only peppered with, but crafted around and systematically involved in the project of the idea's indoctrination.[50] The Puritan rhetoric retained a Christian vocabulary, though it decisively modified the sense of the Christian terms it deployed in its efforts at indoctrination. As we shall shortly see, it was precisely this characteristic that allowed for the opening of the way toward the construction of the conceptual space that came to be called, "America."

The Decay of Gnostic Power in America

Early on, the Puritan strangle-hold on American society's self-interpretation was loosened (though as we shall see, never definitively broken). The cause of the decay in gnostic society, a decay that we can interpret as an element of progress in American civilization, is twofold: firstly, there were the savage, brutal external conditions under which the first gnostic communities in America were forced to operate; second, there was an element internal to the New England Puritan self-understanding that, when coupled with the existential conditions of life on the wild continent, broke the gnostic grip on the American mind before the grip could choke all the spiritual life out of it.

NYU history professor Patricia Bonomi has argued that there was in America a process by which religious attitudes and practices developed, the impetus of which was a tension almost immediately experienced between the doctrinal tenets of the early colonial religious leaders and the colonial experience of life in the wilderness:

> Wherever one stands on questions about the true nature of early American religious culture, it seems clear that a tension existed between colonial leaders devoted to building an orderly

50. For a discussion of this, as well as a helpful bibliography of the historical debate over Puritanism's role in the early colonial settlement vs. other factors that, presumably, could be subsumed under and treated within or as part of a theoretical elaboration of Puritanism's role in early American cultural formation, see Egan, *Authorizing Experience*.

and reverent society, and a people of variant backgrounds, lesser status, and multiform as well as passionate religious convictions. We may never know what proportion of the seventeenth-century settlers shared the religious attitudes of their leaders, but we do know that certain features of the resettlement process itself obstructed efforts by the elite to foster religious uniformity and exacerbated conflicts between leaders and people. Disease, hunger, and Indian wars threatened the survival of the first settlements, diverting attention from spiritual to material needs. Later, when inhabitants ventured out into the countryside, it was more difficult for the newly transplanted sanctions of church and religion to assert their authority. Many colonists scrambled to acquire land and goods, often at the expense of pious habits. Successful colonies attracted new settlers, leading to an ever increasing diversity of population and belief.[51]

Bonomi couches the tension as one between the rulers of colonial society and the ruled, and says the tension is clearly present in colonial life, "wherever one stands on questions about the true nature of early colonial religious culture." The point, however, is that early American culture existed to the extent there was tension, and developed in (sometimes inverse) proportion to the extremity of the tension created in society by the psychic pressures occasioned by the physical hardship and moral barbarism of early colonial life. Said shortly, the immediate necessities of the kind of civilized society in which gnostic forgetfulness can take root were simply not given. The state of perpetual emergency in early America forced the settlers to exercise the kind of practical intelligence that naturally builds up resistance to the spiritual opiate that is gnosticism, severely testing the energies of the Puritan myth-makers.

From Errand to Pilgrimage: American Symbology Develops

The New England Puritan experience originally understood itself as the founding of an eschatological community. This self-understanding was thematized by subsequent generations as an "errand in the wilderness," a symbol first differentiated[52] by the Puritan preacher Samuel Danforth in a 1670 sermon to the Massachusetts General Court:

51. Bonomi, *Under the Cope of Heaven*, 15.
52. Cf. Conforti, *Imagining New England*, 42. Conforti doubts the earliest American

Such as have sometime left their pleasant cities and habitations
to enjoy the pure worship of God in a wilderness are apt to abate
and cool in their affection thereunto; but then the Lord calls
upon them seriously and thoroughly to examine themselves,
what it was that drew them into the wilderness, and to consider
that it was not the expectation of ludicrous levity nor of courtly
pomp and delicacy, but of the free and clear dispensation of the
Gospel and kingdom of God. . . You have solemnly professed
before God, angels, and men that the cause of your leaving
your country, kindred, and fathers' houses and transporting
yourselves with your wives, little ones, and substance into this
waste and howling wilderness, was your liberty to walk in the
faith of the Gospel with all good conscience according to the
order of the Gospel, and your enjoyment of the pure worship of
God according to his institution without human mixtures and
impositions.[53]

The fact that, as early as 1670, Danforth had to remind the people in Massachusetts of the colony's original motivation, suggests that the original
motive had lost its ordering force in the community. This, taken with the
fact that the forgetfulness of the citizenry was manifest most strongly in
people's assiduous attention to the business of living in the world, shows
that New England society's understanding of itself as an eschaton in concrete historical existence was already under serious strain, even if not yet
sufficiently broken.

In the same sermon, Danforth poses the question, "What is it that
distinguisheth *New England* from the other Colonies and Plantations
in *America*?" and answers, "Not transportation over the Atlantick [*sic*]
Ocean, but the *Ministry* of God's faithful Prophets, and the fruition of

---

settlers understood themselves as errant in the wilderness. The term did not exist before 1670. The question is whether Danforth's description of the first settlers' business
in Massachusetts was accurate. Conforti argues that, since the *term* did not exist prior
to 1670, the *description* of the first settlers' self-understanding that Danforth makes to
fall under the term must therefore be unwarranted, anachronistic, false; if this line of
thinking is true, then it follows that, since "regional identity" did not exist in the seventeenth century, there must have been nothing like what we call regional identity in
the minds of seventeenth century Americans; if this holds, however, then the purpose,
the usefulness of Conforti's project is not entirely clear.

53. Emerson, *Puritanism in America, 1620–1750,* 89–90. For the full text of Danforth's sermon, see Danforth, *A Brief Recognition of New Englands Errand into the Wilderness,* available in PDF format at www.digitalcommons.unl.edu, the website of the
University of Nebraska, Lincoln's library science project. Henceforth *Brief Recognition.*

his holy *Ordinances*.[54]" Here, America clearly functions solely as a geo-graphical indicator. In order for New England to emerge as one of the two principal motors of the American Revolution, the conceptual space of America needed to be erected; in order to enter into that conceptual space, indeed, as a principal architect of it, the New England citizenry needed to emerge from its gnostic self-interpretation, and so it did.

Gnostic Failure

As we are beginning to see, the gnostic project failed because existential conditions forced the exposure of its internal contradictions to the de-veloping consciousness of New England Puritans. In the following pas-sage from Danforth's sermon, the doom of the gnostic interpretation of society is spelled:

> The hardships, difficulties and sufferings, which you have ex-posed your selves unto, that you might dwell in the House of the Lord, and leave your Little Ones under the shadow of the wings of the God of Israel, have not been few nor small. And shall we now withdraw our selves and our Little Ones from under those healing Wings, and lose that full Reward, which the Lord hath in his heart and hand to bestow upon us ? Did we not with *Mary* choose this for our *Part, to sit at Christs* [sic] *feet and hear his word*? and do we now repent of our choice, and prefer the Honours, Pleasures and Profits of the world before it?[55]

In the older Christian tradition of which the Catholic Church is the bearer, Mary's portion is imitated in the contemplative life, the life of cloistered monasticism. Puritanism in New England failed because the gnostic au-thorities failed to grasp what the people readily understood by their expe-rience of life there: it is not possible to organize society by quasi-monastic rule; in the face of massive evidence attesting the fact that continued pursuit of the ideal would lead to total social failure (would, in biological terms, be lethal), insisting that society be so organized is madness.

The concrete society that interpreted itself as an eschaton failed in New England because the "not yet" side of the eschaton, as understood in its properly orthodox Christian differentiation, asserted itself to those who had attempted to order society according to such an interpretation.

54. Cooper, *Tenacious of Their Liberties*, 140.
55. Danforth, *Brief Recognition*, 20.

The "not yet" side of the eschaton pressed itself so virulently as to break the psychological pressure of the Puritan leaders' exclusive insistence on the "already" side.[56]

If this had been all there was to the Puritan self-understanding, then perhaps total social disintegration would have been inevitable. As things were, however, the first Puritans also understood themselves as pilgrims. The period of their pilgrimage began in 1607, with the departure for Holland of a group of English "separatists." For nearly a decade, the separatists, or Puritans, as they were derisively styled, eked out an existence in the tolerant quarters of Amsterdam.[57] It was from their travel to a foreign country, in search of a homeland, that the Puritans began to understand themselves as pilgrims. When they came into the American wilderness, they thought they had found a home, and as we have seen, they interpreted their efforts to build that home as the construction of the New Jerusalem. What they discovered was that in crossing the Atlantic, they had not, as a matter of brute fact, escaped the conditions of the world.

Daniel Boorstin's observation to the effect that, for the earliest settlers, the Sea was a path from Babylon to Zion,[58] is another way of saying that the Atlantic crossing was an act of pilgrimage, clearly interpreted as exodus. Finding themselves in a place that was not Zion, at least not yet, and yet relying on the strength of their community for survival, the American wilderness began to appear as a way-stop on the pilgrimage, a place to live out the period of waiting for the Savior's coming on terms of their own choosing, terms of which they certainly believed the Savior would approve, and that is the point. The American experience in the wilderness, while it did not entirely break the power of gnostic fallacy

56. On this side of the *parousia*, the People of God wait in joyful hope for the coming of the Savior, as the Church prays in the liturgical recitation of the Our Father. The mode of waiting in the Catholic formulation is the key to this: As the waiting is joyful, the *eschaton* is already present, for there is joy only in the enjoyment of a thing. The presence of the *eschaton* in history, however, is in and through the Church, which is the People of God and the body of Christ. This body is, further, universal: it exists throughout all time and into eternity. The full achievement of the *eschaton*, through *parousia*, will reveal the Church's full membership. The Church on Earth, in the Catholic tradition, is called the Church Militant. There is the Church Suffering (or Penitent) and in Heaven, there is the Church Triumphant. As things stand now, the most glorious city of God lives in secret, as a stranger here on Earth, which is thematized as Babylon, in light of Babylon's role in salvation history as the place of Israel's captivity.

57. Cf. Emerson, *Puritanism in America, 1620-1750*, 11-36.

58. Cf. Boorstin, *Americans: The National Experience*, 5.

(the symbolism of which, as we have begun to see, has remained with America, as part of America), did succeed in broadening the American mind to a point at which Americans were able to use practical intelligence and draw general conclusions from it; this is the recovery of the idea of the world as *saeculum*, and the beginning of political thinking.

American Humanity Emerges: Gnostic Pressures and Counter-pressures

The religiosity of Americans in the founding generation is not really a matter subject to question, as the primary sources universally attest, and as contemporary scholarship continues to understand more deeply. Forrest McDonald has even gone so far as to say, "Where patriots stood, in the Spring of seventy-six, depended upon whether they believed in Original Sin."[59] While this statement is perhaps hyperbolic, or at least a case of fashionable generality, it helps us toward an understanding of the debate over human nature that was at the center of the ratification debate in 1787–1788. By that time, the debate in America can certainly be seen as one over the effects of Original Sin.

In the early time of the gnostic Puritans, the effects of Original Sin were understood to be total and absolute. Human nature was entirely corrupt, and entirely redeemed by a saving Grace that allowed and required human beings to organize themselves in communities of the elect. By 1787, the Virginia squire-lawyer and revolutionary, James Madison could, under the pen-name Publius (which he took after the Roman Republican statesman Publius Valerius Publicola:[60] an allusion that, importantly, was readily perceived by the allonymous author's readership), write:

> As there is a degree of depravity in mankind which requires a certain degree of circumspection and distrust: So there are other qualities in human nature, which justify a certain portion of esteem and confidence.[61]

That Publius could write this way, not only without fear of offending the religious sensibilities of his audience, but with an eye toward convincing them of the proposed constitution's consonance with human nature, is

59. McDonald, *E Pluribus Unum*, 27.

60. For the most popular life of Publius Valerius in America at the time of the founding, see Plutarch, *Lives of the Noble Romans and Grecians*, 117–30.

61. *Federalist* #55, 273.

a sign of the extent to which the doctrinaire Calvinism of the original colonization had lost its sway over the minds of the founding generation. This had immediate practical repercussions:

> Republican government presupposes the existence of these [good] qualities in a higher degree than any other form. Were the pictures which have been drawn by the political jealousy of some among us, faithful likenesses of the human character, the inference would be that there is not sufficient virtue among men for self-government; and that nothing less than the chains of despotism can restrain them from destroying and devouring one another.[62]

The key term is self-government. To our ears, it is synonymous with democratic institutions or some such. It was not so for the men and women of the founding generation. For those men and women, Self-government named a more basic concept, specifically, the government of one's self. In his 2001 essay on the social forces at play in the debate over declaring independence, Hans L. Eicholz illustrated the point and maintained that this difference is central to our ability to understand the Founders' *forma mentis*:

> In the earliest dictionaries of American English, the definition of self-government was . . . the "government of one's self." This remained true as late as 1959 when the Merriam-Webster dictionary defined self-government as "Self-control; self-command," and self-control meant simply, "control of one's self." The second definition followed, and is the one usually expressed today as majority rule. What was unusual for a dictionary definition was that this second definition was made dependent on the first: "Hence, government by the joint action of the mass of people constituting a civil body; also, the state of being so governed; specifically, democratic government." By the inclusion of "Hence," the dictionary reflected the view that you could not have democracy or the rule of law without individuals capable of governing themselves. The present edition of the dictionary has dropped that beginning, and today, we appear to think primarily of the collective, governmental meaning of self-government. Indeed, many current English dictionaries simply list majority rule as the only definition of the term. To recapture a sense of the older notion, we need to go back to a time when

62. Ibid.

> Americans still maintained a clear conception of themselves as
> a people composed of individuals capable of self-government.[63]

If we take this with our discussion of the existential forces that tended
to challenge the Puritan vision, we can say that, between 1607 and 1787,
the American understanding of human nature had not only changed,
but changed from a doctrinaire Calvinism into something much more
closely akin to the traditional Catholic doctrine of Original Sin, i.e., that
the corruption of human nature through Adam's transgression was not
total and unqualified. There remained in human nature after the fall
something worthy and noble.

What the passages from the *Federalist* serve to show is that there
was, in 1787–1788, a general discussion of "the human character" underway in America. Further, the terms of that discussion were, on one
side at least, if not Catholic in the confessional sense, at least not *prima
facie* inimical to the Catholic understanding of human nature. Thus, the
catholicity (meaning the universality, as indicated by the lower-case initial character) of the discussion of human nature in America admits of
being couched in at least two ways: on the one hand, it could go to show
that America is, as it were, waiting for the Church; on the other, it could
be that America is the Church.

In other words, while it is certain that the Founding Fathers had not
miraculously arrived at the gangway of St. Peter's Barque, comparison of
the texts from Calvin's *Institutes* and the *Federalist* papers shows that the
experience of life in America from the time of the first colonization to the
time of the ratification debate, had effected what we have seen John Adams call, "A change in the religious sentiments of the people." This change
in sentiment was religious, precisely to the extent that it was a change
in the consciousness of concord regarding the principles of society, that
is, a change in the understanding of the experiences that bound Americans together in society. This is especially the case when the comparison
is taken with our discussion of the existential tensions in America and
Voegelin's analysis of the gnostic fallacy at the heart of Modernity.

Before moving to that account, a final word is in order. It regards
the claim to the effect that the debate in America over ratification housed
and in an important sense turned upon the anthropological aspect of the
debate. The general applicability and pertinence of the American debate

---

63. Eicholz, *Harmonizing Sentiments*, 1.

over ratification, i.e., the universal import of the debate underway in America, was commonly recognized by those who were conducting it:

> It has been frequently remarked that it seems to have been re-
> served to the people of this country, by their conduct and ex-
> ample, to decide the important question, whether societies of
> men are really capable or not of establishing good government
> from reflection and choice, or whether they are forever destined
> to depend for their political constitutions on accident and force.
> If there be any truth in the remark, the crisis at which we are
> arrived may with propriety be regarded as the era in which that
> decision is to be made; and a wrong election of the part we shall
> act may, in this view, deserve to be considered as the general
> misfortune of mankind.[64]

Working backwards, then (meaning the last thing Publius said will be the first thing we consider), the (mis)fortune of mankind depends upon the election, that is, the choice, the American people will make in accepting or rejecting the proposed elements of representation. In the first, this means that acceptance or rejection of the proposed Constitution will be grounded in the self-understanding of the men who vote on it. It also means, or could mean, that the proposed elements of representation present themselves as accessible to human beings generally, irrespective of their provenance; that is, the elements of representation proposed in the new Constitution recommend themselves as adequate representative elements for human beings who have an understanding of human nature into which anyone, anywhere might come by consenting to the terms in which Americans express their understanding of it.

Said slightly differently, in order to bring out another aspect of the tension inherent in the claim to American universality: adjudication of the question whether societies of men generally are really capable of establishing good government falls to the people of "this country", i.e., New York and by extension, America (or, in consonance with what we were saying in the last chapter, the people of America in New York, and Virginia, and Massachusetts, and Maryland, and North Carolina, *inter alia*). In order for this claim to bear merit, the society to be represented by the proposed elements of representation must be a society in the membership of which human beings, as such, can take part. So the questions, "What is a man, that he might participate in this society?" and its

64. *Federalist* #1, 1.

converse, "What is this society, that men may as such participate in it?" are centrally, though implicitly present in the ratification debate.

Crèvecœur and the Re-emergence of American Gnosticism

If the early Puritan settlers of John Adams's New England had set out to build a city on a hill, and if the second governor of Virginia could refer to his colony as the New Jerusalem,[65] the situation in 1787 was palpably different, though the threat of gnosticism was hardly defeated. In his 1783 *Letters from an American Farmer*, Michel-Guillaume-Jean (Hector St. Jean) de Crèvecœur gives us a description of American humanity:

> What then is the American, this new man? He is either an European, or the descendant of an European, hence that strange mixture of blood, which you will find in no other country. I could point out to you a family whose grandfather was an Englishman, whose wife was Dutch, whose son married a French woman, and whose present four sons have now four wives of different nations. He is an American, who, leaving behind him all his ancient prejudices and manners, receives new ones from the new mode of life he has embraced, the new government he obeys, and the new rank he holds.[66]

The first thing to note is the terminology Crèvecœur employs to describe the American type. Crèvecœur says the American is a new man. This is an appropriation of the Christian eschatological term for Christ and those who become members of His body through Baptism. The terminology is inescapably Christian and specifically Pauline, rooted in Paul's description of Christ as the second Adam.[67] Crèvecœur's biographical details strongly militate in favour of the idea that he was writing out of a peculiarly Catholic *forma mentis*. Crèvecœur was of the French *petite noblesse*. He had his education from the Jesuits in the middle of the eighteenth century. It is no wonder, then, that he should have had the Pauline language to hand, and all but irresponsible not to read his use of it through a Catholic lens. Why, then, should Crèvecœur have found

---

65. Bonomi, *Under the Cope of Heaven*, 16.

66. Crèvecoeur, *Letters from an American Farmer*, 43. Crèvecoeur's *Letters* were first published at Philadelphia in 1783.

67. Cf. 1 Cor 15:45–9; Rom 5:12–21.

this Catholic theological language so apt to render the American type? Conversely, what is it about America that Crèvecœur expresses when he deploys this terminology?

Persistence of Gnosticism in America

If, in the Puritan project, New England was to distinguish itself from the other colonial enterprises in that it sought to establish the concrete eschatological society, Crèvecœur is now expanding the eschatological society to the point of embracing America. On this reading, however, America would be what a Catholic Christian educated in the *ancien regime* might have called the anti-Christ, that is, the replacement of the Body of Christ, the society that seeks to supplant the Church as the destination of pilgrim humanity and the locus of rebirth into new life. This strong, eschatological reading is a possible one, the presence of which in American culture is palpable. There is a vast literature, scholarly and popular, and in between, of which exhaustive treatment is impossible here.

Apt illustration of the cultural presence of such a conception of America comes from a Hollywood film made in the year 2000, called *The Contender*. The film tells the story of a Senator, a woman named Laine Hanson, who is nominated to fill the unexpectedly vacant office of Vice President of the United States. The Senator's confirmation hearings begin in the midst of a public scandal over her alleged participation in an orgy that took place during her time at university, documentary evidence of which exists in the form of an amateur video that does not, however, allow for clear identification of the female protagonist (not the Senator, as it turns out, though throughout the scandal Hanson refused to comment on her supposed role in the sex party). This, however, was a red herring.

The scandal was concocted by conniving conservative ideologues in the legislature, bent on destroying Hanson's bid for the vice-Presidency. In the climactic scene, Hanson the principled stalwart (we are to believe, if the incidental music and lighting, etc., are any indication of a director's intent or desire to create or elicit emotion, so as to influence judgment) addresses the Senate. After expressing a series of policy stances,[68] she says:

68. Viz. Hanson's support for the right to abortion, her belief that the death penalty ought to be banned, her desire to see the sale of cigarettes to minors made a federal offense, the expansion of the military (which would be used as a tool to stamp out genocide in the world) and the outlawing of handguns in the whole country.

> I may be an atheist, but that does not mean I do not go to church.
> I do go to church. The church I go to is the one that emancipated
> the slaves and gave women the right to vote. It gave us every
> freedom that we hold dear. My church is this very Chapel of
> Democracy that we sit in together, and I do not need God to tell
> me what are my moral absolutes. I need my heart, my brain, and
> this church.

This brief speech contains the falsification of history, the prohibition of inquiry, rejection of transcendence and the apotheosis of the state through the sanctification of the physical spaces devoted to the conduct of the state's business. It seems that, if America is, as the argument has sought from its outset to establish, a conceptual space, then from this reading it is a conceptual space entirely infected by the gnostic civilizational pathology that Voegelin first diagnosed in the *New Science of Politics*.

Through this example, modern gnosticism also shows itself to be built on an inherent contradiction: for all its blustering protestation of the senselessness of existence, and the need to escape the condition of the world (perhaps by re-creating it), the gnostic in America, like the gnostic everywhere else, cannot attempt its work without telling stories. The best stories make sense of the world. The worst are told by idiots; for all their sound and fury, they signify nothing.

The presence of a gnostic element in America is undeniable. Fortunately, however, the gnostic apotheosis of America's democratic institutions is neither the only interpretation, nor the inevitable conclusion of Crèvecœur's American symbology. The other possibility is that Crèvecœur is articulating America as a space in which human beings can encounter each other in a kind of convergence, so far from replacing the Church as the order of society, that it actually recovers an older understanding of society's contemporaneous distinction from and dependence upon the Church, or, at least reasonable (respect for) religiosity. The key to understanding Crèvecœur in this way is in his use of the marriage symbol, to analysis of which we dedicate the next chapter.

CHAPTER 5

The National Importance of Marriage

THE TITLE FOR THIS chapter is taken almost exactly from at least three sources within the body of Stanley Cavell's written work. The earliest of the three is his chapter on *The Philadelphia Story* in his seminal work, *Pursuits of Happiness: The Hollywood Comedy of Remarriage.*[1] The second is the last paragraph of an essay on Alfred Hitchcock's *North by Northwest*, which first appeared in the Summer, 1981 issue of Critical Inquiry and was reprinted in Cavell's collection of essays titled *Themes Out of School: Effects and Causes.*[2] The final source is Cavell's 2004 reappraisal of *The Philadelphia Story* in his book of that year, titled *Cities of Words: Pedagogical Letters on a Register of the Moral Life.*[3]

The central contention of this chapter is that there are certain and well-drawn connections between Crèvecœur's use of marriage as descriptive, in a critically useful way, of the American, whom Crèvecœur calls the New Man, and subsequent cultural developments in American society, developments that take place at significant temporal remove from the founding, and so attest to the presence of a tradition of thinking interchangeably and contemporaneously about things American and human. The principal purpose of the chapter is therefore to bring the connections to light. In illustrating these connections, one strain of American self-interpretation will achieve critical clarity and relief, against which its rival will be more readily visible. The first task of this chapter is, then,

---

1. 147.

2. 172.

3. 40 *et passim.*

to enlarge our discussion of Crèvecœur's use of the marriage symbol. When the central elements of Crèvecœur's understanding of marriage come further into view, it shall be possible to see how the cinematic explorations of marriage that Cavell considers in the aforementioned works of his provide grounds for affirming a tradition of self-interpretation in America that was present as early as Crèvecœur's 1783 *Letters* and as lately as 1949, the year in which the latest of the films definitive of the genre Cavell calls "remarriage comedy" was released.

The Marriage Metaphor in Context

Crèvecœur's use of the symbol was possible and is understandable because of the cultural circumstances in which he grew up and lived, some of which we do well to consider. Nuptial metaphors were commonplace in the eighteenth century. They were idiomatic, and generally understood to have political significance.[4] The sources of the marriage commonplace are, as usual, varied and disparate, ranging from the texts of classical antiquity[5] to the seventeenth century English Puritan revolutionary tracts, most especially John Milton's essay on divorce.[6]

In his 1787 *Defence of the Constitutions of Government of the United States of America*, John Adams describes Lycurgus' Lacademonian constitution in the following terms:

4. By way of example: *La folle journée* could not be staged in Paris until 1784, and Beaumarchais' play was banned from several courts in Europe, including the imperial court at Vienna. Da Ponte's libretto for Mozart's musical adaptation, *Le nozze di Figaro*, stripped the play of political references, thus making the comedy into an *opera buffa*. Cf. Steptoe, *Mozart-Da Ponte Operas*, 113.

5. Xenophon's *Economicus* was widely read and consulted in the eighteenth Century as a manual for domestic life, as well as for its treatment of the relation of the household to the polity. Cf. Hull, *Chaste, Silent & Obedient: English Books for Women, 1475–1640*, 47 et passim. Cf. also Bartlett, *The Shorter Socratic Writings: Apology of Socrates to the Jury, Oeconomicus, and Symposium*. The introduction contains a general discussion of Xenophon's long centuries of esteem and recent decline in stature in the West, generally, and in the English-speaking West, particularly (the editor attributes the decline to the influence of nineteenth-century German scholars, and quotes Edward Gibbon to the effect that Xenophon is one of the two authors (the second being Cicero), whose works Gibbon would first propose to a "liberal scholar."

6. John Milton's tract *On the Doctrine and Discipline of Divorce* was first published at London in 1643, and a second, revised and expanded edition was published in 1644, the year in which hostilities between the crown and the Parliamentary forces commenced. The work was widely read in the colonies.

> This [stability and permanence of government] was effected by
> reciprocal checks and a real balance, approaching nearly to an
> absolute control of the senate [sic], by a marriage between the
> king and people. . . [T]he indissoluble bond that united the king
> and people for ever, was the oath taken by the kings and *ephori*
> every month; the former never to violate the privileges of the
> people, and the latter forever to be loyal to the kings, the descen-
> dants of Hercules.[7]

The context of the text we have just cited is, as the title of the work states
as the broad-strokes description to follow shall illustrate, a defense of
the general systems of government in the United States. Adams's *Defense*
was written at London and designed to influence, so far as possible, the
convention at Philadelphia to take place in that same year.[8] Of particular
note is Adams's equation of "marriage" to an "indissoluble union" that is
effected by an "oath." Now consider Abigail Adams, John Adams's wife, in
a letter to Thomas Jefferson:

> Suppose you give me Miss Jefferson and in some future day take
> a son in lieu of her. I am for strengthening [the] federal union.[9]

This is surely playful banter, but this cannot be an objection; indeed, it is
precisely the point. The seamlessness of the joke is evidence of the depth
to which the metaphor had penetrated the American mind—or at least
Abigail's American mind. Jefferson, however, protested not to understand Abigail's proposal.[10] This, on its own, would go to suggest Jefferson
did not agree with the metaphor's implications for the nature of American fœderal union. Not surprising for a Virginian, Thomas Jefferson had
never thought of the American union under the Articles as indissoluble

7. WJA, 6:112.

8. Cf. McCullough, *John Adams*, 374–79.

9. Abigail Adams to T. Jefferson, in Boyd, *Papers of Thomas Jefferson*, 10:162. Cf.
McCullough, *John Adams*, 364. The importance of this light-hearted epistolary banter
is easily overlooked, since the friendships of John Adams and Thomas Jefferson, as
well as that of Mrs. Adams and Jefferson, are not a matter of diffuse public knowledge
in the present day. The importance of these friendships for America in its founding
generation is therefore not generally known. The thousands of letters comprising the
Adams-Adams correspondence (going back to their courtship) are one of the great
treasures of America, easily on a par with, though far more obscure than the more
famous Adams–Jefferson correspondence, which the two founding fathers began during the revolution, put down, and took up again in old age and retirement.

10. Cf. *TJ* to *JA* in Boyd, *Papers of Thomas Jefferson*, 10:162.

and holy, a single body knit together. The government of the states of America was, in 1787, a fœderal union under the Articles. What is more, the political significance of matrimony ought to be sufficiently suggested by these juxtapositions, especially in light of what we have previously noted about the founding moment of American nationhood, i.e., that it was, in essence, a debate over the kind of *foedus* to have, which is to say a discussion of the proper way to keep faith in America; to discuss this is to ask by what faith is America united.

Crèvecœur and the Typical American

Crèvecœur's use of marriage as descriptive of the American type is tied to his employment of another language symbol, also descriptive of the American, namely, his description of the American as the "New Man". The last chapter ended with a discussion of the importance of Crèvecœur's employment of the term. The passage in which the term appears is well-known to students of American culture, history and society. Nevertheless, a closer reading is in order. Once again, the passage:

> What then is the American, this new man? He is either an Eu-
> ropean, or the descendant of an European, hence that strange
> mixture of blood, which you will find in no other country. I
> could point out to you a family whose grandfather was an Eng-
> lishman, whose wife was Dutch, whose son married a French
> woman, and whose present four sons have now four wives of
> different nations. He is an American, who, leaving behind him
> all his ancient prejudices and manners, receives new ones from
> the new mode of life he has embraced, the new government he
> obeys, and the new rank he holds. He becomes an American by
> being received in the broad lap of our great Alma Mater. Here
> individuals of all nations are melted into a new race of men,
> whose labours and posterity will one day cause great changes
> in the world.[11]

The passage contains language that could be construed as modern, as well as language that can be taken as indicative of those civilizational elements, which are most resistant to modernity. On the side of modernity, Crèvecœur apparently makes being or becoming American a matter of abjuring roots, of abandoning tradition. Also on the side of modernity is the appropriation of Christian eschatological and soteriological

11. Crèvecoeur, *Letters from an American Farmer*, 43.

symbolism in the language of the "New Man," which we analyzed in the last chapter. If Crèvecœur's description of the American type is possibly an extension of the American gnostic to the whole of society and each of society's members, it is nevertheless only possibly so.

Crèvecœur's language is amenable to at least one other interpretation, for *homo novus* is a term that comes from another vocabulary, more ancient than the Pauline one we analyzed in the last chapter, and in important ways tied to it. The term, *homo novus*, like the term, *fides*, is a technical term in the Roman political lexicon. *Homo novus* may connote something akin to "upstart" or *enfant terrible*. Often, the *homo novus* was what we would call, "The coming man," in English. Strictly, however, *homo novus* names the first son of a family to reach consular rank.[12]

Crèvecœur inquires rhetorically into the character of the American, asking, "What then is the American, this new man?" and answers with a description of his nuptial habits. According to Crèvecœur's description, the American, the new man, is one who is free to wed a woman who, in the Old World, could not have been but a stranger to him—beyond his reach, unless he was one of the first citizens of his country, i.e., a high nobleman, of royal blood (or its equivalent), and therefore not only free but beholden to marry a person of his social station, wherever she might be found. Crèvecœur's American typology therefore contains the monarchical principle of social or political organization. When we take his use of the Roman language, together with his description of the American as universally marriageable, we see that Crèvecœur is describing the American type as one in which the principle of monarchy is present in each member, that is, diffuse throughout society.[13] When each citizen is a new man, that is, of equal station with those who hold the highest rank in the government that is given for society, and yet beholden to no illustrious ancestor for his place in society, then the responsibility for ruling, for the care of the whole people, rests equally with every member of

12. The term was by extension sometimes applied to the first man of any family to sit in the Senate. A good survey of the *novi homines* is found in Wiseman, *New Men in the Roman Senate, 139 BC–AD 14*.

13. The reader will recall that, in America, the monarchical principal was not understood as limited to the institution of an hereditary king. The president was understood (not always approvingly) to be essentially an elected king during his term of office, as were the *consules* of the Roman republic and the Lacademonian *archontes*. John Adams discussed the matter in an exchange of letters with Roger Sherman of Connecticut. The letters are published in *WJA* 6:427–442. See also Novak, *Choosing our King: Powerful Symbols in Presidential Politics*.

society.[14] Hence, there are in America—in principle—neither imperme-
able boundaries of social station, nor endogamic restrictions.

Crèvecœur does indeed say that the American leaves behind him all
his ancient prejudices and manners, and that he receives new ones. The
central importance of this observation, however, is understandable in
light of Crèvecœur's subsequent description of the sources of the American's new prejudices and manners, namely, the new mode of life he has
embraced, the new government he obeys, and the new rank he holds. The
new mode of life he has embraced is, that of the small farmer, in a word,
the husbandman. The new government he obeys is of his making, and his
rank in it is second to none, which is to say, consular. Thus, the new man
receives what were his ancient prejudices and manners anew, through
the mediation of the social and political order of which he has become
a member. This is transformation of tradition, not the destruction of it.
The key to this is in the following: when Crèvecœur says that in America,
individuals of all nations are melted into a new race of men, the founding
agent is marriage, for it is through marriage that the strange mixture of
blood is achieved. In this sense, the work of founding America belongs
to each new generation. In turn each generation must assess the terms
and conditions of the assumption of assuming the burdens of the work of
founding—must find the grounds of—its aptness to—consent; this is at
once the condition of marriage, and of legitimate government.

Marriage in History

Crèvecœur's use of marriage is important for another, further and closely
related reason. While subsequent revolutions sought to remake society
utterly, that is, to establish new bases for the legitimacy of power in and
over society, the American revolution justified itself as a preservation of
society's traditional order. Crèvecœur's use of marriage attests to this,
and to another, related truth. Marriage is a natural social institution that

14. The symbolism admits all the ambiguity of a symbol at work in political reality, e.g., Louisiana Governor Huey Long's "Every Man a King!" motto, around which
he organized the Share Our Wealth Society, and to which he gave expression in song
and, perhaps less famously though more fulsomely, in a speech to voters on February
23, 1934. Long's basic insight was that no person who is systematically denied access
to the means requisite for the acquisition of life's basic necessities, including the mini-
mum amenities of civilized living, can be independent in any politically or socially
meaningful way. From this insight, however, Long attempted unsuccessfully as a U.S.
Senator to argue the soundness of certain wealth redistribution policies. The policies'
unsoundness, however, does not necessarily impeach the insight.

preserves and guarantees the basic stability of society in history. If the historical existence of a society is interpreted as having been overcome, that is, if a given society interprets itself as an *eschaton*, as having entered into the end-phase of history, then the institutions that traditionally provided for the stability of that society while it was, so to speak, on pilgrimage, will appear superfluous. Thus, Crèvecœur's use of the marriage symbol attests to his understanding of American society as a society in historical existence, i.e., a society in eschatological tension.

More to this: an understanding of the importance of marriage and its consequences for America serves to dispel one of the most oft-repeated misrepresentations of the American, namely, the American as the "rugged individual." The problem with the picture of the American as the rugged individual is not so much with the words, as with their association. The "rugged individual" is generally understood to be a single man, further identified as an isolated, an atomic unit. This is historically inaccurate. In early America:

> The thinness of community life put a heavy burden on the family. Everywhere during the colonial period the family fulfilled many more functions than it does today, but among farmers, especially in the early years, it might be everything—factory-, church, school, hospital, tavern. The farmer and his wife had to make everything they could not buy. Without a school, they had to teach their children to read; without a church, to worship at home; without a doctor, to care for the sick. Children were plentiful and made more hands to do the endless work. Some might take over the farm as their parents grew old, but most of them would eventually leave to carve out new farms.[15]

The family is the basic American unit. The family in America, though often physically isolated, is by its very composition, let us say its constitution, not only social, but cosmopolitan. Its constituents come out of the Old World's disparate realms and regions; they bequeath to their posterity the tradition of becoming one in America. An examination of the structure of marriage will bring the issue further into view.

The Structure of Marriage

Marriage is a public institution. To speak in a language borrowed from the time in which the *Federalist* papers were written and published, marriage

15. Blum, McFeely, et al., *National Experience*, 71.

is a matter interesting the public weal. Think about what happens at a wedding. Who is there, what do they do, where do they do it, when do they do it, how do they do it? Most basically, there are the spouses, the witnesses and the agent of the state. The agent of the state speaks formal words and asks the spouses a question, each in turn, the same question *mutatis mutandis*; the spouses give their answers, their consent to be married; it does not strictly matter where the agent and the witnesses and the spouses convene to do what they do, though it often takes place in a house of worship or a civil courthouse; typically, a marriage takes place after a courtship, and agreement, and preparations including the spouses' appearance before a clerk or other person competent to issue a license to marry, and sundry other preparations. The presence of an agent of the state may be taken to represent government's recognition of its duty to protect the well-being, let us say the safety and happiness, of those under the sway of its power.

The presence of witnesses, no less necessary to the validity of a marriage, may be taken to show the social importance of the institution, as well, though in a slightly different way. The necessary presence of witnesses, i.e., persons who, precisely as members of society, stand to attest the marriage, goes to show there is an underlying juridical structure of human existence in society, to which the representative element, the civil authority, is responsible, and on which it depends.[16] The marriage ceremony is not *per se* civil, but may happen, *per accidens*, before a civil magistrate, who only gives recognition of the civil effects of the marriage ceremony. Like the people, and the people's membership, the institution of marriage is temporally and ontologically prior to the state.

The Timing and (Onto)Logic of Marriage

The temporal priority is easy to see: it is a fact of history that the institution of marriage pre-exists the state. The ontological priority of the institution is more problematic, though the grounds of the claim are easy

16. When the persons who would act as witnesses are not citizens, some jurisdictions require them to obtain permission from the civil authority, in order that they might act as witnesses. Far from impeaching our claim, this fact actually goes to confirm it; for, the civil authority has, among the reasons for its existence, the duty to protect the citizenry in the exercise of voice. A visitor, or stranger, say, an alien, is therefore required to obtain specific permission to act as society's surrogate in witnessing the marriage.

enough to state: persons who espouse themselves are not created by the state; properly speaking, the state is their creature. The consequences of the ontological priority of marriage with respect to the state, as well as the central philosophical importance of affirming it, are apt to come into view through attention to another area of the work of Stanley Cavell, specifically, Cavell's consideration of what he calls the genre of remarriage comedy in America's cinematic tradition, for in the thought of Cavell on the Hollywood comedy of divorce and remarriage, the institution of marriage becomes a symbol of American political life.

The National Importance of Marriage

In his series of pedagogical letters on a register of the moral life, titled *Cities of Words*, specifically in the chapter on a Hollywood comedy of divorce and remarriage that starred Katherine Hepburn and Spencer Tracey and bore the title *Adam's Rib*, Cavell considers that the issues at stake in Adam's Rib are related to, and their treatment a continuation of issues also at stake in an earlier film, which also starred Katherine Hepburn, called *The Philadelphia Story*, of which he also treats in the same volume. The essays on these two films, which appear in *Cities of Words*, are themselves critical reconsiderations of ideas Cavell first put forward in an earlier collection of essays, called *Pursuits of Happiness*, in which Cavell first differentiated the genre of remarriage comedy. This is not the place for a fulsome discussion of all the features by which a film may be identified as belonging to the genre. A direct discussion of all the features by which the internal relations of the films belonging to the genre communicate with each other and contribute to the genre's development is therefore impossible. Our purposes do, however, require a word about the essential distinguishing feature of remarriage comedy as a genre unto itself.

Essential Features of Re-marriage

The essential feature of remarriage comedy, the feature that distinguishes remarriage comedy from both Old Comedy and New Comedy, is that the argument, in Cavell's words, "the drive of its plot" is neither the young male suitor's overcoming of obstacles posed by what Northrop Frye has called a senex figure (New Comedy), nor the discovery (perhaps literal, as she is often disguised as a boy) of the heroine as the comedy's cardinal character (Cavell, following Frye, will call her the key-bearer), which is to say the revelation of the heroine as marriageable.[17] The remarriage comedy rather seeks, "not to get the central pair together, but to get them *back* together, together *again*."[18] One need only recall the situation of the United States at the time of the convention at Philadelphia, in order to see that remarriage comedy's aptness to serve as a metaphor for the reconstitution of the United States explains itself, especially if taken with the commonplace use of marriage as a metaphor for political life in the eighteenth century.

The present concern is therefore with what, if anything remarriage comedy has to say about the conceptual space that orders the people's life and informs the people's institutions. A way toward an answer to this question is to observe, with Cavell, that remarriage comedy is peculiar to American culture. This, however, if taken on its own, is merely *petitio principii*. The necessary, further question is therefore twofold: its first part regards what contribution, if any, remarriage comedy makes to the self-understanding of the people that calls itself American; its second is concerned with how, if at all, that contribution is connected to the American self-understanding at the moment of the founding.

Marriage-ability and Remarriage-ability: (Re)Creating the Human

The connection with the American self-understanding in the founding generation is located in certain thematic observations Cavell makes about the genre of remarriage comedy at the beginning of *Pursuits of Happiness*, observations that invoke, perhaps without the author's awareness, the symbolism of Crèvecœur:

> The year of the earliest member of our genre, 1934, is early enough for that film to have had a decisive say in determining the creation of Hollywood sound film. The genre it projected, on my interpretation, can be said to require the creation of a new woman, or the new creation of a woman, something I describe as a new creation of the human.[19]

17. Cf. Frye, "Argument of Comedy." Cf. also Cavell, *Pursuits of Happiness*, 1.

18. Cavell, *Pursuits of Happiness*, 2.

19. Ibid., 16.

The vastness of the interpretative possibilities opened by these few lines will most certainly not be exhausted in the discussion to follow. The present and immediately pertinent issue is the nature of the new creation the genre requires, and supposedly supplies, namely, a new woman, i.e., a person, or a character, which, in the American register, is immediately identifiable as the spouse, the development, the completion of the New Man. For interests of economy, we will concentrate exclusively on two of the films Cavell discusses in his articulation of the genre. Once again, they are *The Philadelphia Story* (1940) and *Adam's Rib* (1949).

The Philadelphia Story is an account of the re-marriage of an already divorced couple. The title of the film, however, immediately calls our attention to the story of what happened at Philadelphia, which is to say in American terms, *the* Philadelphia story, or the drafting of the documents of American independence and national unity, most importantly the Constitution of the United States. A few plot and character observations are in order. To begin with, the film proper opens with *Spy* magazine editor-in-chief Sydney Kidd noting the impending nuptials of Tracy, the eldest daughter of one of Philadelphia's leading families, the Lord family—which is to say that the film is concerned with the Lords of Philadelphia. Next, Kidd assigns a reporter, Macauley "Mike" Connor and a photographer, Elizabeth "Liz" Imbrie to cover the wedding, which has been closed to the public. Mike and Liz are guaranteed access to the proceedings by the underhanded agency of Tracy's ex-husband, C.K. Dexter Haven. This plot detail is significant, for the story of the founding was told in newspapers and pamphlets; the proceedings of the Constitutional convention were secret, i.e., closed to the public, precisely in view of the importance of the public business being conducted. The object of the convention was to re-forge the union. The journalists' attempt to access the wedding may be taken as an attempt to access the secret business of the convention. *The Philadelphia Story*, then, is at once the story of a couple's re-marriage, i.e., in the presence of other potentially viable alternatives, their discovery of each other as apt partners, and an allegory of the work at Philadelphia that expresses a culturally diffuse, let us say, common American claim regarding the nature of the federal union planned at Philadelphia in 1787. It is also, and simultaneously, an exploration of the kinds of beings for whom that federal union was made, in the first place.

Again, Cavell understands that in remarriage comedy, the female lead requires a kind of transformation, a turning into marriage-ability, which Cavell calls a creation of a new woman. The female must take on humanity in order to be an apt spouse. Cavell places the matter as follows:

> In *The Philadelphia Story* the narrative emphasis on identity takes the form of the question whether the heroine is a goddess made of stone or of bronze, or whether a woman of flesh and blood; and its cinematic occasions for studying Katharine Hepburn's [Tray Lord's] body take their cue from the presence of water, first watching her trained dive into her swimming pool, and second. . .sensing her weight and her pliancy as James Stewart [Mike Connor] enters carrying her in a bathrobe falling open at the knees. . . We will hardly avoid seeing the carrying posture, if only in retrospect, as symbolic of her death as a goddess and rebirth as human.[20]

The heroine's rebirth to humanity, and hence to marriage-ability, is instantly recognizable as the complement of Crèvecœur's understanding of America as the *locus* of the creation of a new man, whose principal characteristic is the range—in principle, universal—of his eligibility for marriage. Thus, the genre is, as an American phenomenon, involved in the tradition advanced in and through Crèvecœur's writing.

Marriage in the American Tradition

If the founding of a political society is, as we have been arguing, an analogue of marriage, and if this story is a metaphor for the founding of American political society, then the specific claim that this film is making for or about American political society is that American political society is founded on shared experience, a common history, metaphorically expressed in the protagonists' having grown up together.[21] Cavell places the matter explicitly in reference to *The Philadelphia Story* in *Cities of Words*, where he writes:

> The importance is, according to our concerns with these films, not simply that a happy marriage has been found, but that its happiness, showing marriage to require a double ratification (by itself, by its being chosen out of experience not alone out of innocence; and by its acquiescence in allowing itself to become

20. Ibid., 140–41.

21. Viewers are first informed of this when Tracy's once and future husband, C. K. Dexter Haven, informs Mike Connor of it in the offices of *Spy* magazine. The information is relayed to other characters inside the drama at least twice.

news, open beyond the privacy of privilege, ratified by society) in effect ratifies its society as a place in which happiness and liberty can be pursued and, to whatever extent such a thing is possible, preserved.[22]

Claims to the effect that the integrity of society depends on the integrity of the family, are commonplace. The claim the remarriage comedies generally, and this film specifically advance, is, on Cavell's reading, that the integrity of society is a function of the integrity of marriage, and vice versa, i.e., that they are actually functions of one another.[23]

Cavell notes that of the seven films definitive of the remarriage genre, *The Philadelphia Story* is the only one in which the pair's happiness is rediscovered in the larger world in which they divorced, literally in the place they grew up together, rather than in a place of remove, a world of their own making, he says, "of adventure.[24]" This is, at least, further confirmation of the political significance of the film, and also confirmation of the American interpretation being developed here. Again, the key to this is that the States and the people in the states grew up together, that is, came into their own, into independence together. They made a first attempt at union, the terms of which proved weak and frail; at Philadelphia in September of 1787, it was anything but clear that the states would stay together. Parting was likely as not.

Essentially at stake in the ratification debate was the future of the American conversation. This question is dramatized in *The Philadelphia Story* by the presence of not one, but three suitors, or potential suitors. Tracy Lord is set to marry an up-and-comer, George Kittredge, who is presented or discussed as having "political timber," and who, in an early sequence of the film, asks Tracy what would happen if he should decide to go into politics. "You'd be elected president," Tracy answers, establishing George as nothing less than presidential timber[25], which is to say he

22. Cavell, *Cities of Words*, 75.

23. Cf. Cavell, *Pursuits of Happiness*, 194

24. Cavell, *Pursuits of Happiness*, 146.

25. Cf. ibid., 136. In the plot sketch Cavell gives at the beginning of his chapter on *The Philadelphia Story* in *Cities of Words*, Cavell describes Kittredge as "a rising, wooden man of the people" (35). In light of Cavell's interest in encouraging his readers to consider certain intentional relations among several of the remarriage comedies and several plays of Shakespeare (cf. ibid., 45). Cf. also Cavell, *Pursuits of Happiness*, 141–45, and especially considering the advancements of that encouragement in the essays of Cavell, which are very much involved in our present reflections, it is worthwhile to note that timber is wood, and then to recall the line that Shakespeare puts in Marc

has the mettle, at least, to attain to consular rank. After witnessing a scene involving a drunken and quite possibly morally-compromised Tracy in the arms of an equally inebriated Mike Connor, Kittredge declares his willingness to proceed with the nuptials, since the (just announced) presence of *Spy* magazine publisher Sydney Kidd attests to the "national importance" of the impending marriage. Cavell elaborates:

> Tracy had toward the beginning defended George to Dexter by claiming that he [George] is already of national importance, in response to which Dexter winces and says she sounds like *Spy* magazine. Yet George and Tracy may be wrong not in the concept of importance but in their application of the concept. What George had said was that Sidney Kidd's presence *gives* [my emphasis] their wedding national importance, and this leads George to put aside his doubts about the woman he is involved with and go ahead with the ceremony. It is to this that Tracy finally says, "And goodbye, George."[26]

George reveals that he is unsuited to Tracy because he fails to recognize the inherent importance of his impending nuptials. It does not, perhaps because it cannot, occur to George that marrying Tracy is important for him precisely because—and for no other reason than that—he is marrying Tracy. Cavell has described George's as an "outside-in" in existence.[27] Tracy, for her part, although she has yet to consent to living "inside out", has in any case been awakened to the "fires within" her, fires that Mike Connor identifies as "hearth fires and holocausts," right after telling her, "You're lit from within, Tracy—you've got fires banked down in you." This awakening, we may suppose, has brought her to recognize that she is not interested in being the source of George's outside-in (pseudo?) happiness; she is not interested in ratifying his place in society; she would not be a goddess-wife to the stuffed man, presidential as his stuff may be. On the other hand, Mike Connor proved his aptness as a suitor, as much by the ease and grace with which he engaged Tracy in conversation, as by his refusal—even while under the influence of intoxicating liquor himself— to take advantage of Tracy's own condition. This leaves Dexter.

Antony's mouth, to the effect that the Romans are neither wood, nor stones, but men. If there is in this association further illustration of the reasons for George's ineligibility as a spouse for Tracy, who, in order to acquire the capacity for true marriage, must die to her wooden or bronze divinity, in order to rise in flesh and blood, then the better.

26. Cavell, *Pursuits of Happiness*, 147.

27 Cf. ibid.

In *Pursuits of Happiness*, Cavell finds that Dexter's claim to Tracy is grounded in his and Tracy's having grown up together, a fact that earlier served to illustrate the political significance of the drama. Rather than provide any sort of answer, this biographical particular raises the question as to the reason of the failure of their first attempt at union.

Marriage as Remarriage

Cavell locates the failure of their first attempt at marriage in their failure to establish a conversation. Dexter was given to excessive drinking, and Tracy attributes the failure of their marriage to his drunken boorishness (an episode of which serves as the film's prologue, thus showing that the charge is not, as such, groundless). Addressing the accusation, Dexter says to Tracy, "Granted [drinking was my problem]. But you took on that problem when you married me. You were no helpmeet there, Red. You were a scold." The biblical allusions are clear as day. Eve is made as Adam's helpmeet. Further, in the American tradition, Milton's tract on divorce argues that "a meet and happy conversation is the chiefest and noblest end of marriage.[28]"

The film establishes the connection between willingness to converse and being a helpmeet in an exchange between Dexter and Tracy, in which Tracy says, "Oh, Dext, I'm such an unholy mess of a girl," to which Dexter replies, "Why, that's no good, that's not even conversation." This exchange illustrates three central political and anthropological issues in remarriage comedy, to wit: Tracy, in recognizing herself as an unholy mess of a girl, has embraced her humanity, though she has not as yet become marriageable, i.e., she is not quite ready to converse; Dexter's prodding presence at once encourages Tracy toward conversation, and shows that to talk in turns is not necessarily to converse; finally, it illustrates that willingness to converse is not immediately translatable into aptness for conversation—it is a necessary, though not a sufficient condition.

Before going any further, it is necessary to recall MacIntyre's observation to the effect that conversation is the form of human transactions in general. Marriage is, on this reading, and like citizenship (itself a form

---

28. Someone may object that the unity of the spouses in the openness to and care of offspring are in fact the ends of marriage. This, however, is not so much an objection as an alternative formulation. The embrace of sexual intercourse and the welcoming of its consequences are modes of marital conversation, elements in the form of life that is marriage.

of membership in society), a form of conversation, which means it is a form of human life. It will require two human beings, two beings sufficiently similar as to be able to speak with one another, and sufficiently different as to make their speaking a conversation, and a specific kind of conversation. Arguably, Dexter has achieved his humanity by conquering his addiction to alcohol, and this he accomplishes by reading.[29]

Precisely[30], Mike is surprised to learn that Dexter has his book, telling him, "C.K. Dexter Haven, you have unsuspected depth," and goes on to ask Dexter whether he has read the book. Dexter answers, "Well, I—I was trying to stop drinking. I read anything." Mike asks, "Did you stop drinking?" and Dexter replies, "Yes—but yours didn't do it for me." Through reflections in an earlier chapter with Cavell with Emerson with Thoreau, an understanding emerged, according to which philosophy is reading whatever is before you. In the right ear, "I read anything," will sound like an echo, or a paraphrase (perhaps even an imperfect quotation) of philosophy thusly construed. Add to this that Mike's book "didn't do it" for Dexter, i.e., didn't cure him of a reliance on a foreign substance—the very kind of reliance that disqualified George as a suitor—and Dexter's suitability as a suitor appears as grounded in his assumption of philosophy—his achievement of self-reliance that does not disdain to know itself, its incompleteness, as a work in progress—as though achieving true self reliance were a matter of being dispelled, disabused of the idea of self-reliance as synonymous with self-sufficiency (a matter of knowing, with Martin Luther King, that *we* cannot walk alone—and of understanding, at the same time, that there is no guarantee you *can* walk together). To do so, to be so dispelled, would be at once to assume the risk of loneliness and ignorance (perchance to form a more perfect union?).[31]

---

29. Cf. Cavell, *Pursuits of Happiness*, 145–46. Cavell understands Dexter's act of self-mastery as one by which Dexter acquires a certain power to control events, and compares Dexter to Oberon. The reading presently under offer is not meant to contest Cavell's reading. The extent to which it may rely on Cavell's reading must remain open.

30. Cavell reports the exchange somewhat imprecisely. The possible implications of misquotation are discussed *super*, 126–28.

31. After Dexter has arranged to marry Tracy, and right before Tracy gives herself over to Dexter's arrangements, she asks him, "Are you sure?" to which he replies, "Not in the least, but I'll risk it for you."

Between Privacy and Publicity:
Classifying Marriage in America

At another, earlier point in the film, in connection with the recollection of an incident from their first attempt at marriage, in which Tracy drank to excess and danced naked on the roof of their house, Dexter tells Tracey that, despite her protestations to the contrary, the episode was, and remains, "Enormously important," and goes on to tell her, "you'll never be a first-class person or a first-class woman until you've learned to have some regard for human frailty." Cavell finds the idea of a "first-class person" to be morally dangerous.[32] He locates the moral danger in something he calls snobbery, to which he understands most of the principal characters in remarriage comedy are exposed.[33] He further locates the issue in the American tradition, having been debated under the question of the existence of a natural aristocracy in the correspondence of Thomas Jefferson and John Adams.[34] Cavell notes that Adams and Jefferson engaged in that debate in order to speculate on the conditions for the Union to survive and flourish, and discovers in the exchange between Tracy and Mike regarding the relative merits of Tracy's uncle Willie (a wealthy, bottom-pinching lecher) and Mac the night watchman (a prince among men), intimation of the film's thematic preoccupation with the same question.[35]

The call for Tracy's completion, the naming of the need for her to become a first-class human being in order for her successfully to enter into marriage, is a call for the completion of what Cavell calls, roughly, the repudiation of the hierarchies and enforcements of the European past and the making of a new beginning, a reformation of the human condition.[36] In the American register presently under construction, to demand that the woman become a first-class person is to demand that she attain to consular rank, i.e., that she recognize herself as man's equal in humanity, and so demand recognition as such. The film responds to the call for a new creation of the human by dramatizing the creation of a new woman to be a helpmeet, an apt conversant for the new man. As such, the film is a dramatic appeal for the completion of the American revolution.

32. Cf. *Pursuits of Happiness*, 156–57; cf. also *Cities of Words*, 47–48.
33. Cf. *Cities of Words*, 78.
34. Cf. *Pursuits of Happiness*, 155.
35. Cf. ibid.
36. Cf. ibid., 156.

With this observation, the work is arrived at the cusp of consideration of the second remarriage comedy, *Adam's Rib*. Before engaging
that film directly, however, a final series of observations on the political
significance of the *Philadelphia Story* is in order. First, there is the outstanding matter of the location of Dexter's and Tracy's remarriage. We
saw that Cavell notes a peculiarity in the film, namely that, unlike the
other definitive members of the remarriage genre, the heroic couple in
The Philadelphia Story rediscover their happiness in the larger world in
which they grew up together and in which they divorced. Cavell goes on
to observe that this odd feature would reach what he calls "a satisfactory
equivalence" if we could understand Tracy and Dexter as having come
to regard their own larger society as itself world enough, itself the scene
of adventure.[37] Earlier in our investigation, we saw that philosophy and
gnosis are basically opposite attitudes toward the world. If Cavell is correct in attributing the couple's rediscovery of happiness in their world
to be a sign of their discovery of that world as one of adventure, that is,
worth experiencing and endlessly knowable, then the couple's discovery
that happiness is worth pursuing together in their world, the world of
Philadelphia and its story, is a discovery that places what we have been
calling America further in the way of what we have been calling philosophy. Cavell puts the matter as one of the couple's discovery of their
marriage as exemplifying or symbolizing their society at large[38], "quite as
if," writes Cavell, "they are its royalty; and their society itself is embarked
on some adventure.[39]" The knowledge to which the film attests, i.e., that
164 years after the signing of the Declaration of Independence, America
still exists[40], does not foreclose, but urgently presses the question as to
what legitimizes American society. At the same time, and precisely insofar as the integrity of society and the integrity of marriage are functions
of one another, the legitimacy of marriage is exposed to doubt, and so,
as it were, from within. The question of the legitimacy of marriage is no
longer avoidable.

37. Cf. ibid., 146–47.
38. Cf. ibid., 147.
39. Ibid.
40. Cf. Cavell, *Cities of Words*, 75.

The Law of Marriage

A 1949 work also directed by George Cukor, *Adam's Rib* tells the story of a couple approaching middle age, both of whom are practicing attorneys, he in the District Attorney's office and she in private practice. The pair become aware of a threat to their union when the DA appoints the man, Adam Bonner, to the prosecution of a woman who shot and wounded her husband, whom she caught *in flagrante delicto* with another, younger and decidedly more glamorously beautiful woman. Adam Bonner's wife, Amanda Bonner, takes the case of the accused. The ensuing courtroom drama provides the framework in which an investigation of nothing less than the promise, the possibility of America is tested. *Nota bene*, the courtroom, and its drama, provide the framework, the stage, as it were. The testing ground is the Bonners' marriage.

In explaining to her husband, who has been assigned the prosecution of the case, why she has agreed to defend the accused, Amanda says she wishes to dramatize an injustice, like the Sons of Liberty, who (in) famously held a Tea Party in Boston. This places the film in the American revolutionary register. Precisely, Amanda says, "Take the Boston Tea Party. What did they do? They dramatized an injustice. That's all I'm trying to do." It is not clear whether Amanda intends to compare whatever injustice she intends to dramatize with the injustice that occasioned the Boston Tea Party, or whether she intends to say that her mode of dramatizing the injustice will be similar to the mode the Sons of Liberty chose to dramatize the injustice of East India Co.'s tea being under-sold with parliamentary collusion. Which, or whether she fully means one or the other, is a question for the film, and for the reader of it.

On the first day of trial, Amanda declares in open court that "all women are on trial here." "Here" names the courtroom, and by extension, society. Amanda's is a complex claim. It implies that all women are victimized by a systematic injustice that has become so heinous as to justify (not merely to excuse[41]) an attack on an otherwise legitimate institution, because of the institution's participation in the injustice. If, however, this is not a gross *non sequitur*, it calls for an account how suffering victimization is, on its own, an indictment of women. Victimization would, on its own, place women in the condition of an aggrieved party. One direction toward an answer that the film offers us is Amanda's analogical invocation of the Tea Party, which places women in the condition of the colonists

41. Cf. Cavell, *Pursuits of Happiness*, 192–93.

under the tyranny of Parliament; it also places society—men and women together?—in the position of Parliament, i.e., the position of a foreign legislature tyrannically exerting power over a whole people, and so under color of right. Roughly, and preliminarily, the claim amounts to something like the following: women in such a condition as the analogy claims they find themselves, are without a voice. They haunt their society. They are prepared, therefore, indeed compelled to assert their voice at gunpoint, so as to inhabit their society. Adam, for his part, both in and out of court, will claim that Amanda's conduct has placed their marriage on trial, and by extension, the institution of marriage, which, as we shall see, he equates with the law. Amanda will counter this claim on the second day of the trial, essentially saying that Doris Attinger's duty to protect her domestic tranquillity is a sacred obligation. It remains unclear, to say the least, how shooting her husband effects the protection it is her sacred duty to provide. In any case, the court's acquittal of Mrs. Attinger must somehow stand for society's acceptance of Mrs. Attinger's claim to the effect that she was not seeking to kill her husband, which is to say, that she is not guilty of attempted murder. Fine. There remains outstanding, however, at least the issue of Amanda's placement of her own marriage on trial. Having achieved vindication of the equality of men and women, by securing the acquittal of Mrs. Attinger (here we are left to assume that no jury would convict a man for shooting his wife or her *paramour*, having caught them *in flagrante*—not an entirely implausible assumption in 1949), it is left for her and Adam to work out together whether her assertion of sameness as necessarily synonymous with equality is one that can, or must hold, if society (Amanda's and the genre's word for it is marriage) is to flourish. In other words, at issue is the significance of Amanda's achievement of the same treatment for a woman as that supposedly reserved for a man accused of the same crime as Doris Attinger. In short, what is at stake is not the fact of her courtroom victory, but its meaning.

Names and Places in Marriage

The film's title further locates the ground for the testing of America, namely Adam Bonner's capacity to give and take a ribbing;[42] it claims, as

---

42. Cavell will place this variously as Adam's ability to submit to low comic indignities, in victory to swallow his anger together with his pride, his capacity to be humbled by words. Cf. *Cities of Words*, 79; cf. also *Pursuits of Happiness*, 214.

if with the author of the *Federalist*, that a wrong election of the part Adam and Amanda are to play will be for the general misfortune of mankind.

Adam quite literally stands for humanity, i.e., it is an anglicized Hebrew word for "man". Amanda is Latin for "she, who is to be loved". The narrative drive of *Adam's Rib* achieves its crisis when Adam Bonner says, "I'm not sure I want to be married to the New Woman." We are prepared for the new man to wonder about such a thing. That we are dealing with an issue that could be tragic is intimated by the fact that the new woman is named as someone to be loved, so that the question becomes, by whom? Is this Adam made to be her mate? Is the completion of the American Revolution possible, are the terms and conditions of its completion given? Cavell has discussed the matter as one of tension between the private and the public:

> [I]ntimacy is not sufficient for marriage, which requires beyond this the open declaration of this exclusive privacy. Openness is required as a condition both of asking for the public sanction of the marriage, admitting society's stake in it; and of expressing the need for this stake, that their bonding requires a decision or contract, and power to have it enforced, that it is not natural, not, so to speak, a family matter. The simultaneous establishing and transcending of intimacy, say as from strum to ear, is a way of putting the point of *Adam's Rib* generally, its interpretation of the dialectic of remarriage, why it is good to think of the necessity of remarriage as the necessity of taking marriage to court: you must test it in the open or else mutual independence is threatened, the capacity to notice one another, to remember beginning, to remember you are strangers; but it is only worth subjecting to this examination if the case is one of intimacy, which you might describe as the threat of mutual independence.[43]

Cavell's problematic invocation of the natural at this point helps to place the discussion in the American register we have been elaborating from the outset. Specifically, it allows us to understand the problem of marriage as essentially, intrinsically involved in the problem we have thematized as the discussion in America, of the question whether government is naturally limited in the scope of its power. Recall Alexander Hamilton's argument to the effect that all powers of government are by their nature sovereign, and include by force of the term a right to employ all means

43. Cavell, *Pursuits of Happiness*, 215–16.

fairly applicable to the attainment of the ends of such power, and that the powers are limited only by morality and the essential ends of political power.[44] If marriage is, as Adam says, a contract, the law, then the limit of its legality is the nature of the institution. Cavell is certainly correct in asserting that *Adam's Rib* forces upon us the question, whether courts are capable of assessing the validity of marriage.[45] The answer the film gives, however, is rather more, or differently complicated than he suggests in asserting that marriage is not natural.

The dialogue of *Adam's Rib* raises the issue explicitly under the rubric of the contract. When the principal pair find each other at home following the third day of the trial, Adam says, "What is marriage? It's a contract, it's the law," and goes on to say (as he had begun to say in the scene of the film in which the Bonners are introduced to us) that Amanda's manifest disrespect for the law (Adam characterizes his wife's advocacy as turning a courtroom into a "Punch and Judy" show[46])—meaning at least her attempt to justify attempted murder in open court—will leave nothing to respect.[47] The precise placement of this invocation of the idea of marriage as a contract is telling to Cavell:

> The word, "contract," at this climactic moment, to my ear names the social contract that was to replace the divine right of kings. Here again the fate of the marriage bond in our genre is meant to epitomize the fate of the democratic social bond, as more or less explicitly in the aristocratic equations of marriage and society in *The Philadelphia Story*, . . . the linking of fates that underlies. . .Milton's argument for divorce.[48]

Courts as they stand cannot assess the validity of marriage for two reasons. In the first, they have no access to the space in which the conversation of marriage takes place, to the space created by their consent to each other, and maintained by their continued engagement in the conversation. This space is called the home, specifically the bedroom, and more specifically, the marriage bed, in, or over which the argument of *Adam's Rib* is joined, and from which the viewers of *Adam's Rib* are originally and finally excluded, as were citizens from the transactions that took place

44. See also 174–76.

45. Cf. ibid., 193.

46. Cf. ibid., 194.

47. Cf. ibid., 193.

48. Cf. ibid.

behind the closed doors of the Philadelphia State House (also known as Independence Hall), from May to September, 1787—not, it turns out, because what they are doing is private, but precisely because the public weal depends on the success of their conversation. In the second, the authority of the courts does not extend to the realm of nature (often called, to Cavell's confessedly unending delight, "Connecticut,"), which is the *locus* in which the hero and the heroine exchange anew their consent to be bound together in the institution of marriage, which they now recognize as the propitious space for the formation of a more perfect union.

Contracting Marriage

The film's final exchange illustrates the importance of considering what are the terms of the union of the new man and the new woman:

> **Amanda Bonner**: there's no difference between the sexes. Men, women, the same.
>
> **Adam Bonner**: They are?
>
> **Amanda Bonner**: Well, maybe there is a difference, but it's a little difference.
>
> **Adam Bonner**: Well, you know as the French say...
>
> **Amanda Bonner**: What do they say?
>
> **Adam Bonner**: *Vive la différence!*
>
> **Amanda Bonner**: Which means?
>
> **Adam Bonner**: Which means hurrah for that little difference.

Certainly, no Bryn Mawr and Yale-educated lawyer (such as Amanda Bonner) would in 1949 require a translation of the French phrase, *vive la différence!* So, Amanda's question was inquiring into, or after, what the difference between men and women means.[49] This exchange occurs at the end of the film, when the two have decided to bear their marriage together, to face its trials and promises together. If we recall Dexter's rejoinder to Tracy's remark to the effect that she is a girl, and all messed up, i.e., his deflection of her words as not being for or in conversation, we now recognize that Dexter's rejoinder essentially charges Tracy's remark

---

49. Cf. Cavell, *Cities of Words*, 77.

with not being for or in the kind of conversation that marriage is. The final exchange of *Adam's Rib* tells us that marriage is essentially a celebration, through mutual acceptance of a common invitation to conversation about the differences between men and women, whatever they are or might be. To press the issue further: as a symbol of and metaphor for polity, specifically American polity, the films dramatize the idea that crisis in society occurs when, faced with the awareness or at least confronted with an intimation of ignorance of, possibly occasioning doubt regarding the origins, the grounds of society's legitimacy, the parties suspend or refuse conversation until such grounds can be established. To be sure, one way to do this would be to fall back on an axiom, that is, axiomatically to assert something, e.g. that men and women are the same, and that there is no difference between them. Since establishing such grounds is what both the conversation of marriage, and public discourse are all about, in the first place; since finding oneself in marriage, and finding oneself in America are both a matter of discovering oneself a participant in an endless conversation; the couples' choice to bear marriage is a choice to remain in each other's society, to legitimize the conversation by refusing to disengage with it. This decision against disengagement from the conversation that constitutes the union is at once a decision for America and for philosophy.

Marriage in and for a Free Society

Our project now demands that we trace the implications of our investigation, and move toward a conclusion of the discussion we began regarding the defensibility of the American claims, which required that we rediscover what they are and begin to recover the tradition in which they constitutively participate. This task, or series of tasks, will require a series of general observations regarding the contribution of the film comedies we have been considering, to our understanding of the American tradition. Beginning with the question of equality, of the meaning of it, we shall move to a final consideration of the importance of government by consent, and what America understands it, and its limits, to be.

In *The Philadelphia Story*, we saw the creation of a new woman who is the helpmeet of the new man: her becoming "a first-class person, a first-class woman," which we understood to be her attainment to equal station with the new man, her coming to share in consular rank suggested her creation, and their aptness for each other. *Adam's Rib* tested the implications of her attainment, her possibilities, responsibilities, requirements and limits, and explicitly questioned, or tried the essential continuity of the story of the human in America with the biblical history of humanity's progress. Adam Bonner's initial questioning of his desire to be married to the New Woman, and final resort to a typically female form of manipulation, namely, crocodile tears, as he says, in order to "get her back" (which is, at once, to say, win her back again, and get back at her, implying she has wronged something that was his, call this the difference on which what Cavell has called the bargain of their marriage is based[50]), when coupled with his assertion of marriage as a contract, as the law, and his vindication of the proposition that no one has the right to break the law, suggests that marriage is indissoluble. To break the conversation that constitutes marriage is at once to break faith with one's word, with one's interlocutor, and with the society before which, and behind which the married couple stands.

The frailty of the human condition, and our duty to be mindful, understanding of it, may indeed make it necessary to create legal avenues for those who require release from the bonds created by the giving of their words of consent. The law, on such a reading, is marriage. To break the latter is to break the former. A court of law may say when a contract has been breached, or fraudulently entered, or improperly or imperfectly executed. In short, a court may say who is not married. The kind of people the American people are, however, or at least, as these films attest, legitimately aspire to be, is one that does not despair of the human capacity, the capacity of men and women equally, though differently, to give their word, and to keep faith with it. They do not believe they require the chains of despotism in order that they be kept from destroying and devouring one another.

Government by Consent

The Declaration of Independence tells us that in America, the time has come for dissolution of political bands that bind peoples together. It further tells us that in America, peoples have the right to form governments, which, in their estimation, are likely to secure the safety and happiness of their members. The Declaration also tells us that in America, people

50. Cf. Cavell, *Pursuits of Happiness*, 194.

hold in the equal creation of all human beings, which is the font of their inalienable rights, among which are life, liberty and pursuit of happiness, to be self-evident truth. Americans also hold to the self-evident truth of the proposition that governments derive their just powers from the consent of the governed. The Declaration takes no positive action toward the establishment of governments for the American political societies that subscribe to it. It is a statement of the common ground upon which the peoples in America base their claim to dissolve their allegiance to the positively constituted authorities by which they were previously governed. In this sense, it is an act establishing the American understanding of the natural limits of positively constituted authority, and declaring the commitment of Americans to a common understanding of the meaning of their experience together.

The Constitution of the United States provides a frame of government for a single people, articulated in several political societies, a people dedicated to the propositions advanced in the Declaration. It is an instrument, by which the people locate and determine the exercise of the powers of government. The Constitution is, in this sense, entirely conventional.

If there were only the Declaration, America would be entirely based upon a claim to the self-evidence of the propositions to which Americans cling as true. If there were only the Constitution, then America would be entirely conventional, a constituted government among several others. No means of establishing the justice of the institutions created by the Constitution would be available, beyond the document itself. As things stand, however, America has both the Declaration and the Constitution. As a result, Americans find themselves in tension between evidence and convention. The convention is to be understood in light of the evidence declared in the Declaration, while the rectitude, the rightness of the Declaration is, on this reading, proved by the ability of the new American people to do what it said it could do, i.e., by the success of the society that has given itself a new Constitution.

American society has faced many crises during the course of its history, all of which somehow involved, and continue to involve, the practical consequences of America's commitment to the idea that human beings are created equal, even though they are different. The crisis of the female voice in American society was a crucial one, in which the equal station of women in America claimed and received recognition within and because of the social framework the government of the country had been established to protect.

American society in history discovered the equality of all human beings, created as male and female, and came to understand their institutions of government as necessarily equally protective of the different persons and the public institutions based on the difference of persons as essentially expressive of the fullness of humanity, which is at once always male and female, even though each individual can only be either male or female. The role and responsibility of citizens is precisely that of making sure their governing institutions effectively represent their differences. Failure properly to exercise this duty is, here and there, inevitable. Failure in commitment to doing it, is failure in fellowship. At the end of *Adam's Rib*, it is Amanda Bonner who confirms her marriage and confirms that the New Woman is a political animal, too, that her voice is to be heard in the public square (and perhaps never more strongly than when united with her husband's), when she says, "No more deductions. We like to pay taxes." There is no more American expression of consent to society. In this understanding is the American synthesis of convention and self-evidence.

The practical consequences of destroying, whether by collapsing or exploding the tension between evidence and convention, the tension that creates the space for the conversation of America, the space for fellowship, are readily identifiable. If Americans ignore the need for convention, then society is exposed to the deleterious effects of momentary passion. If Americans ignore their tradition of inquiry and nationhood, then all society's members, become creatures of the state. The danger is real and present. Questions regarding the aptness of the institutions designed by the founding fathers must be returned to the context of the larger question regarding the kind of people for whom they designed them, the kind of people that ratified those institutions. Failure to recover the order of the larger conversation will have consequences.

Concluding Review

AT THE END OF this work, there are three points that require critical visitation, so as to take a sounding of its accomplishments and a measure of that, which it has left undone. The three points were raised explicitly as questions in the introduction, and though not all of them received thematic attention during the course of the work, each in its own way was a concern of the writer on every page. The first question regards the role of history—the concept and the discipline—in America. The second question is whether the work has proved the claim entered in the introduction, according to which Voegelin, MacIntyre and Cavell are in conversation with one another in and over and about America. The third question is whether the work has made progress toward a recovery of an understanding of the American Founders' *forma mentis*—and whether that progress is sufficient to justify the effort expended in the doing of the work. Each of these three shall receive proper treatment, in turn, and move us toward a general appraisal of the work's success in sustaining the work it set out to do.

The Question of History

The explicit discussion of the historical discipline as practiced by historians of America in the American academy, which appeared in the methodological introduction, did not receive any further direct treatment in the ensuing five chapters. A reader might take the conspicuous absence of a thematic discussion of the academic discipline in the body of the work as a consequence, or a function of its having basically been a piece of intellectual cartography, provided for the benefit of the eventual reader. At worst, it might merely have been one of the many disappointing—or relieving, (depending on how one approaches the issues raised in this essay)—episodes of "throat clearing" encountered in academic writing.

The question of history was nevertheless a key point of focus in and throughout the work. Even though the academic discipline called history did not receive explicit thematic treatment during the course of the work's five chapters and more, the relationship of a people's—indeed humanity's—past to its present was central to the theoretical plant of the work; as the work unfolded, this question emerged as a crucial one in the debate over the meaning of America, and so from America's very beginning.

The first and the fourth were the chapters that most heavily relied on available historiography. Appropriate use of the available material allowed us in the first chapter to establish the political society present along the Eastern littoral of the North American continent in the second half of the eighteenth century as an appropriate field for inquiry into the general problem of order, which we articulated with Eric Voegelin as the problem of representation. The fourth chapter used some of the historiographical materials most commonly available, though in a manner at once integral and critical. By the time the work had progressed far enough to approach the beginnings of America, it had become possible to understand those beginnings as moments in a debate that was primarily over the constitution of man and society, and only secondarily (I mean second in order: remember Publius' claim, which we saw in chapter 3, to the effect that government is the greatest reflection on human nature, so that to decide on a form of government is to enter a claim about the nature of man) over the form and substance of the institutions—Voegelin calls them elements—to be erected for the governance of men in society. Where one stands in relation to that debate—what side one takes, or is on—is and must remain open to informed decision to be taken in intellectual liberty. The achievement of this part of the work is the recovery of the debate, and the use of the materials available in the historical record were the stuff with which the work was achieved.

In other words, where one stands in relation to the question whether America has escaped or is (constituted as or predicated on a claim to be) an escape from the conditions of man in history, will determine in large part how one understands the American contribution to the debate over the relationship of humanity's present to its past. For example: if one accepts the expression, "Never look back!" as what we saw the late Arthur Schlesinger Jr. call, "America's unspoken motto," then one is going to have an inexhaustible plethora of interpretative questions arise, before one can even begin to apply the maxim to the reading of events. A sampling of such questions might be: how can something be unspoken and still be a motto (let alone the motto of a political society, the members of which entirely stake their claim to nationhood on an act of declaration); how, given Americans' broad and penetrating reading in and use of history in the debates that attended and, as we argued in the second and third chapters, really informed the decision to sever ties with England and the work of founding their present constitutional order, ought we to understand Schlesinger's claim—in other words, assuming we are to take him seriously, what are we to understand his maxim to claim? Only after historians have sufficiently entertained at least these questions, can they begin to debate how and how far they might be prepared to let that historian's maxim govern their reading in and into the events of America's past.

Indeed, the second chapter of Schlesinger's book is titled, "History the Weapon"—and a weapon is what history becomes when those who are its professors practice their profession from one side or another of the question regarding the relation of humanity's past to its present, without recognizing the presence and importance of the question to, for and in their work—or worse—when they unconsciously or uncritically take and work from one side or the other of the question.

This work has shown that the people whose history provided the field of its inquiry cannot be understood by a discipline that does not recognize the centrality of the question of humanity's past to its present in the life of that people. Not only: it has shown that historians cannot approach America without recognizing the question's centrality to their own practice and work in it (in America and in the history of America).

Historians of America, to the extent that they are or may be able to internalize such a question, might escape the fetters of foreign methods (I mean methods that are foreign to the study of history as such—or are they?) and bring their study (the word, *historia*, means "study" or "investigation" in the first place) into its own. Those who practice the discipline of history would continue to investigate, debate the relative merits of, and construct narratives based on more-or-less qualified commitments to sociological, economic and religious factors and elements. After internalizing such questions as those articulated above, however, they would arguably be free from dependence upon the methodological constraints of those branches of human knowledge, which have hitherto constrained them. This project may not have inspired the question; one could take the essay merely to have occasioned a particular formulation of it.

The work, however, has arguably and even demonstrably done more than this. One of the central elements of the analytical and interpretative method that it has been the business of this project to construct, is Eric Voegelin's conviction to the effect that the existence of man in political society is historical existence, so that a science of politics, which penetrates to principles, must at the same time be a philosophy of history. One of the things this work has brought into focus is the way in which national commitment to living a science of politics "inside-out"—as we saw Cavell describe the existential vector in the case of Tracy Lord, whose marriage was in, about and for America—operates on the persons who write the story of the people to which they belong and at the same time, on the stories they tell, and on their telling of them (though I will not now insist on this as an achievement, in America, of Cavell's desire to see the literary and the philosophical conjoined anew).

Let a brief reconsideration of Schlesinger's motto illustrate the point, and move us within range of summary: the work has given a way for us to understand Schlesinger's proclamation of an American motto (as such unspoken except by his pen), as an expression of history's desire to become philosophy in America—to speak for America and not just about it. Said another way: the work has shown that, and how historians of America have begun to understand that, in order to tell the story of the American people, one needs to penetrate to the principles of political science, for it is by these that there is a people in America.

In sum, the work has shown that writers of American history are concerned with questions of order in a way, a manner, that is—or has been and may again be—proper to a kind of writing that has been called philosophy; it has done this by showing that the kind of writing that is called historical has found itself in America to be necessarily concerned with the kinds of questions that concern philosophers. This is one major part of the evidence the work has offered in favor of the broad claim with which the work began, i.e., that America is essentially a philosophical problem, so that the working out of the one will necessarily involve the working out of the other. At the same time, it is an intimation, an inkling of an answer to the query through which we approached that claim, i.e., the question whether there is an American inflection of philosophy.

Voegelin, MacIntyre and Cavell
in Conversation about America

The concluding considerations of last section shade perceptibly into those of the present one, for the question whether there is an American inflection of philosophy is one we found in, or inherited from, Stanley Cavell—one of the three authors with whom we were principally engaged throughout the work. In the methodological introduction, there was a description of the program of the work, according to which we would find Voegelin, Cavell and MacIntyre (to be) in conversation with each other regarding the problem of America.

Had the claim been merely that each of the three spoke to, or about America, then the work almost would have accomplished itself—as indeed it almost did in the Cavellian conjunction of texts that occurred in Chapter Four. The claim was more ambitious, however, and in retrospect, was one that perhaps left the work most exposed to criticism. The reason for this is the extreme difficulty involved in attempting a substantiation of the claim without appearing, at least, to enter a *petitio principii*: their being involved in conversation with one another regarding the problem of America depends on there being an America in the sense we have claimed—and this was precisely what was at stake in the project. How, in other words, could it have been possible to say anything about the matter without presuming either America or the conversation?

There are (at least) two answers, or ways to (an) answer. Neither is likely to be entirely satisfactory to anyone; some readers might even find both entirely inadequate. The most I can claim for them is that they are reasonable, whether as answers or as ways toward one.

The first answer (assume from this point, forward, that "answer" stands for itself, *sic et simpliciter*, and also for "way toward an answer," unless otherwise specified) is that the conversation about the meaning of America was already underway when Voegelin, Cavell and MacIntyre engaged it, so that their contributions are just that: contributions. There is (and we saw introduced) ample evidence to support this line of answer, e.g. Cavell's invocation of Emerson and Thoreau as the originators of an American tradition of thinking, or the opening considerations of MacIntyre's *Whose Justice? Which Rationality?*, which rehearse what we observed Cavell calling, "The headline moral issues of the day," issues that are undoubtedly even if not exclusively the stuff of American headlines, or Voegelin's perhaps shocking claim to the effect that the United States represents (with mother England) the oldest and most consolidated stratum of civilizational tradition. These at least prove that the three authors thought of themselves as engaged in a conversation both older and broader than their own participation in it. What it does not prove is that they knew they were talking to one another—and such awareness would seem to be a necessary condition for conversation.

While I would not say that the preceding remarks have followed the first line of answer as far as it might lead, they have nevertheless followed it to a point at which it appears, anyway, to encounter the second line of response. Specifically, the answers meet in conversation—in the concern of the work with the idea of conversation, under the specific kind of conversation called "argument", a type of which is tradition. The reader will recall that, in the fourth chapter, we observed MacIntyre describing conversation as the form of human transactions in general. Earlier, in the methodological introduction, we observed that same author describing tradition as an argument extended through time, the progress of which is measured both in terms of its engagement with external critics and enemies, and in terms of the internal debates through which the meaning and rationale of the fundamental agreements come to be expressed and by the progress of which a tradition is constituted.

Now, through the unfolding of this work, the conceptual space called America has begun to appear as one that has at least provided instances of concern common to Voegelin, Cavell and MacIntyre. If this were all the work had achieved, then this is all we could claim. The work thus far advanced, however, has also shown that the conversation constitutive of the conceptual space called America is itself constituted by the concerns the three authors share; their contributions to the discussion of those concerns are internal to America in conversation, and not merely or simply occasioned or instanced by it. A brief rehearsal of the work we have done will help bring the matter further (back) into view.

In the first chapter, we engaged the conversation called America through Voegelin, specifically over the problem of representation, which presented itself as at once the basic problem of theoretical politics, and the motive problem behind the political crisis in British colonial order. In the second, we restated the problem with Cavell, from the side of anthropology, and found Cavell and Voegelin agreeing that politics is essentially and inextricably and basically concerned with human nature; we saw that this idea is present in the American self-understanding that began to emerge in the period of the imperial crisis, and also that the American response to that crisis was essentially a recovery of an older way of think-ing about political problems, which takes man to be a *zoon politikon*, as the human ability to speak attests (let this be a point of community with MacIntyre, as well), most authoritatively in the act of declaration. The third chapter followed the implications of the reading accomplished in the first and the second, and allowed for a further recovery of the Ameri-can founding, specifically in the debate over ratification of the proposed Constitution of 1787—a debate that appeared in light of the earlier work as really concerning the constitution of man and society, under the guise or in the clothing of a political argument over whether to have a people of the United States of America. The fourth chapter showed the concerns of Voegelin, Cavell and MacIntyre converging in the earliest history of America, and allowed for an articulation of the question of America in terms that would be measurable in further study. The fifth chapter began the further study for which the fourth chapter called (I do not say this is all the fifth chapter did, but only that it did do this).

One might insist that this is all fine and good, but it does not prove that Voegelin, MacIntyre and Cavell are in conversation with one another. Anyone arguing a case like the one here presented would have to grant this, though he would be free to provide that proof of a conversation can-not be given outside of it, or antecedently. If one is willing to entertain the possibility that the three are in conversation with one another, and prepared to listen to what they have to say—say, as we have presented it in the five chapters of this work—then one would have to judge the merits of the presentation itself. I claim nothing more than that, in light of the work conducted according to the hypothesis that Voegelin, MacIntyre and Cavell are in conversation with one another about America, it is reason-able to characterize America as an argument extended through time, in which certain fundamental agreements are defined and redefined in terms of two kinds of conflict: those with critics and enemies external to Amer-ica who reject all or at least key parts of those fundamental agreements, and those internal, interpretative debates through which the meaning and rationale of the fundamental agreements come to be expressed and by the progress of which America may be said to continue in existence; and if such internal debates may on occasion destroy what had been the basis of common fundamental agreement, so that either America divides into two or more warring components, whose adherents are transformed into external critics of each other's positions, or else America loses all coher-ence and fails to survive; and if it can also happen that two understandings of America, hitherto independent and even antagonistic, can come to recognize certain possibilities of fundamental agreement and reconstitute themselves as a single, more complex mode of ordering life, then America is the name of a tradition of inquiry that is also a nation, or a tradition of nationhood. The reasonability, the defensibility of this claim is what emerged from the treatment of Voegelin, Cavell and MacIntyre as though they were in conversation with one another.

The Founders' *forma mentis*: A Progress Report

Another basic task of this work has been the recovery of what we have variously called the founders' *forma mentis* and the *forma mentis* of the founding generation. The purpose of the present remarks is to recapitulate the evidence for that claim and then to measure the claim against the accomplishments of the work.

If we take seriously the idea that Jefferson and Adams thought representatively, that they were, in the words of their mutual friend and fellow founding father, Benjamin Rush, "[T]he poles of the revolution," and that, while others wrought and fought, "[They] thought for [them] all, (Letter to Adams, October 17, 1809)" then their thinking with and against one another will have a claim to being the first expression of an American tradition of thinking. That claim was substantiated when we found, in the subsequent history of America, the presence of the arguments that constituted their conversation.

The literary original of American thinking, which Cavell claimed to have found in Thoreau and Emerson, we located in the founding generation, represented in Adams and Jefferson, and epitomized in the documents of foundation, themselves. Jefferson and Adams engaged each other in a discussion of the meaning of the claim to the self-evidence of human equality, in light of the tension in society among persons of different fortune and ability, and they have left us a record of their thinking in the letters they exchanged. The conversation they started, however, is one that continues to the present. We saw the questions they raised and articulated in American terms return in the cultural expressions of American cinema a century and a half's remove and more from the founding act. We observed those questions at issue in the movement for civil rights.

What the present work has done is to pay attention not only or even primarily to the points of agreement and disagreement within the debate in which Adams and Jefferson were representatively engaged (it has done that), but to the fact that the debate took place among people who were committed to the self-evident truth, "All men are created Equal." This work has therefore recovered the founders' own understanding of their project, which is to say, brought back into view the project that the founders understood themselves to have been undertaking: the creation of a political order that would preserve and nurture the existential conditions in which the conversation about the meaning of the propositions in the common dedication to which there may be said to be an American people, might continue to flourish.

One specific contribution to philosophy that this work has made is therefore its indication of a way of listening and responding to America that allows for progress toward an answer of the original question: "Is there an American inflection of philosophy?" *Nota bene*, the claim is not that the work answers the question. The claim is that the work has shown what an answer to the question will look, or sound like, by recovering what it looked and sounded like in the founding generation of America. This work has been accomplished most especially in the work's showing how the conceptual space called America is, or animates, an exercise in managing existential tensions that, while they inevitably arise in and under institutions of government, nevertheless bear principally on the constitution of the society for which those institutions are given.

In providing a conceptual framework that allows the vision of the priority of anthropological and social-constitutional questions to inform and direct the search for answers to institutional questions—i.e., to inform the institutions themselves, America provides a reply to, and possibly, a way to overcome the basic political problems of Modernity. At the same time, the history of order in and under America shows how there is no ultimately or perfectly effective institutional guarantee against the decay of a society's spiritual health. In other words, the general idea of freedom to pursue the good together in society, which America represents, can degenerate into post-modernity, and this possibility cannot be institutionally arrested or curtailed - at least not without violating the human freedom on which the experiment is based. The project's success is in the balance.

AMDG

Bibliography

Adams, Charles Francis, and John Adams. *The Works of John Adams, Second President of the United States With a Life of the Author.* 8 vols. Boston: Little, Brown, 1851–1857.

Angle, Paul M. *By These Words: Great Documents of American Liberty, Selected and Placed in Their Contemporary Settings.* New York: Rand McNally, 1954.

Appleby, Joyce, and Terence Ball, eds. *Thomas Jefferson, Political Writings.* Cambridge: Cambridge University Press, 1999.

Bailyn, Bernard. "The Central Themes of the American Revolution: An Interpretation." In *Essays on the American Revolution,* edited by Stephen G. Kurtz and James H, 3–31. Hutson. Chapel Hill: University of North Carolina Press, 1973.

———, ed. *The Debate on the Constitution.* 2 vols. 1981. 8th printing, New York: Library of America, 1993.

Ball, Terence, ed. *The Federalist with Letters of Brutus.* New York: Cambridge University Press, 2003.

Bancroft, George. *Literary and Historical Miscellanies.* New York: Kessinger, 1855.

Bartlett, Robert C., ed. *The Shorter Socratic Writings: Apology of Socrates to the Jury, Oeconomicus, and Symposium.* Ithaca, NY: Cornell University Press, 1996.

Barzun, Jacques. *From Dawn to Decadence: 500 Years of Western Cultural Life, 1500 to Present.* New York: HarperCollins, 2000.

Basler, Roy P., ed. *Abraham Lincoln: His Speeches and Writings.* Cleveland: World, 1946.

Benveniste, Emile. *Le vocabulaire des institutions indo-européennes.* 2 vols. Paris: Les Editions de Minuit, 1969. Page references to the Italian translation by Mariantonia Liborio, *Il vocabolario delle istituzioni indoeuropee.* Milan: Einaudi, 1976.

Bergh, Albert E., et al., eds. *The Writings of Thomas Jefferson.* 20 vols. Washington, DC: Thomas Jefferson Memorial Association of the United States, 1903–1904.

Blackstone, Sir William. *Commentaries on the Laws of England.* Facsimile of the 1st ed. 4 vols. Chicago: University of Chicago Press, 2002.

Bloom, Harold. *The American Religion: The Emergence of the Post-Christian Nation.* New York: Simon & Schuster, 1992.

Blum, John M., William S. McFeely, et al., eds. *The National Experience: A History of the United States*. 8th ed. Fort Worth, TX: Harcourt Brace Jovanovich, 1993.

Bonomi, Patricia U. *Under the Cope of Heaven: Religion, Society, and Politics in Colonial America*. New York: Oxford University Press, 1988.

Boorstin, Daniel J. *The Americans: The Colonial Experience*. New York: Random House, 1958.

———. *The Americans: The National Experience*. New York: Random House, 1965.

———. *The Americans: The Democratic Experience*. New York: Random House, 1973.

———. *The Genius of American Politics*. Chicago: University of Chicago Press, 1953

———. *The Lost World of Thomas Jefferson*. 3rd ed. Chicago: University of Chicago Press, 1993.

Boyd, Julian et al., eds. *The Papers of Thomas Jefferson*. 34 vols. of 60 vols. Princeton: Princeton University Press, 1950–.

Burnett, Edmund Cody. *The Continental Congress: A Definitive History of the Continental Congress from Its Inception in 1774 to March, 1789*. New York: Macmillan, 1941.

Calvin Jean. *Institutes of the Christian Religion*. Translated by by Thomas Norton. *Institutes of the Christian Religion*. London: A. Hatfield, 1599. Available online through the Center for Reformed Theology and Apologetics at www.reformed. org/master/index.html?mainframe=/books/institutes/. London: A. Hatfield, 1599. Available online through the Center for Reformed Theology and Apologetics at www.reformed.org/master/index.html?mainframe=/books/institutes/

Cappon, Lester J., ed. *The Adams-Jefferson Letters*. Chapel Hill: University of North Carolina Press, 1959.

Carpenter, Frederick I., ed. *Ralph Waldo Emerson: Representative Selections, with Introduction, Bibliography and Notes*. New York: American Book, 1934.

Cavell, Stanley. *Cities of Words: Pedagogical Letters on a Register of the Moral Life*. Cambridge: Belknap of Harvard University Press, 2003.

———. *The Claim of Reason: Wittgenstein, Skepticism, Morality and Tragedy*. New York: Oxford University Press, 1979. Reprinted with a new preface by Oxford University Press, 1999. Page references are to the 1999 edition.

———. *In Quest of the Ordinary: Lines of Skepticism and Romanticism*. Chicago: University of Chicago Press, 1988. Page references are to the paperback edition by Chicago University Press, 1994.

———. *Pursuits of Happiness: The Hollywood Comedy of Remarriage*. Cambridge: Harvard University Press, 1981.

———. *The Senses of Walden: An Expanded Edition*. Chicago: University of Chicago Press, 1992. First published 1981 by North Point Press.

———. *Themes Out of School: Effects and Causes*. Chicago: University of Chicago Press, 1988. First published 1984 by North Point Press.

———. *This New Yet Unapproachable America: Essays after Emerson after Wittgenstein*. Albuquerque, NM: Living Batch, 1989.

Cicero, M. Tullius. *De re publica. De legibus*. Loeb Library edition with translation by C. W. Keyes 1928. Reprint, Cambridge: Harvard University Press, 1994. Page references for both *DRP* and *De legibus* are to the 1994 reprint.

Colapietro, Vincent. "Striving to Speak in a Human Voice: A Peircean Contribution to Metaphysical Discourse." *The Review of Metaphysics* 58 (2004) 367–98.

Conforti, Joseph A. *Imagining New England: Explorations of Regional Identity from the Pilgrims to the Mid-Twentieth Century.* Chapel Hill: University of North Carolina Press, 2001.

Cooper, Barry. *Eric Voegelin and the Foundations of Modern Political Science.* Columbia: University of Missouri Press, 1999.

Cooper, James F. *Tenacious of Their Liberties: The Congregationalists in Colonial Massachusetts.* New York: Oxford University Press, 1999.

Crèvecœur, Hector St. John De. *Letters from an American Farmer.* London: Dutton, 1912.

Crick, Bernard. *The American Science of Politics: Its Origins and Conditions.* Berkeley: California University Press, 1959.

Decaen, Christopher A. Hughes, Glenn, Stephen A. McKnight, and Geoffrey L. Price, eds. "Politics, Order and History: Essays on the Work of Eric Voegelin." *The Review of Metaphysics* 56 (2002) 425.

Diggins, John Patrick, ed. *The Portable John Adams.* New York: Penguin Classics, 2004.

Egan, Jim. *Authorizing Experience: Refigurations of the Body Politic in Seventeenth-Century New England Writing.* Princeton, NJ: Princeton University Press, 1999.

Eicholz, Hans L. *Harmonizing Sentiments: The Declaration of Independence and the Jeffersonian Idea of Self Government.* New York: Peter Lang, 2001.

Eldridge, Richard, ed. *Stanley Cavell.* New York: Cambridge University Press, 2003.

Ellis, Joseph J. *American Sphinx: The Character and Legacy of Thomas Jefferson.* New York: Knopf, 1997.

———. *His Excellency, George Washington.* New York: Knopf, 2004.

———. *Passionate Sage: The Character and Legacy of John Adams.* New York: W. W. Norton, 2001.

Emerson, Everett. *Puritanism in America, 1620–1750.* Boston: Twayne, 1977.

Farrand, Max, editor. *Records of the Federal Convention of 1787.* 4 vols. New Haven: Yale University Press, 1937.

Fiske, John. *The Critical Period of American History, 1783-1789.* Boston: Houghton Mifflin, 1897.

Fite, David. *The Rhetoric of Romantic Vision.* Amherst: University of Massachusetts Press, 1985.

Fliegelman, Jay. *Prodigals and Pilgrims: The American Revolution against Patriarchal Authority, 1750–1780.* Cambridge: Cambridge University Press, 1982.

Ford, Worthington C., ed. *Journals of the Continental Congress.* 34 vols. Washington, DC: U.S. Government Printing Office, 1904–1937.

Freeman, Joanne B., ed. *Hamilton: Writings.* New York: Library of America, 2001.

Frye, Northrop. "The Argument of Comedy." In *English Institute Essays: 1948,* edited by D. A. Robertson Jr., 58–73 New York: Columbia University Press, 1948.

Haraszti, Zoltán. *John Adams and the Prophets of Progress.* Cambridge: Harvard University Press, 1952.

Hart, George. *A Dictionary of Egyptian Gods and Goddesses.* London: Routledge & Kegan Paul, 1986.

Herberg, Will. *Protestant, Catholic, Jew: an essay in American religious sociology.* 2nd ed. with an introduction by Martin E. Marty. Chicago: University of Chicago Press, 1983.

Hill, W. S., editor. *The Folger Library Edition of the Works of Richard Hooker.* 7 vols. Cambridge: Belknap of Harvard University Press, 1977–1998.

Hobbes, Thomas. *Leviathan: Or, the Matter, Forme & Power of a Commonwealth, Ecclesiasticall and Civill.* Edited by A. R. Waller. Cambridge: Cambridge University Press, 1904.

Houck, Davis W., and Amos Kiewe, eds. *Actor, Ideologue, Politician: The Public Speeches of Ronald Reagan.* Westport, CT: Greenwood, 1993.

Hull, Suzanne W. *Chaste, Silent & Obedient: English Books for Women, 1475–1640.* San Marino, CA: Huntington Library, 1982.

Hume, David. *Essays: Literary, Moral, and Political.* London: Routledge, 1870.

Jefferson, Thomas. *A Summary View of the Rights of British America.* 1st ed. Chicago: The Caxton Club, 1976.

Kermode, Frank, and J. Richardson, eds. *Stevens: Collected Poetry and Prose.* New York: Library of America, 1997.

Kerr, Hugh T., ed. *A Compend of the Institutes of the Christian Religion.* Philadelphia: Presbyterian Board of Christian Education, 1939.

Kersh, Rogan. "The Rhetorical Genesis of American Political Union." *Polity* 33 (2000) 229.

Kinsella, W. P. *The Iowa Baseball Confederacy.* 1986. Reprint, New York: Marriner, 2003.

Koch, Adrienne. *The Philosophy of Thomas Jefferson.* Gloucester, MA: Peter Smith, 1957.

Levine, Lawrence W. *The Opening of the American Mind: Canons, Culture, and History.* Boston: Beacon, 1996.

Lucas, Stephen E.. "Justifying America: the Declaration of Independence as A Rhetorical Document." In *American Rhetoric: Context and Criticism,* edited by Thomas W. Benson, 67–130. Carbondale: Southern Illinois University Press, 1989.

MacIntyre, Alasdair. *After Virtue.* 2nd ed. Notre Dame, IN: Notre Dame University Press, 1984. Reprint, 2003.

———. *Three Rival Versions of Moral Inquiry.* Notre Dame, IN: Notre Dame University Press, 1990.

———. *Whose Justice? Which Rationality?.* Notre Dame, IN: Notre Dame University Press, 1988.

McCullough, David. *1776.* New York: Simon & Schuster, 2005.

———. *John Adams.* New York: Simon & Schuster Paperbacks, 2004.

McDonald, Forrest. *Alexander Hamilton: A Biography.* New York: Norton, 1979.

———. *E Pluribus Unum: The Formation of the American Republic, 1776–1790.* 2nd ed. Indianapolis: Liberty Fund, 1979.

———. *Novus Ordo Seclorum: The Intellectual Origins of the Constitution.* Lawrence: University Press of Kansas, 1985.

———. *States' Rights and the Union 1776–1976: Imperium in Imperio.* Lawrence: University Press of Kansas, 2000.

———. *We the People: the Economic Origins of the Constitution.* 1958. Reprint, New Brunswick, NJ: Transaction, 1992.

Middelkauff, Robert. *The Glorious Cause: The American Revolution, 1763–1789.* Revised, expanded edition. New York: Oxford University Press, 2005.

Miller, Perry. *The New England Mind: The Seventeenth Century.* New York: Macmillan, 1939.

Montesquieu, Charles Louis de Secondat, Baron de. *The Spirit of the Laws.* 2 vols. Rev. ed. translated by Thomas Nugent with special introduction by Hon. Frederic R. Coudert. New York: Appleton, 1900.

Mulhall, Stephen. *Stanley Cavell: Philosophy's Recounting of the Ordinary*. Oxford: Oxford University Press, 1994.

Novak, Michael. *On Two Wings: Humble Faith and Common Sense at the American Founding*. San Francisco: Encounter, 2001.

———. *Choosing our King: Powerful Symbols in Presidential Politics*. New York: Macmillan, 1974.

Peterson, Merrill D., ed., *Thomas Jefferson : Writings : Autobiography / Notes on the State of Virginia / Public and Private Papers / Addresses / Letters*.

Plutarch. *Lives of the Noble Romans and Grecians*. Translation by John Dryden. Edited by Arthur H. Clough. New York: Modern Library, 1932.

Pocock, J. G. A. *The Machiavellian Moment: Florentine Political Thought and the Atlantic Republican Tradition*. Princeton, NJ: Princeton University Press, 1975.

Prebish, Charles S. *Religion and Sport: The Meeting of Sacred and Profane*. Westport, CT: Greenwood, 1993.

Prest, Wilfrid. *Albion Ascendant: English History, 1660–1815*. Oxford: Oxford University Press, 1998.

Rahner, Hugo. *Man at Play or Did You Ever Practise Eutrapelia?* London: Burns and Oates, 1963.

Richards, Leonard L. *Shays's Rebellion: the American Revolution's Final Battle*. Philadelphia: University of Pennsylvania Press, 2002.

Ritter, Kurt, and David Henry. *Ronald Reagan: The Great Communicator*. New York: Greenwood, 1992.

Savarese, Paolo. *Il diritto nella relazione*. Torino: G. Giappichelli, 2000

———. *La possibilità nella regola: il diritto nel mondo comune*. Torino: G. Giappichelli, 2004.

Schlesinger, Arthur M., Jr. *The Disuniting of America: Reflections on a Multicultural Society*. Rev. ed. New York: Norton, 1995.

Smith, William, ed. *Dictionary of Greek and Roman Antiquities*. 2nd ed. Boston: Little, Brown, 1870.

Stark, James H. *The Loyalists of Massachusetts and the Other Side of the American Revolution*. Boston: J. H. Stark, 1910.

Steptoe, Andrew. *The Mozart-Da Ponte Operas: The Cultural and Musical Background to Le Nozze Di Figaro, Don Giovanni, and Cosi Fan Tutte*. Oxford: Clarendon, 1990.

Stevenson, William R. *Sovereign Grace: The Place and Significance of Christian Freedom in John Calvin's Political Thought*. New York: Oxford University, 1999.

Storing, Herbert J., ed. *The Complete Anti-Federalist*. 7 vols. Chicago: University of Chicago Press, 1981.

Strauss, Leo. *Natural Right and History*. 7th ed. with preface. Chicago: University of Chicago Press, 1971.

———. *The Political Philosophy of Hobbes: Its Basis and Its Genesis*. Translated by Elsa M. Sinclair. Chicago: University of Chicago Press, 1952.

Strauss, Leo, and Joseph Cropsey. *A History of Political Philosophy*. 3rd ed. Chicago: University of Chicago Press, 1987.

Szatmary, David P. *Shays' Rebellion: The Making of an Agrarian Insurrection*. Amherst: University of Massachusetts Press, 1980.

Thomas Aquinas. *Expositio librii Boetii de Hebdomadibus.* In *Sancti Thomae de Aquino, Opera Omnia,* iussu Leonis XIII P.M. edita, tomus L. Romae–Paris: Commissio Leonina–Cerf, 1992.

Thoreau, Henry D. *The Variorum Walden.* Edited by Walter Harding. New York: Twayne, 1962.

Trapè, Agostino, ed. *La città di Dio.* 3 vols. Roma: Città Nuova, 1978–1989.

Turner, Frederick Jackson. *The Frontier in American History.* New York: Holt, Rinehart and Winston, 1921.

Voegelin, Eric. *The Collected Works of Eric Voegelin.* 34 vols. Edited by Paul Caringella, Jürgen Gebhardt, et al. Columbia: University of Missouri Press, 2001–2004.

Waldo, Dwight, et al. *On Political Science in the United States of America.* Paris: UNESCO, 1956.

West, Delno C., and Sandra Zimdars-Swartz. *Joachim of Fiore: A Study in Spiritual Perception and History.* Bloomington: Indiana University Press, 1983.

Weston, Corinne Comstock. *English Constitutional Theory and the House of Lords, 1556–1832.* New York: Columbia University Press, 1965.

Williams, Michael Allen. *Rethinking "Gnosticism": An Argument for Dismantling a Dubious Category.* Princeton, NJ: Princeton University Press, 1996.

Wiseman, T. P. *New Men in the Roman Senate, 139 BC–AD 14.* Oxford: Oxford University Press, 1971.

Wittgenstein, Ludwig. *Philosophical Investigations.* Translated by G. E. M. Anscombe. Oxford: Blackwell, 1997.

Xenophon. *The Shorter Socratic Writings: Apology of Socrates to the Jury, Oeconomicus, and Symposium.* Edited with introduction by Robert C. Bartlett. Ithaca, NY: Cornell University Press, 1996.

Zank, Michael, ed. *Leo Strauss: The Early Writings.* Albany: SUNY Press, 2002.

Index

www.ingramcontent.com/pod-product-compliance
Lightning Source LLC
Chambersburg PA
CBHW070406270326
41926CB00014B/2730